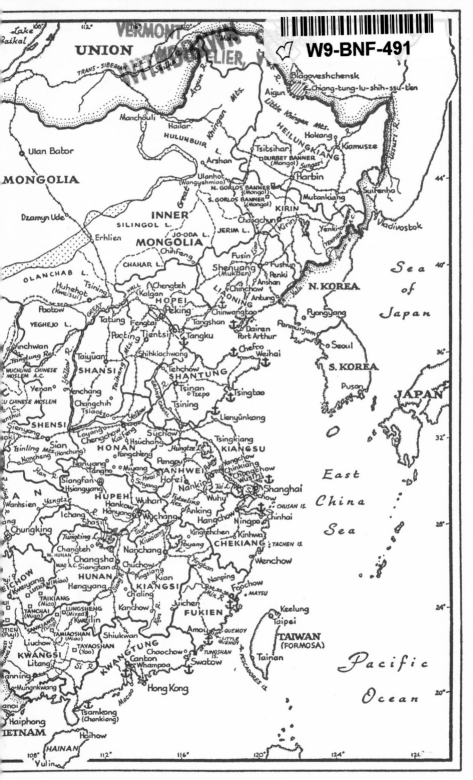

W9-BNF-491

H. TANG, COPYRIGHT 1957 BY FREDERICK A. PRAEGER, INC.)

China's Politics in Perspective

HAROLD S. QUIGLEY

China's Politics in Perspective

THE UNIVERSITY OF MINNESOTA PRESS
Minneapolis

TO MARGARET, ANN, AND KATHLEEN

PREFACE

THIS book is not addressed to specialists but to readers who feel a need for a concise introduction to Chinese politics and policies today. It seeks also to contribute to an understanding of present-day China by recalling briefly her background of political ideas and the development of imperial and republican government. Its hope is to aid toward perspective at a time when many observers dwell only upon omens of disaster.

My debt to scholars in the East Asian field, to statesmen, journalists, and common people, and to my students in American and Chinese universities who have discussed this subject with me for some forty years, is beyond telling. I am especially grateful to my wife for constant interest and keen comment, to Professor John E. Turner for assistance in selecting and assembling pertinent documents, to the *Virginia Quarterly Review* and the Extension Division of the University of Minnesota for permission to include writings previously published, to Frederick A. Praeger, Inc., for the map of China used on the end papers and to the director and staff of the University of Minnesota Press.

HAROLD S. QUIGLEY

INTRODUCTION

GRANTED that we Americans are emotional rather than logical in foreign relations, we want to be fair to other peoples, and to meet our responsibility, as citizens in a democracy, to aid in the formulation of foreign policy. Popular understanding of peoples with whom our government must deal is essential if we are to build a foundation of public opinion on solid rock rather than shifting sand. This brief inquiry into how China came to be what she is today seeks to contribute toward a more realistic view than has been evidenced in American policy toward her during the past decade. It is not an argument, it does not attempt to reach an editorial conclusion. Rather it is offered in the belief that a long-time student of a great civilization so different from our own has an obligation to call to mind basic facts likely to be overlooked in a period of severe tension, and that readers will welcome a presentation of such facts, written with no other intent than to be informative and readable.

The narrative is primarily descriptive of how, over many centuries, Chinese politics was marked by application of the ethical tenets of Confucius and other classical thinkers who lived and taught, and in many instances served in government, in the time of Socrates, Aristotle, and Plato. The Chinese sages taught obedience to absolute monarchy but their teachings imposed upon rulers obligations to govern virtuously, with due regard for the personal dignity and economic welfare of their subjects, and with hospitality toward strangers within the gates. The great mass of illiterate people could not read the books of their revered philosophers but they learned to live morally through listening to the village schoolmasters and practicing the ceremonies which were so intimate a part of their lives. They viewed the distant Emperor in his magnificent palace as the vicegerent of

God, endowed with Heaven's mandate. But Chinese history is full of rebellions against tyrannical rule. Time after time dynasties were overthrown when an enduring but self-respecting people were led by insufferable economic depressions to turn to new leadership. But not until a half-century ago did apostles of democracy arise to challenge benevolent despotism. The story of why this is true, as revealed under the long-lived empire, is brief but deserves reading both for its own interest and for what it adds to our capacity to diagnose China today. Inevitably, a people so long accustomed to being treated as children, unprovided with free schools, and inexperienced in politics above the village level, though cultured in the fundamental sense of regard for moral, artistic, and scholarly standards, have found it difficult to estimate the value of political ideals which have yet to reach full fruition in Western democratic systems. Inevitably the early republican hopes of popular support were disappointed. Absolutism took new forms, liberal leaders were frustrated. External as well as internal pressures engendered the centralization of authority and retarded the transfer of liberal principles from paper to practice. Yet the seed sown by Sun Yat-sen and his co-revolutionists did not die. Throughout the past fifty years its vitality amidst the quack-grass of warlordism, reactionary lip-service to democracy, and Communist totalitarianism is documented in this survey. The tardiness of Western governments in recognizing the latent resentment of the Chinese people toward residual aspects of nineteenth-century imperialism, the advantage taken by Soviet propaganda, and the paralyzing effects of Japan's program of "cooperation," are reviewed.

Has democracy a chance in China? I believe that it has, and I discuss the factors favorable to its ultimate success and likely to mold its character. A major influence upon its progress can be exerted by the government and people of the United States. For that reason this introduction to a subject so worthy of our thought concludes with an appraisal of current American policy toward China. This country has an enviable record of friendly, helpful relations with that nation. No people other than those of the British Commonwealth has been more sincerely and consistently regarded as entitled to our concern. The Chinese people have, until recently, shown corresponding confidence in us. Today the Communist leaders revile us as their chief enemy. Why has this reversal taken place? Our concern for the Chinese people has not diminished. Today we face the necessity of devising a policy that will reflect a perspective of Chinese political development. I hope that this all too brief but, I believe, dispassionate look at the record will be helpful to that end.

THE ROMANIZATION OF CHINESE

THE system most generally used in writing Chinese words in English was invented by Sir Thomas Wade, British minister to China from 1871 to 1883. The Wade system uses the apostrophe after some consonants and omits it after the same consonants to distinguish hard from soft sounds. Exceptions occur in words frequently printed, such as Peiping. Some writers are less meticulous than others in consistent use of the Wade system, which has been criticized as unnecessarily complicated. In this book the Wade system is used except with words now regularly written without apostrophes by writers in English. Listed below are the principal consonant and vowel sounds romanized.

CONSONANTS (pronounced as in English with the following exceptions)

ch = j	k' = k
ch' = ch	p = b
hs = hs preceded by aspirate	p' = p
j = r	t = d
k = g	t' = t

VOWELS

a = ah	ao = ow as in owl
e = u as in fun or e as in yen	ia = eeah
i = ee or short i	ei = long a
o = uh, like u in hull	ua = wah
u = oo; with umlaut, short i	iu = eeyou
ai = long i	ui = way

ou = long o

TABLE OF CONTENTS

China's Politics in Perspective

EARLY POLITICAL THOUGHT: THE CLASSICAL HERITAGE

CHINESE historical records begin in the twelfth century B.C., though scholars date the origin of Chinese society between twelve and eighteen centuries earlier. The earliest of the recorded dynasties which ruled China before the Republican Revolution of 1911 was the Chou (1122–255 B.C.). Known as the Classical Age, this long period saw the development of moral precepts which were codified unofficially in the writings ascribed to China's greatest philosopher, Confucius (K'ung Futze – the Master, K'ung). In the actual process of Chou administration the authority of the emperors was slight after the eighth century B.C., when *wangs* (kings), divided the country and became feudal rulers. Their relations with one another are suggested by the description of the era as the "period of warring states," but they professed to recognize principles that remind us of the inter-state law of ancient Greece.

Confucius

Confucius was born in 551 B.C. and died in 479 B.C., dates which are approximate in the absence of definitive records. It is of interest that Confucius lived about a hundred years before Socrates (469–399 B.C.), a hundred and fifty years before Plato (427–347 B.C.), and two hundred years before Aristotle (384–322 B.C.). Thus the classical ages of China and Greece were roughly contemporaneous. We have, however, no evidence that the writings of Confucius were known to the Greeks. Actually, we lack evidence as to these writings. Scholars have proved that much of the philosophy he taught was not written down by him but by his disciples after his death. Other works at one time ascribed to him we now know to be in the nature of historical annals. He also has been given credit which he would not have claimed for some of the work of other classical theorists. Also, men who wrote many centuries after his time sought to support their own works by quoting as Confucian writings ideas of their own or of other early sages.

Confucius did not attempt to lay down a complete theory of government, nor did he claim originality. Rather he regarded his teachings as the embodiment of historical experience, a modest deprecation of himself quite characteristic of the best Chinese scholarship. Neither he nor any other classical theorist attempted to set forth a theory of state structure distinct from that of the families within the state. To them the state was the family writ large: the emperor was the father, the people his children. However, Confucius, like Socrates, sought to find a formula for good government. Both asked: "What should men do to govern well?" In answering this basic question Confucius began with the premise that men are by nature neither good nor bad. This led him to make goodness, or virtue, the supreme *means* as well as the supreme *end* of political action. He did not neglect the importance of intelligence and reason, but he held that if the ruler were virtuous his rule would minister to the people's welfare and happiness. To quote briefly from the *Great Learning*, not written by him but believed to embody his doctrine:

The ruler will first take pains about his own virtue. Possessing virtue will give him the people. Possessing the people will give him the territory. Possessing the territory will give him wealth. Possessing wealth he will have resources for expenditures.

In the *Doctrine of the Mean* occurs this sentence relating to government, also written after but ascribed to Confucius:

All who have the government of the empire with its states and families have nine standard rules to follow: the cultivation of their own characters; the honoring of men of virtue and talents; affection toward their relatives; respect toward the great ministers; kind and considerate treatment of the whole body of officers; dealing with the mass of the people as children; encouraging the resort of all classes of artisans; indulgent treatment of men from a distance; and the kindly cherishing of the princes of the state.

Confucius inculcated observance of *li* — conduct laid down in his formulation of classical moral ideals. He was conservative, distrusting innovations. Thus he turned men's minds to the past, bound them to be uncritical of ancient precepts and opposed to change as by nature bad. His influence promoted learning but hindered progress and encouraged smugness. It affected the youth who sought entrance into the civil service; they were required to memorize the classics and to compose essays and poems on the models found therein. While their preparation insured a scholarly bureaucracy, it also held them in well-worn intellectual grooves and hindered objective analysis of new ideas. This attitude was destined to slow China's appreciation of Western thought when contact began in later centuries. Yet we cannot overlook the fact that Chinese classical political theory was on a high ethical plane. Nor can we doubt that in permeating Chinese society it inspired even the humblest people with ideals that have contributed to their remaining strong throughout their long record of continuous statehood.

Obviously, there was no hint of democracy in the thinking of classical China. In this respect it differed profoundly from that of classical Greece. Absolute monarchy was the premise of all Chinese sages; even those who justified rebellion against an unjust ruler assumed that a monarchy overthrown would be followed by a new absolutism. Just as the father of a family was supreme over the wife and children, so was the emperor supreme over the people — his "children." The entrance into Asia of the concept of democracy awaited the impact of Western thought, which came in the nineteenth century.

Confucius gave limited attention to inter-state relations. We have noted that in his time China was a congeries of states loosely associated within the Chou empire. His thinking had to do with these communities rather than with the world at large, much as Roman thinking developed the *jus gentium*, the law of the tribes within the Roman Empire. Like the Romans, Confucius did not conceive of universal fraternity but of reciprocal rights and duties, collaboration, and good faith between peoples. He condemned imperialism, terming it a combination of pride and violation of the rights of others. He summed up foreign policy concisely: "to satisfy strangers already within the country and to attract others." Apparently his motive was to develop trade. Although not a militarist, neither was he a pacifist. He approved of armies, preparedness, heroism, and patriotism. War, he believed, both offensive and defensive might be undertaken in exceptional circumstances.

Confucius was one among the philosophers of history who advocated an international organization. He proposed a "Great Union" of all Chinese states, of which the principal agency would be a commission composed of representatives chosen by virtuous and capable citizens. The functions of the Union would be to promote respect for international agreements and peaceful settlement of disputes, to encourage relations among states, to develop natural resources, and to promote the distribution of goods for the benefit of all peoples. This proposal reflected his desire to substitute a more rational order for the feudal warfare of his time.

Like many scholars of classical China, Confucius held positions in government. His writings reveal that this experience gave him a practical point of view without weakening his faith in the ethical basis of good administration. He urged his students to go into government service even when they regarded the ruler as corrupt, since only thus could bad rule be rectified. When asked by a student why he had served under a corrupt ruler he replied: "Is it not said of the really hard that you may grind it and it will not grind down; also of the really white that you may dye it and it will not turn black? Am I indeed a bitter gourd? Must I, like it, be hung up and never eaten?" (Taken from *The Analects,* conversations recalled by his disciples after his death.)

As above noted, we cannot be certain as to which classical works were written by Confucius. But the following may be regarded as embodying his political ideas. All of them may be read in English translation. The standard translations are those of James Legge: *The Analects* (*Lun Yü;* dialogues with disciples); *The Spring and Autumn Annals* (*Ch'un Ch'iu;* annals of the state of Lu, of which Confucius was an official); *Memoirs on Customary Duties of States* (*Li Ch'i*); *Constitutional Law of Chou* (*Chou Li*); *Maxims of Ancient Emperors* (*I*); *Edicts* (*Ch'u*).

Mencius

Mencius (Mengtze), 372–289 B.C., was the foremost interpreter of and commentator upon the ideas of Confucius — ideas he spent his life in clarifying and popularizing. Like Confucius, he served in government but left that career to teach and write. His chief contribution was in the field of political theory. He too accepted monarchy as divinely ordained but even more emphatically than Confucius he taught the doctrine that a ruler's chief responsibility was to promote public welfare. Said he: "The people are the *end*; the emperor is the *means*. The people are the most precious, the spirits second, the ruler third. The ruler should consult the people on policy and appointments, and his prime obligation is to maintain peace. Heaven sees as the people see, and hears as the people hear." His aphorism reminds us of the Western challenge to absolutism: "The voice of the people is the voice of God." Mencius is a forerunner of John Locke in his belief that the people were justified in revolting against a tyrannical ruler, though he did not advance the concept of a contract between ruler and people.

Mencius also was liberal on economic issues. He opposed tariffs and advocated freedom of trade between states. "Formerly," he said, "tariffs were imposed to protect the people from brigands. Today they serve the policies of brigandage" by facilitating illegal trade in arms. However, he opposed the concept of universal love as likely to weaken patriotism. While admitting the justice of war when demanded by the whole people, he distinguished between just and unjust wars. A just war he defined as one undertaken to vindicate the rights of a state. He condemned aggressive violence as destructive of the people and contrary to morality.

Classical Pacifists

In order of the degree of their condemnation of war we may fairly describe Laotze (604–? B.C.), Chuangtze (330–275 B.C.), and Motze or Moti (born about 500 B.C.) as pacifists. All of these men were influential in the development of the traditional Chinese distaste for the military profession. Laotze's doctrine of *tao,* the way, was a religion of quietism. He held that virtue was acquired not by frenzied striving but by getting back to nature. He opposed all talk about the classical rules of ceremonial, *li,* holding that ceremony worked toward substituting mere form for sincerity. Men should cast off desire and the complexity of culture, and should contemplate the simplicity of nature. He was opposed to governmental regulation, preferring to trust in the natural goodness of men. He held that no war was just unless dictated by necessity, i.e., presumably, in honestly conceived self-defense. Weak states he advised to be content with their weakness, saying: "do things that no one thinks of doing; enjoy things no one thinks of enjoying; be as water, which always, by seeking the lowest place, makes itself useful to all and has no enemies."

Chuangtze was an interpreter of Laotze, and like him an exponent of quietism, goodness, and non-regimentation. He was at first a steward of a king but later turned to philosophy and teaching. His wit was famous and his profound ideas were expressed in fables. His first concern was to inculcate universal love, and he applied his doctrine to both individual and state relations. Filial piety, strongly urged by many predecessors of Chuangtze, he compared to the affection of tigers and wolves for their young. His counsel to governments was to avoid war by renouncing comfort and wealth. His teachings might be compared with those of Christ.

Motze, whose influence was powerful in later Chinese culture, was a convinced pacifist. He took a practical rather than a purely ethical approach to his doctrine of universal love, maintaining that it could be realized only if men appreciated its value in their own lives and only if peoples practiced it reciprocally. But he condemned war as immoral. His stinging attack upon war was unqualified:

The whole world condemns robbery and wounding between individuals and calls them immoral. But war, on the contrary, leads to the praise and glorification of such acts. One who kills a man is an assassin of the first degree; one who kills ten men is ten times an assassin; one who kills one hundred men is one hundred times an assassin. Wherefore a conquering hero is an assassin to the degree he has gone in destroying life. Why does this arch assassin admire himself? Why do others admire him? What a perversion of the moral sense! Is it that evil, multiplied to infinity, becomes good? As well attempt to prove that a black point, multiplied to infinity, becomes a white surface. Every war is a crime, whatever belligerent or conscienceless people may say.

The Legalists

The classical age of political thought produced not only the moralists, of whom the five already briefly characterized were the most notable, but also other thinkers usually described as legalists. Two of the ablest of these were Hanfeitze and Yinwentze. Although the legalists drew some of their inspiration from the moralists, they differed from them in their emphasis upon the necessity of law, which they held to be superior to morals in the conduct of government. They maintained, as we do in the Western world, that virtuous rulers cannot ensure good government. As one of them, Kwantze, phrased it: "a saint may be able to produce law but he cannot ignore it and also have successful government." We note here the conflict between ideas of which is the more important, good laws or good men, a conflict that is probably only to be reconciled by recognizing that we cannot have one without the other. To trust to rulers' goodness alone is to open the way to scoundrels; on the other hand, to trust to law is to risk totalitarianism. Until the evolution of representative government, which has not yet come to pass in China, there is no assurance that law will embody the popular will. The Chinese have preferred, therefore, to trust classical ethical principles. Confucius and his disciples have won over the legalists. This does not mean that China has been ruled without law but rather that law has been regarded as secondary to morals. China has had good rulers and bad. Dynasties have been overthrown for failing to heed the "mandate of Heaven," that is by failing to rule as Heaven, representing the right of the people to be ruled in the interest of the people's welfare, decrees. The Chinese are a practical people. They gauge goodness in government less by a government's pretensions to virtue and more by what it accomplishes for their economy. In this they are not unique.

The Formulation of Confucianism

In the centuries since Confucius lived and taught, numerous interpreters and commentators have sought to understand him. They have not only formulated what may be termed a Confucian canon or body of doctrine but have added ideas which he did not espouse, just as the would-be interpreters of Christ and the Buddha have put words into their mouths. Out of the great quantity of writing has emerged what is called Confucianism. It embodies much of the philosophy of Confucius himself, but it also has elements that have emanated from his disciples and been attributed to him. The influence of this body of doctrine has varied from age to age, but even today, under communism, it continues to be respected.

After the introduction of Buddhism from India about the time of Christ, the influence of that great religion spread throughout China. It did not displace Confucianism but for a time it ranked with it. We also find Confucian scholars introducing Buddhist concepts into Confucianism. Others attempted to find in the words of Confucius concepts similar to but superior to those of Gautama, the founder of Buddhism; these writers are described as Neo-Confucians. Most influential among them was Chu Hsi (A.D. 1130–1200). A later Neo-Confucian, who held high office, was Wang Yang-ming (1472–1529). Since the writings of these theorists were concerned mainly with nonpolitical subjects we need not deal with them.

Ultimately Chinese scholarship rebelled against Neo-Confucianism. The reason for the opposition lay in the desire of intellectual leaders to rid Confucianism of the unorthodox elements which had submerged the essential humanitarianism and high moral ideals of classical thought under an overlay of deference to absolutism. A reformer sometimes described as socialistic, Wang An-shih, had denounced this tendency in the eleventh century, but the height of the back-to-Confucius movement came in the eighteenth century. It came in spite of the antagonism to it of the Manchu rulers who ascended the throne after the Manchu conquest of China. Some of the reformers suffered imprisonment or death for their ideas. They criticized both the philosophers who spent their time in metaphysical discussion, neglecting to apply themselves to practical matters, and the rulers who failed to exhibit virtue and were hated by the people. Outstanding among the reformers was Tai Chen (Tai Yung-yüan), who lived from 1724 to 1777. Had these modernists succeeded in ousting the restrictive interpretation and obsequious formalism of the Neo-Confucians, China might well have escaped a century of misfortune brought on by its failure to understand the impact of the West. Unhappily the Neo-Confucian doctrines persisted until close to our own day.

The Chinese are notably eclectic — that is, they incline to "examine all things and to hold fast to that which is good" as they see it. Today their philosophy has elements of classical thought, of Buddhism, Christianity, democracy, and Marxism. But like Christianity in the West, so given to materialism, Confucianism in China seems to answer man's need for guiding moral ideals. Confucianism differs from Christianity in that it is not concerned with life after death. But no religion deserves the name which is not founded on ethics, and in its ethics Confucianism *is* a religion. This central fact underlies its continued influence today.

IMPERIAL GOVERNMENT

CHINA emerged from feudalism in 221 B.C., when the ruler of the state of Ch'in brought the many principalities of the defunct Chou Empire under his control and established himself as the first Emperor of a unified China. He took the title Ch'in Shih Huang Ti, the first Emperor Ch'in. The state of Ch'in embraced present-day Shensi and part of Kansu; the Empire comprised the area between the Yangtsze River and the Great Wall, built in part by Ch'in Shih. From the fourth century A.D. onward the Chinese moved south, driving out the original inhabitants and ultimately occupying the whole expanse of China as we know it today.

Although there have been many periods of civil strife since then, China has not relapsed into feudalism throughout her long history. We shall discover, however, that the term "unitary" as applied to the government of China does not imply close administrative control from the capital. Rather it distinguishes the system inaugurated in 221 B.C. from the preceding feudal freedom to disregard Imperial decrees. Mainly for reasons of geography and primitive means of communication the problem of governing so vast a country as China was tremendous. But in theory China was ruled by a succession of dynasties, twenty-four in all, until, in 1911, the Ch'ing, or Manchu, monarchy was overthrown by the Republican Revolution. Of the twenty-four the most significant, in historical order, were the Ch'in, Han, Sui, T'ang, Sung, Yuan, Ming, and Ch'ing. Most distinguished for cultural excellence were the T'ang (618–907), and the Sung (907–1279). Throughout its history the Chinese thought of their Empire as universal, not national, until the military power of Western invaders forced them to recognize other states as distinct and independent. Not until then did they begin to think of themselves as a nation.

From the Ch'in period (221–207 B.C.) onward, the central government was administered, under a theoretically absolute emperor, by ministers and councils, aided by a civil service. Though there were variations from dynasty to dynasty in the powers enjoyed by these officers, the numbers and titles of their positions, and the degree to which official appointments were determined by civil service examinations, the general character of the system remained constant. We may, therefore, confine ourselves to a survey of the system at its highest point, under the last of the dynasties, the Ch'ing or Manchu. The Manchus were alien conquerors. But they, like the Mongols of the Yuan dynasty (1279–1368), which was also alien, respected and adopted the essential features developed by the Chinese. It may safely be assumed that monarchy is gone from China, never to return; but a system which was successful over a vast territory, inhabited by many races, for more than two thousand years, deserves our study.

The Nature of Imperial Rule

There was no written constitution until the republican era. One of the writings ascribed to Confucius, the *Ch'un Ch'iu* (*Spring and Autumn Annals*), contains many rules for the organization and administration of an ideal state. Sometimes referred to as a substitute for a constitution, it was in fact a composite of historical experience and moral principles. Many imperial decrees and precedents set by custom also provided a kind of unwritten constitution. But the recognized right of an emperor to repeal decrees and ignore custom evidences the absence of binding fundamental law. The strength of the classical moral code, which had been reformulated in the Han period (206 B.C.–A.D. 220), was, however, binding upon emperors and ministers as a general rule. It operated much as the bill of rights operates in a democracy.

The most powerful and able Manchu emperors were K'ang Hsi and his son Ch'ien Lung, whose reigns covered most of the eighteenth century. The absolutism of their power was reflected in K'ang Hsi's dictum: "There is but one ruler, myself," which is roughly contemporaneous with Louis the Fourteenth's famous *"L'état c'est moi"*—"I am the State."

Europeans of the time were acquainted with Chinese ideas and institutions as revealed in the writings and translations of missionaries, and the civilizations of China and France were attractive each to the other and reciprocally influential. In both countries royal power was unquestioned, but the great sovereigns of China sought to live up to the Confucian code of ethics. Weaker rulers were largely controlled by court favorites — male and female — eunuchs, relatives, and corrupt officials. Peking, perhaps the most magnificent city in the world, was a grand setting for the central government. Within its great walls, broken at intervals by splendid gates, the palace buildings, painted red and roofed with glazed tile in blue, green, or yellow, symbolized to the people the superior culture and strength of an eternal polity. Here, in the early morning — the time believed best for clear thinking — the emperors held audience with their officials. Their robes of the finest silk were decorated with embroidery of striking designs and colors. Outside the walls were the temple and altar of Heaven, where the emperors worshiped in token of their vicegerency of God.

There were no representative legislature, no voting. At the apex of administration two small bodies, the Grand Council and the Grand Secretariat, advised the emperors about policy. The Grand Secretariat was an older body used by the preceding Ming emperors as advisers on general matters. The Grand Council, on the other hand, though originated by the Manchus to deal with military policy, gradually encroached upon the field of the Grand Secretariat, which remained a distinct body but became little more than a keeper of archives. Each body consisted of five or six of the most able and influential officials — all, of course, imperial appointees — and each was divided equally between Chinese and Manchu nobles. The idea underlying this division was the desirability of having the Chinese as a check upon the Manchus, and vice versa. Manchu leverage was, however, strengthened by their longer terms in office and by the allotment of chairmanships to them. Often an especially powerful man would serve on both bodies. Thus the central authority was monopolized by a handful of experienced and capable mandarins.

The Administrative Boards

The administrative functions were carried on by six boards — Civil Office, Rites, Revenue, War, Punishments, and Works. At times the heads of the boards were also members of the Grand Council or the Grand Secretariat or both. Each board had two presidents, one a Manchu, the other a Chinese. They were legally equal in authority, and each was intended to be a check on the other. However, the Manchu president tended to have greater influence since the turnover among the Chinese heads was more frequent and Manchu emperors tended to favor their own race. But able emperors realized that too marked favoritism toward the Manchu heads would cause a breakdown of the check and balance system of control, thereby undermining their own power. They also could not overlook the fact that as a rule the Chinese heads had greater experience and knowledge.

Briefly, the boards' functions were as follows: The Board of Civil Office controlled — subject to imperial approval — the appointment, promotion, and removal of members of the civil service. It did not conduct the examinations; thus favoritism was kept within reasonable bounds. The Board of Rites (or ceremonies) conducted the civil service examinations. It also supervised the highly complicated system of ceremonies, a very important responsibility in a land so observant of the traditional rules of conduct. A third function of the Board of Rites was the conduct of negotiations with Western states. The Board of Revenue was the treasury, receiving and disbursing the national revenues, and also the final court of appeal in civil cases sent up from lower courts. The Board of War administered military affairs except those relating to the Manchu army, a separate force largely stationed about Peking but with some units in areas of doubtful loyalty. This force was under the direct administration of the imperial household. The Board of Punishments was the department of justice. The Board of Works supervised the construction and repair of public buildings, roads, canals, and bridges, and the care of river channels and dikes.

We note the absence of a board of education. Such part as the government took in this field was within the purview of the Board of Rites, but this part was small since China had no system of public education. Nor were there boards of commerce, agriculture, postal administration, labor, or public welfare. However, in some degree the existing boards provided for certain services which we assign to these special departments. Moreover, provincial and local agencies supplied some additional services. And the family system accepted responsibilities for family members to an extent not customary in Western countries.

Auxiliary Agencies

In addition to the Grand Council, Grand Secretariat, and the six boards there were a few less exalted but important central organs of administration. The Mongolian Superintendency dealt with the vassal states, of which there were many, extending from Korea and Mongolia in the north to Annam, Burma, and Siam in the south. China was suzerain over these peoples, her relation to them was not that of a sovereign state over colonies but rather that of an elder toward a younger brother. Obviously we observe here another aspect of the family system enjoined by the Confucian code of conduct. The vassal states were independent but they paid tribute to China, followed the Chinese calendar, asked her approval of a new sovereign and of royal marriages, and so on. In return they benefited from the right to trade with China and to ask for protection against an attacker. Another agency was the Court of Censors, a group of fifty-six official critics assigned to various localities. The Censors were authorized to report upon the conduct of officials. Theoretically the emperors themselves were subject to their criticism, but it took great courage to criticize an absolute monarch. Censors of such courage there were, and some paid for it with their lives. The Censorate served as a valuable source of warning, enabling the government at distant Peking to take timely action against a corrupt official who was arousing public resentment.

The Hanlin (Forest of Pencils) was a national academy of eminent scholars, similar to Great Britain's Royal Academy. It was not a teaching group, but its members wrote the history of a dynasty after the dynasty had ended, thus avoiding pressure to omit unfavorable facts or to praise where blame was due. The work of the Hanlin resulted in the preservation of an exceptionally complete historical record, which is supplemented by documents national, provincial, and local.

The Civil Service

Under the central government ramified throughout the country a remarkable civil service. All officials except those of the villages were centrally appointed. As a rule entrance and promotion were obtainable only upon examination. China thus had a merit system before the West did, a system which attracted her ablest young men. Unfortunately, the education needed to pass the examinations was not provided for from public funds. Consequently poor boys were kept out unless their home community or a wealthy patron financed their education. This meant that the great majority of officials came from the land-owning class, the gentry. To our way of thinking the examinations were impractical. They required intensive knowledge of the classical literature rather than of political, economic, and social data or of principles of contemporary public administration. A candidate had not only to have memorized the major classical writings: he had also to write prose and poetry in classical style. To a Chinese youth this was what writing in Greek or Latin would be to an American candidate. The classical language was very different from ordinary speech. The number of ideographs required might run to thirty thousand. Not only were the examinations difficult, the conditions under which they were written were severe. Each candidate was locked in a tiny cell; his food was pushed through a hole in the wall; he slept on a bare board and stayed in his cell until the examinations, which took several days, were completed. Only the most earnest hopefuls would endure such a test and the successful ones were the most highly honored people in the land. While there were exceptions to appointment on merit, they were too few to affect the normally high quality of Chinese officialdom.

Successful candidates received appointments. Salaries were low and were usually supplemented in a demoralizing fashion by the acceptance of commissions from persons seeking official action. This practice was known as "squeeze," i.e. graft. Squeeze became an accepted thing and was tolerated within limits. Tax collectors remitted less to the treasury than they collected. Even judges expected squeeze, as is indicated in the Chinese proverb: "When the doors of the magistrate's court open wide, he without money does better outside." We should note, however, that the practice of squeeze also permeated the rest of Chinese society. Buyers for business firms expected it from wholesalers; even house servants who bought the family groceries squeezed both the grocer and the housewife. Of course this was unhealthy, but whether it was more so than Western practices such as the overcharging of the government by great business firms; accepting gifts of mink coats, purebred cattle, and hotel expenses; or favoring campaign contributors with diplomatic appointments and protective tariffs may be doubted. Corrupt Chinese officials who went beyond the customary limits of squeeze might be imprisoned or executed. Those favored as to the manner of execution might receive a silk cord with an order to bore two holes in a wall, run the ends of the cord through the wall, insert their necks between the cord and the wall, and have a friend pull the ends until they choked. This was unpleasant, but preferable to the "death by a thousand cuts" they might suffer if they disobeyed the order.

Judicial Administration

The courts were staffed by administrative officers and no distinction was made between executive and judicial functions. Also no formal distinction was made between civil and criminal law. In practice, however, the Board of Revenue was the highest court for what Western law would term civil cases — those in which there was no alleged offense against public authority, and in which the penalty was not imprisonment or execution. The Board of Punishment had appellate jurisdiction in what the West would term criminal cases. The Board also might take original jurisdiction in cases where the death penalty was not possible. In capital cases not dealt with provincially or by the district court, as they normally were, a body of ex officio judges known as the Commission of Revision had jurisdiction. In capital cases the emperor, advised by the Commission of Revision, was the ultimate judge.

Provincial Government

Under the Manchus China was composed of eighteen provinces of varying size and population, plus outlying areas. One of the latter was Manchuria, ancestral home of the Manchus; this area consisted of three provinces which, until 1907, were administered somewhat differently from the eighteen. The eighteen provinces were largely autonomous though not legally so. They were ruled by governors and viceroys, the latter having authority over two or three provinces each. These officials and their subordinates were members of the civil service, appointed and removed by the central government. In practice, so long as the governors sent in the expected revenues in grain, silk, tea, and so on, they were not likely to be disturbed by Peking. Special commissioners were sent out in cases involving misgovernment. Thus China was a kind of confederation rather than a highly unitary system. The viceroys and governors were highly able men, comparable to the members of the central boards. They were military commanders as well as civil administrators. They could inflict capital punishment, subject to appeal. Under them and carefully selected were the provincial treasurer, the judge, the salt controller, and the grain intendant. These four formed an advisory council to the governor, but their principal jobs were the administration of departments suggested by their titles. The treasurer, in his capacity of lieutenant-governor, dispensed patronage within the scope of the prefectural civil service examinations. These were conducted by a director of education, who conferred the lowest of the literary degrees. The treasurer or the judge or both conducted the bureau of foreign affairs in provinces having dealings with foreigners. The salt controller supervised the manufacture and sale of salt, which was a government monopoly. The grain intendant levied and received the grain paid in lieu of taxes.

Local Government

The provinces were composed of circuits (*tao*), which were subdivided into prefectures (*fu*), which were subdivided into *hsien* (districts). Within the districts were walled towns (*ch'eng*), district towns (*t'un*), and villages (*li*). The prefectural heads had judicial functions and in some instances were associated with the customs service and the salt gabelle. Most important were the districts and the localities — the towns and villages. Administration of the towns was carried on as for groups of villages. For most purposes the villages were self-governing, although the district magistrate, the *hsien chang*, had legal authority over them. Their governing bodies were groups of elders, men held in respect by the villagers and selected by them upon a plan of rotation so that each head of a well-to-do family might have his turn. A demonstration of ability and interest in local affairs often gained an elder a practically permanent position. The chairman of the elders was the headman, whose selection had to be confirmed by the *hsien chang*. Generally speaking the conduct of village affairs was entrusted to the headman, in consultation with the other elders.

In the villages and towns we find the vital element in China's political system. Here we get close to the people. Here the taxes were collected, entertainment for officials provided, materials found for dike-building, road patrols and constables appointed, walls repaired, wells dug, markets and fairs supervised, theatrical entertainments provided. A bronze gong hung before the village hall, upon which the constable beat during the night hours, warning robbers to keep away. Village government was a patriarchal aristocracy, not shared with the humble farmers who lacked education and wealth. It was paternal in spirit but it was unconcerned, as was the central government, to educate the individual or to give him political experience, a fact which worked against subsequent efforts to create a republic.

The keystone of the arch of local government was the district magistracy, the office of the hsien chang. It was the principal link between the villages and towns below and the provincial office above. The magistrate was expected to perform all political functions and to devise plans for the improvement of economic and social conditions. With him were associated a number of subordinate officials who did clerical work for him. He was district judge, hearing the great majority of cases not settled by the village elders. He was responsible for the collection of taxes, the registration of land titles, measures against famine and plague, and the preservation of walls and buildings. Road maintenance, police, care of the temple, public morals —

everything for which an official could be responsible within the hsien — was included in the magistrate's burden. Customarily, however, he sought and heeded the suggestions of the gentry, reminding us of eighteenth-century England. The hsien chang often was referred to as "the father and mother of the people."

Although we might assume that in a so-called Oriental absolutism every administrative function was performed by officials, we would be mistaken. It would also be wrong to think of the people as closely regulated. The merchant guilds in the towns took upon themselves the gathering of information about the economic status of their members, and sought to promote industry and trade. In the localities minor disputes between individuals were settled by "peace-talkers"— respected elders who mediated between them. Groups similar to our fraternal societies extended aid to members in distress. When public order was threatened, vigilantes were organized by men of high standing to supplement the regular police and army. On the less pleasant side we note the influence of court favorites during periods of weak or corrupt rule. As for the attitude of the masses toward the government, the best word for it is indifference. Sun Yat-sen described China as "a sheet of loose sand." To the masses the "Son of Heaven"— the emperor at Peking — was almost as remote as Heaven itself. They took or were given no part in government, and they felt its influence very slightly. Consequently their attitude toward it is well illustrated in an incident related by the Abbé Huc in his delightful book, *The Chinese Empire*:

In 1851, at the period of the death of Emperor Tao Kuang, we were travelling on the road from Peking. One day, when we had been taking tea at an inn, in company with some Chinese citizens, we tried to get up a little political discussion. We spoke of the recent death of the Emperor, an important event which of course must have interested everyone. We expressed our anxiety on the subject of the succession to the imperial throne, the heir to which was not yet publicly proclaimed. "Who knows," said we, "which of the three sons of the Emperor will have been appointed to succeed him? If it should be the eldest, will he pursue the same system of government? If the younger, he is still very young, and it is said that there are contrary influences, two opposing parties at court; to which will he lean?" We put forward, in short, all kinds of hypotheses, in order to stimulate these good citizens to make some observation. But they hardly listened to us. We came back again and again to the charge, in order to elicit some opinion or other on questions that really appeared to us of great importance. But to all our piquant suggestions they replied by shaking their heads, puffing out whiffs of smoke, and taking great gulps of tea. This apathy was really beginning to provoke us when one of these worthy Chinese, getting up from his seat, came and laid his two hands on our shoulders in a manner quite paternal and said, smiling rather ironically: "Listen to me, my friend! Why should you trouble your heart and fatigue your head by all these vain surmises? The mandarins have to attend to affairs of state; they are paid for it. Let them earn their money then. But don't let us torment ourselves by what does not concern us. We should be great fools to want to do political business for nothing." "That is very conformable to reason," cried the rest of the company, and thereupon they pointed out to us that our tea was growing cold and our pipes were out.

TRANSITION AND REVOLUTION: THE COLLAPSE OF MONARCHY

THE Manchu dynasty (1644–1912) attained the zenith of its power and prestige during the reign of Emperor Ch'ien Lung in the latter half of the eighteenth century. At that time some aspects of Chinese culture rivaled the accomplishments of the great eras of T'ang and Sung. Europeans, among them Voltaire, regarded Chinese society as well ordered and governed by beneficent rulers on moral principles. Among the states of East Asia, many of which accepted Chinese suzerainty, China was recognized as their mentor and model in cultural, political, and commercial fields. The omens were favorable for the attainment of still greater distinction. Yet within a few years after the death of Ch'ien Lung in 1796 a rebellion against the dynasty occurred. It was provoked by economic distress, the usual signal to Chinese minds that Heaven would welcome a new regime.

In his later years Ch'ien Lung weakened mentally. Corrupt courtiers and officials took advantage of his loss of vigor to raise tax rates, and to neglect measures against famine, floods, and disease. The population was increasing faster than the food supply, with resulting impoverishment. Military suppression of the rebellion saved the dynasty but lessened its hold upon the people still further. In the first half of the nineteenth century conditions failed to improve and in mid-century a tremendous uprising, the T'aip'ing Rebellion, broke out. In fighting throughout a decade this attempt to unseat the Manchus was put down, with foreign aid. From it the dynasty emerged permanently discredited. It persisted for another half-century but was forced by the Republican Revolution to abdicate in 1912. Since 1911 the Chinese have been trying to find their way to representative democracy under a republican system.

The Impact of Western Imperialism

It is not my province here to write a history, but we should note the relation between the downfall of the Manchu dynasty and the Industrial Revolution in Europe. China had traded with European countries and permitted their missionaries to preach and teach from the sixteenth century on. These contacts had not cost her humiliation or loss of territory. Her self-confident assumption that the Europeans were tributaries seeking to profit from her superior culture and products — rice, silk, and tea — had been maintainable. When, however, England set out to find raw materials for her factories and markets for her textiles the assumption came face to face with a very hard fact: English military power. In 1839–1842 the Opium War demonstrated that power and forced China into her first unequal treaty. The loss of the war forecast the dynasty's fate. The following eighty years were a long era of tragedy marked by seizures of territory, establishment of many types of alien control, and the reduction of the great empire to what Sun Yat-sen truly called a hypo-colony. This was the last age of imperialism. Many states of Asia became colonies of one power or another. China was too big to swallow, so she remained independent, though her sovereignty was trampled upon. The agony of that experience bit deeply into the Chinese soul and is reflected today in Chinese submission to a doctrine and system that have restored China's dignity as a nation. Whether that doctrine will continue to be accepted depends upon its leaders' realization that their tenure hangs upon their appreciation of the Chinese individual's belief in himself. It will not endure if it continues to substitute military control over the individual for concern with his welfare and his personal dignity.

It is often said that the Chinese, unlike their neighbors the Japanese, failed to discern the futility of resisting the West's determination that the world should be brought into one international community and failed to take measures that would satisfy the West. This is not wholly borne out by the facts of nineteenth-century history. The pace of change was slower in China, but there were reasons for that — among them great size, a rapidly increasing population, disbelief in Western superiority. Not all of the Manchu emperors of the nineteenth century were unworthy, though some of them were corrupt and dissolute. Truly distinguished Chinese statesmen and scholars sought to save the monarchy through political, economic, social, and military reforms. The time allowed by the West and by the Japanese was too short. The Republican movement, aided by betrayal within the imperial oligarchy, and by the long-cherished Chinese hatred of the Manchus, overtook the reformist program.

Beginnings of Political Reform

Let us briefly trace the transition to the Republic in terms of governmental change. The first change was the creation in 1861 of a new agency, the Board of Foreign Affairs, which gradually developed into a cabinet, displacing the older Grand Council. It functioned so deliberately that foreign states came to label it, in the words of Dr. Arthur Smith, a missionary, "an Oriental circumlocution office, not to transact but to prevent the transaction of business" (*China in Convulsion*, New York, 1901). It was reorganized in 1901 to deal only with foreign affairs.

In 1890 a Board of the Navy was added, to be replaced in 1910 by a ministry. In 1898 Emperor Kuang Hsü was persuaded by two eminent scholars, K'ang Yu-wei and Liang Ch'i-ch'ao, to inaugurate a sweeping reform of administrative organization and to promise a constitution. These reforms were designed to preserve the monarchy and the dynasty. They were nullified by the powerful Empress Dowager Tz'u Hsi, who had been the real ruler since giving birth to a son while concubine of the weak Emperor Hs'ien Feng; this accomplishment raised her status to that of consort and subsequently Empress Dowager. Not until the allied intervention against the Boxer Rebellion, which was anti-Manchu as well as anti-foreign, did Tz'u Hsi see the necessity of reform. From 1901 on paper reforms were instituted. The old titles of the imperial councils and boards gave way to new ones similar to those of the West. The distinction between administrative and judicial functions was recognized and separate courts were set up. The most genuine change was the abolition of the classical civil service and its replacement by one modeled upon Western lines.

The beginnings of advisory national and provincial assemblies preceded the revolution of 1911. Members were chosen by voters highly qualified educationally or financially. These assemblies were surprisingly critical and reformist. Their members expressed opinions freely, opinions dangerous to autocracy. Had not the Revolution come so soon, there is good ground for questioning whether China might not have evolved a liberal government gradually while retaining the unifying element of monarchy. One may not answer this question in view of what actually happened. The Manchu mandate had run out. Instead of a new dynasty — the traditional replacement — a Republic was launched upon a stormy sea.

The "Principles of the Constitution"

Tangible progress toward a formal constitution began in 1905, when a special commission was set up to study foreign constitutions and their operation. The Old Buddha, as Tz'u Hsi was called by the people, intended to make the constitutional movement the means of maintaining the dynasty forever. Naturally, therefore, her commission gave most attention to the constitutions of Germany and Japan. Both of these had been handed down from the throne; neither ruling house showed ill effects in consequence of its generosity, while its international standing had improved. It seemed wise for China to imitate them. A constitution was promised for 1917. For the interim the Court issued a document entitled "Principles of the Constitution," which were in fact the application to proposed institutions of the single principle that the "Great Pure Dynasty" was to continue forever. The Principles were in essence a transliteration of the Japanese constitution, with the slender financial powers of the parliament reduced to the mere right of protest. Three years later a more liberal instrument, the "Nineteen Articles" was issued in the midst of revolution as a last-minute effort to meet the demands of the apprehensive national assembly, which had drafted the document. The Articles were designed to maintain the dynasty but strip it of power. They placed supreme power in a parliament and, in general, were modeled upon the British system. They were never brought into operation. The southern provinces had set up a Republic and convened a representative national council at Nanking. October 10, 1911, was the revolutionists' Fourth of July. Dr. Sun Yat-sen, provisional president of the new regime, demanded the abdication of the dynasty. In February, 1912, abdication was promulgated. Monarchy had lost the mandate of Heaven.

Anti-Manchu Currents of Opinion

Three major currents joined to form the torrent which overwhelmed the Great Pure Dynasty. These were as follows: (1) The long-standing resentment of the Chinese people toward the Manchus, whom they regarded as aliens of inferior culture who ruled by virtue of military conquest. (2) The opposition of the provincial gentry to the growing centralization of authority at Peking, largely induced by the government's dealings with foreign governments and bankers for economic development, particularly the building of railways. These dealings had led to the increase of taxation, and also involved embarking upon projects which the provincial gentry preferred to undertake themselves. (3) The movement for a republic. The combination of mass feeling, conservative self-interest, and magnetic liberalism gave the revolution a degree of strength which could not have been mustered by the liberal leadership alone. It had, however, the weakness of its strength. The masses and the gentry had no genuine interest in a republic. The liberals' problem was to maintain a kind of government undesired and but little understood. Only a miracle could have solved this problem. It remains unsolved today.

The Abdication

Why did the Manchus abdicate? Our answer lies in part in the decline of the Court, in part in the ambition of its principal military officer, Yuan Shih-k'ai. From the Opium War onward the only strong Manchu ruler had been a woman, Tz'u Hsi. She may be compared in vigor and intelligence to her contemporary, Queen Victoria. Tz'u Hsi, as Empress Dowager, ruled from behind the throne, not on it. Apparently she was revered by the masses, who were ignorant of her cruelty to any who dared to go counter to her will. Her weakness lay in her refusal to recognize the necessity of accommodating policy to new conditions both domestic and foreign. These conditions called for governmental leadership to strengthen the Chinese economy and to build a modern army and navy, and also for the carrying out of the treaties peaceably until the country grew strong enough to demand their replacement by relations of equality. Because of failure to recognize these necessities China lost wars with the West, territory, sovereignty, and respect. After her defeat by Japan in 1895 there was doubt at home and abroad that the country would survive as an independent state. The influence of the United States, supported by Great Britain, exerted in the Open Door doctrine, may have saved China, but it did not save the monarchy.

Tz'u Hsi died in 1909, and in the same year Emperor Kuang Hsü died, leaving a baby emperor theoretically on the throne when the Revolution broke out. Shortly thereafter the Regent resigned. The central power was held by Yuan Shih-k'ai, a man of long political experience and high ability, but a Chinese who had suffered humiliation for a period and had small reason to feel personal regard for the dynasty. He had, however, been recalled to high office and had built a new army and officered it with men trained by and personally loyal to him. Undoubtedly he could have defeated the revolutionary army, which was headed by Li Yuan-hung, sometimes dubbed "Old Lady Li." A story of the day related that Li did not want the headship but was dragged from under a bed and persuaded to take command. It is probable that Yuan already saw an opportunity to set up a new dynasty when he accepted from the revolutionists the office of President and advised the Manchus to abdicate.

Yuan Shih-k'ai versus Sun Yat-sen

The Republic was considerate of the fallen monarchy. The "Little Emperor" was allowed to hold the title of a foreign sovereign, a portion of the palace was reserved for his occupancy, and an annual appropriation from public funds was made for him and his household. The livelihood of his military retainers, the Manchu bannermen, was guaranteed. Unfortunately these provisions could not be fully honored, as Republican finances were diminished by civil strife. The Emperor remained in the palace until 1925, when he was forced by the so-called Christian General Feng Yu-hsiang to flee to the Japanese legation. Subsequently he was placed on the puppet throne of Manchukuo by the Japanese.

It is difficult to understand why Sun Yat-sen, who had devoted his adult life to raising money and organizing the movement for a Republic, assented to resigning the provisional presidency in favor of Yuan. He could hardly have believed that Yuan agreed with his principles, whatever promises Yuan made. Sun was an idealist but he faced harsh reality in the military power which Yuan could bring to bear. He also faced foreign fears that if war became widespread, opportunities for investment would be postponed. Foreign governments of the West wanted strong central administration, and foreign bankers were willing to lend money to China under such an administration. These factors determined Sun and his colleagues to risk placing Yuan in power. He took office, biding his time before attempting to realize his monarchical dream. When that time came he betrayed the Republic, as he had betrayed the dynasty.

POLITICAL IDEAS OF SUN YAT-SEN

SUN YAT-SEN is venerated in China as the Father of the Chinese Republic. His tomb on the slope of Purple Mountain near Nanking is a magnificent monument, more so than the tomb of Napoleon Bonaparte at Les Invalides in Paris. He was a man of magnetic personality and deep earnestness. He was small of stature but of great dignity. His fine eyes were kindly and thoughtful. His features were not pronouncedly Chinese and his approach to problems was cosmopolitan rather than Oriental. One who conversed with him even briefly felt that he was a truly dedicated man with a sense of destiny. He did not impress one as a visionary, though often pilloried as such by more cynical politicians. He spoke gravely to foreign visitors upon the failure of the democracies of the West to support his liberal leadership. He died in 1925, apparently defeated, but not acknowledging defeat. In death his spirit lived on to challenge his own and other peoples to remove feudal and foreign shackles from his countrymen. He was a man before his time, such a man as China needs today.

Sun was born to a peasant family in 1866, in a village near the city of Canton. At the age of thirteen he went to Hawaii, where he was entered in Punahou school, a missionary institution in Honolulu. Here he began his study of democracy and Christianity. After completing high school there he did his college work at Queens College, Hong Kong, then took the first medical degree granted by Hong Kong University. He entered the practice of medicine in his native province but left it shortly afterward to engage in his lifetime effort to overthrow the Manchu monarchy. He was convinced that only through the establishment of a republic could China get rid of corruption and foreign controls. The agitation which he began with a few friends led the government to put a price on his head but he got out of the country, fleeing to Japan and subsequently to England. In London he was kidnapped and held prisoner in the Chinese legation. He managed to inform an English friend, Dr. James Cantlie, of his plight, and Dr. Cantlie aided him to escape. He went to Europe where for several years he studied Western ideas while soliciting funds to carry on his cherished program of revolution. During these years in Europe he sketched out his "Three Principles of the People," but he did not formulate them in writing until 1924. In 1905 he organized, in Tokyo, the first liberal Chinese political party, the Tung Meng Hui [1] or Nationalist Society, dedicated to a republican revolution. We know this party today as the Kuomintang, the Nationalist Party. By 1905 the revolutionary idea had found numerous adherents both within and outside China, and was receiving financial support from Chinese living abroad. Several attempts were made at revolution, only to be foiled, and many revolutionaries were executed. As we have noted earlier, a combination of forces antagonistic to the dynasty brought ultimate success in 1911–1912.

The Three Principles of the People

We turn now to Sun's Three Principles of the People, which embody his political ideas. He had gathered materials for several books in the field, all of which had been destroyed by a militarist attack upon his office in Canton. Undaunted, he delivered his ideas in lectures, which were published and have been translated into English and other languages. If they suffer from the loss of his source materials they remain lively reading. His purpose was practical, not to display his erudition as a scholar and theorist, but to stimulate popular realization of China's situation and offer his inspiration toward change. They deserve not criticism for deficiencies but appreciation for their merits. They evidence Sun's study of Western liberal writers: Rousseau, Montesquieu, Henry George, Marx, and others.

The Principle of Nationalism

Sun's three principles, which he described as the fundamentals of national reconstruction, are nationalism, democracy, and livelihood.

---

[1] Also spelled Tungminghui, having the same meaning, "the society of all the people."

He identified nationalism with racial unity, which he defined as homogeneity of blood, language, religion, and customs. China has many races, it would become a nation by the fusion of the races into one. He argued that the great majority of China's four hundred million people were of the Han race; the problem of fusing the other races — the Mongolians, Manchus, Tibetans, and Turks — was not the obstacle to nationalism. Rather it was the fact that

the unity of the Chinese people has stopped short at the clan and has not extended to the nation. . . . The Chinese people have shown the greatest loyalty to family and clan with the result that in China there have been familism and clanism but no real nationalism . . . for the nation there has never been an instance of the supreme spirit of sacrifice . . . there is no national spirit. Consequently, we are in fact but a sheet of loose sand.

Sun continues bitterly:

We are the poorest and weakest state in the world, occupying the lowest position in international affairs; the rest of mankind is the carving knife and the serving dish while we are the fish and the meat. Our position now is extremely perilous: if we do not earnestly promote nationalism and weld together our four hundred millions into a strong nation, we face a tragedy — the loss of our country and the destruction of our race. . . . The European powers, to a large extent, are near the frigid zone. China has the mildest climate and the most abundant natural products of any country in the world. . . . If the powers some day subjugate China, it will be large numbers overcoming a smaller number. And when that time comes, they will have no need of us: then we will not even be qualified to be slaves.

Sun thus suggests one incentive to national unity — the danger from population pressure in the West and in Japan. He then brings forward the danger of political pressure, instancing China's losses of territory through foreign conquest. He asserts that this danger remains, though the contemplated partition of his country between 1895 and 1911 had been prevented by the Republican Revolution. He gives no credit to the Open Door doctrine. A third danger, economic pressure, he regards as still facing the country. China, he declares, is "being crushed by the economic strength of the powers to a greater degree than if we were a full colony. . . . I think we ought to be called a 'hypo-colony,' . . . our real place is below Annam." To evidence his charge of inferiority he describes foreign control of the customs service and of tariff rates. He contends also that China's industry has been ruined by the import of foreign manufactured goods: that foreign banks in China, issuing their own currency, have caused depreciation of Chinese money; that they are receiving huge Chinese deposits which should go to Chinese banks; that freight rates to Europe from China, levied by foreign companies with no competition from non-existent Chinese shipping, are higher than those from Japanese ports, since the foreign companies must compete with Japanese lines; that taxes on Chinese residents of foreign settlements in China, and land prices and rents therein, are higher than in areas administered by Chinese; that the numerous foreign business companies in China are robbing the Chinese under protection of the unequal treaties. By these economic means, Sun concludes that foreign domination cost China an annual loss of $1,200,000,000. His figures are estimates, relevant to conditions in 1924. They may be grossly exaggerated and he takes no account of economic advantages accruing to China from foreigners' activities. The significance of his denunciation is not, however, in the accuracy or inaccuracy of his estimates. It is rather in the fact that he made the justifiable charge of economic imperialism. In so doing he does not lay the whole blame on foreigners. He blames his own people for being submissive to the point that they engage in many dealings with foreign concerns and administrators in preference to dealing with their own tradesmen, bankers, and government. He seeks in this way to awaken a spirit of nationalism.

Sun's View of Communism

In developing his case against Western imperialism, Sun refers favorably to the Soviet Union. While acknowledging that its doctrine of self-determination of all nations was similar to that of Woodrow Wilson, he argues that Wilson was unable to influence the powers to apply it. The Russian revolution, he says, engendered "a great hope in the heart of mankind." This and other references to the revolution have been used by his critics to brand Sun a Communist. Such a charge cannot be sustained by historical data, as Mao Tse-tung pointed out during his rise to power. In his desperate effort to liberate the country Sun turned to the Soviets after the democratic states refused their aid. He also was willing to make concessions to Japan and to ally himself with Chinese militarists who would agree to cooperate. Does this opportunism reflect personal ambition? To a degree, it does. Sun had supreme confidence in himself. He saw himself as the only man capable of freeing his country. But his ambition was not primarily to gain personal power. Rather it was to establish the Republic on a solid foundation. Shortly before his death he wrote or dictated his will, a document of but two paragraphs. The first paragraph reads:

For forty years I have devoted myself to the cause of the people's revolution with but one end in view, the elevation of China to a position of freedom and equality among the nations. My experiences during these forty years have firmly convinced me that to attain this goal we must bring about a thorough awakening of our own people and ally ourselves in a common struggle with those peoples of the world who treat us on the basis of equality.

The Principle of Democracy

Sun's second principle of the people was democracy. He envisaged democratic government as the ultimate form of government toward which men progressed through three earlier forms: force, theocracy, and monarchy. He rejected the idea that men are born free and equal, holding that they obtain freedom and equality through historical circumstances. For China the essential prerequisite to democracy, he declared, was not individual liberty but national unity. He maintained that the individual in China already was relatively free; he "does as he pleases," feeling governmental controls only when they required payment of taxes or were used to suppress rebellion. Sun insisted that the advocacy of individual liberty by certain Chinese intellectuals was mere imitativeness, the consequence of too much reading of Rousseau. Apparently he was thinking mainly of the position of the country in relation to foreign controls, since he urged that "for us nationalism may be said to correspond to their [i.e., Western] liberty, because putting the people's nationalism into effect means a struggle for the liberty of our nation." He could hardly have mistaken individual indifference to government for individual liberty. Undoubtedly his emphasis upon nationalism goes far toward explaining his seeming readiness to collaborate with militarists and his deferment of democracy to the indefinite future.

Democracy by Stages

It is of interest to note that after World War II many new Asian states, after experimenting with democratic institutions, reverted to "strong man" government. In fairness to Sun, his opportunism may better be interpreted as realism than as deprecation of democracy. He was an egotist, but what great political leader has been humble? His desired end was democracy. He took risks to acquire the power needed to attain that end. Had he lived and received the support of a strong army who can say that he would not have reached it?

We have noted that Sun also rejected the idea that men are born equal, which, we know, is an idealistic belief in their moral right to equal treatment before the law, not a contention that they are equal intellectually, physically, or socially. Sun urges the necessity of cooperation among men of different talents — seers, executives, and others — with the common aim of service to the community. Let each contribute in proportion to his abilities. To assert, as Sun's disparagers do, that he was a believer in totalitarianism is ridiculous. It is true that in discussing the problems of administering a democratic government, he refers to Bismarck's opposition to democracy and suggests that China go slowly in imitating the West. He points out that Western natural science has gone beyond its political science, and regards this as a warning to China. He argues that for China democracy would be advanced through the recognition of ability as a requisite for official life. The people, he says, should be shareholders and should choose able managers. If the people possess the rights of suffrage, initiative, referendum, and recall, they may safely leave actual administration to experts. He advocates five rather than three governmental divisions, adding to the usual executive, legislative, and judicial powers those of supervision and civil service. The supervisory power, which would observe and control official conduct, is a borrowing from the imperial censorate. The civil service power should, Sun believed, be separate, to guard against favoritism in appointments.

Political Tutelage of the People

Although Sun does not attack the problem of inducing a citizenry equipped with political rights to select able officials, he approaches the problem with his program for a period of "tutelage." During this period he foresees government by a self-constituted political party backed by strong military forces. Democracy would be established by regions in proportion as the people therein became enlightened by tutelage. Ultimately it would become nation-wide. When we consider this program in the context of ninety per cent illiteracy we cannot dismiss it as undemocratic. But it had to operate against the inclination of men in power to hold control. We will be observing subsequently the barriers which have slowed the realization of the program, barriers from within and from without China.

The Principle of Livelihood

We come now to the principle of livelihood, which many commentators view as socialism or communism. Sun's exposition of it is specifically non-Marxist, since he rejects the Marxian doctrine of the class struggle. Yet he is not afraid of words. He calls his program "practical communism." He calls the class struggle "a disease arising during the process of progress," which he regards as a social process, with the struggle for a living as its central force. At some length he discusses the book of an American, Maurice William, whose *Social Interpretation of History* was published in 1921. Sun states that his ideas had not been borrowed from William, and that he had preached them for twenty years. But textual comparison shows clearly that Sun owes a debt to William for the detailed analysis of the differences between the social and the economic interpretation of history. There is no basis, however, for the claim that William's book turned Sun away from belief in communism, which he had never advocated during his long struggle against feudalism and imperialism. Sun advocated a revolution not to overthrow capitalism but to replace absolutism with democracy. He had not viewed revolution as the attack of the proletariat upon the dominant economic forces but as a means of cooperative action to bring about a regime of political freedom under which all men would benefit. He himself is partly responsible for his thought's being misunderstood because his speeches in 1924 were ambiguous in some respects. At that time, also, he had lost hope of getting recognition from the democracies, and had turned to the Soviets. We should note, nevertheless, that Sun took no part in the organization, in 1921, of the Chinese Communist Party.

Sun pointed to such evidences of his basic thesis of the attainment of livelihood through social processes in Western states as direct taxation and public ownership of transportation systems, water, gas, electricity enterprises. He denied that these changes had resulted from class war. He held that "society progresses . . . through the adjustment of major economic interests rather than through the clash of interests." This adjustment, he thought, comes about by recognition of common interests.

Proposed Economic Reforms

In applying the principle of livelihood to China, Sun proposed the equalization of land ownership and the regulation of capital. He called for two fundamental reforms: appropriation of the unearned increment of land by the state, and control of capital by state ownership of large natural monopolies. His plan included giving land to tenant farmers, as well as loans, irrigation, and the reclamation of waste land by the government. He also advocated unemployment relief for urban workers. Sun did not contemplate expropriation of land holdings, but an owner who undervalued his land for tax purposes was to be subject to the government's exercise of its right to purchase the land at the owner's valuation. Moreover, the unearned increment of any rise in land value due to public improvements or social progress should accrue to the state after the original valuation had been made. In conjunction with his proposals for democratic government, his principle of livelihood may be best defined as democratic socialism.

Criticism of the Sages

Sun's early enrollment in an American school in Honolulu and his continuing there through high school precluded his acquiring the knowledge of classical philosophy which youth educated in China received. That he had read the great books of Confucius, Mencius, and later commentators is demonstrated by his occasional references to them; but he referred to them chiefly to point out their errors. A major error he found in the generally-held conception that "action is difficult, knowledge is easy," which had achieved the status of an axiom or proverb. Sun devoted a lengthy book to repudiating this idea and to arguing that, on the contrary, "action is easy, knowledge is difficult" (*Psychological Reconstruction*, translated into English under the inappropriate title *Memoirs of a Chinese Revolutionary*, published in 1919 or shortly thereafter by McKay in Philadelphia; the book is undated, but Dr. Sun dates his preface December 30, 1918). In this work Sun advances ten "proofs" of the primary necessity of knowledge before action. Such an effort would seem gratuitous, yet to Sun it was made necessary by his countrymen's inclination to condemn his post-revolutionary program as impractical. He says that even his comrades in the overthrow of the dynasty were deserting him; that many of them had expected that the Republic, having been established, would be immediately operative without the necessity of planning the many reforms needed. Confronted by this necessity, they had lost heart and had turned to "action" of a selfish kind which was nullifying the Republic. They were, he argued, quite competent to get the needed knowledge and to act upon it, but were mentally too much tied to the ancient axiom to believe that the key to the problem was the attainment of knowledge. Although he does not say so, Sun was striking at something more than an axiom. His aim was to present the importance of Western science and techniques to a people accustomed to thinking of China as the most cultured nation, altogether able to meet new problems with old principles and techniques. He was also seeking to reinforce his colleagues against the onslaught of reaction, to give them the courage to fight on. Equipped with new knowledge, they would be able to crush forces ignorant of the scientific findings and methods of the West.

Sun was honest in admitting that he too had failed to appreciate the necessity of knowledge until after the Republic had been established. Out of consideration for his party members he does not dwell upon another failure — failure to realize their tendency to use their easily-won victory in their own interests. Too many had joined his movement as politicians, not as liberals. It may be doubted that his appeal for the reversal of an ancient maxim would have influenced such men except as it seemed likely to profit them. The campaign against the maxim was, however, effective in drawing younger men to Sun and it played a part in the later rejuvenation of his party.

THE PARLIAMENTARY REPUBLIC

No APOLOGY need be made for a brief survey of the early stages of the struggle for a republic in China. We cannot comprehend the present without studying the steps, the forward and backward motions, that led to it. We should not be contemptuous of early failures. If Sun Yat-sen and his co-believers in democracy aimed at a shining target, if they tried to move too rapidly, where did they find their inspiration? Where but in the French and American revolutions? If the first Republic collapsed after a few years, why did it collapse? Is the complete answer to be found within China? Why did communism come to power? We throw light on these issues by observing the course of Republican history. We find that interesting, too, in itself. The ways of the Chinese people are their own. In utilizing borrowed ideas they are eclectic; they adapt rather than adopt their borrowings. As a civilization they are old and wise. In the study of differences lies more interest than in the study of similarities.

The Constitution of 1912

Upon the abdication of the dynasty a provisional constitution was promulgated, in March, 1912. This document was drafted by the revolutionary council at Nanking, with the anticipation that it would soon be replaced by a permanent constitution. In fact, the adoption of a permanent instrument was delayed until 1923. Consequently the provisional constitution remained the formal fundamental law until that year. It was honored more in the breach than in the observance but deserves mention in view of its expression of the liberal spirit of the Revolution. It boldly and definitely asserted that the Republic of China had been established by the people, and that in them sovereignty was vested. The chapter on popular rights declared that all citizens were equal, and were endowed with the freedoms customarily recognized in democratic states, including both civil and political rights. It provided for a parliament of one chamber — the sitting national council — but authorized that body to pass laws creating a permanent parliament. The powers of the parliament were broad, comparable to those we are familiar with in the West. In addition to legislative power, they included the right to question cabinet members, to impeach them, to approve appointments of superior officials, and to ratify treaties and declarations of war. The parliament was further empowered to elect the president and vice-president and to impeach them for treason. It was competent to pass laws over a veto but not to require the resignation of the cabinet by a vote of lack of confidence, as is usual in a strictly parliamentary or cabinet system. On the other hand, the parliament could not legally be dissolved by the president, as is normal in such a system. In these latter inconsistencies lay the weakness of the provisional constitution, one which conduced to deadlock. This weakness was the result of the contradictory views of President Yuan Shih-K'ai and of the revolutionaries who had reluctantly elected him president. It gave the document the nature of a cross or mixture of presidential and parliamentary government, somewhat similar to France's at that time.

The president and vice-president were elected by the parliament. The presidential powers were those found in Western presidential systems. Beyond the normal executive powers were those of introducing bills into the parliament, issuing ordinances to implement statutes, and the suspensory veto power. The vice-president was assigned no functions beyond attending to the duties of the president when the latter was absent or incapacitated. A cabinet primarily responsible to the president but jointly responsible with him for executive bills was composed of the ministers who headed the executive departments. The judiciary was to be an independent branch of government, guaranteed against interference by the usual safeguards, though appointed by the president.

Finally, the provisional constitution authorized the parliament, which was to be convened within ten months in accordance with laws to be passed by the provisional parliament or council, to adopt a permanent constitution.

Deficiencies of the System

We note that the provisional document was designed along the lines of the Western three-branch systems, not the five-branch system advocated by Sun Yat-sen; also that it contained no articles about provincial relations with the central government. These apparent deficiencies were explained by the haste with which the instrument was drafted and the intention that it should operate briefly while the permanent constitution was in process of adoption. This process was delayed far beyond expectation, bringing the weaknesses of the provisional constitution into stronger relief. In operation it did not furnish an easy-running machine. The parliament felt compelled to stretch its approval and impeachment powers in order to compensate for its inability to overthrow a cabinet or minister by censure. The impeachment provision was vague; charges of "failure to perform official duties" could easily be trumped up where criminal offenses were not involved. When impeachment was attempted in such cases, the president could, and did, refuse to remove his appointee. Also, the large quorums required for legislative business made it easy to block executive bills and difficult to complete action upon a member's bill. The situation was that regularly observable in a presidential system, aggravated by the reciprocal jealousies of president and parliament.

The "Old Parliament"

In accordance with its authorization, the provisional parliament, which moved from the revolutionary center, Nanking, to Peking in April, 1912, and held office until April, 1913, passed laws for the establishment and election of a two-chamber national assembly, which was convened on April 8, 1913, at Peking. That body usually is referred to as the Old Parliament, though the accepted English translation of its title is National Assembly. It was a large legislature: there were 274 members in the Senate, 596 in the House of Representatives. Both houses had members from the twenty-two provinces and also from Tibet, Mongolia, and Kokonor, regarded as parts of the Empire and of the new Republic, though not integrated closely with the rest of China. In addition the Senate had 8 members elected by the Central Education Society and 6 from abroad chosen by an electoral college. The term of Senators was six years, one third retiring every two years; that of Representatives was three years. The electorate was composed of male citizens who possessed low qualifications based upon education or ownership of property. Each provincial assembly elected 10 members to the Senate; the number elected for the House by the provincial assemblies varied from 46 to 18, depending upon population. The Assembly did not hold its sessions in the palace but in a modest building of cheap grey brick. A beautiful grove of cedars gave its location some aesthetic quality but the contrast between it and the President's offices in the palace was striking.

Early Political Parties

Political parties had appeared before the Republican Revolution and were active in the new National Assembly. We have noted previously that in 1905 the Nationalist Society, the T'ungminghui, was organized by Sun Yat-sen and others in Tokyo. Its platform was anti-Manchu and embodied Sun's three principles of the people. In 1912 it joined with other groups to form the Nationalist Party, the Kuomintang (*tang* meaning "party"). The leaders were strongly in favor of the Republic and many of them were sincere liberals. Sun Yat-sen was their recognized chief, and supporting him were men whose names appear prominently in the checkered history of the first Republic: Wang Ch'ung-hui, a distinguished legal scholar; T'ang Shao-yi, first premier appointed by President Yuan Shih-k'ai; Hu Han-min, a conservative politician but reliably republican; and others. The Kuomintang was the largest in Assembly membership, having a majority in each house. Other parties included the Kung Ho Tang (Republican Party), composed of leading supporters of Yuan; the Ming Tzu Tang (Democratic Party), organized by the Confucianist scholar, Liang Ch'i-ch'ao, which favored gradualism, occupying a position midway between that of the Kuomintang and that of the Kung Ho

Tang; and smaller groups. All parties were parliamentary rather than popular since the citizenry was not yet concerned with politics.

Expulsion of the Kuomintang

Relations between the Assembly and President Yuan were stormy from the outset. Yuan showed immediately that he was determined to have his way, constitution to the contrary notwithstanding. On the other hand, the majority Kuomintang refused to submit to arbitrary disregard of the legislature. The major focus of disagreement was the procedure to be followed in drafting a "permanent" constitution. The Assembly insisted that the drafting should be entrusted to a committee of sixty, half of its members coming from each house of the Assembly. Yuan wanted to appoint some members and to have the others chosen by the provincial assemblies. The Assembly had its way and its committee met in the old imperial Temple of Heaven, a beautiful building, calculated to impress the deliberations with the values of tradition, symmetry, and perfection. The discussion of the draft was marred by wrangling with President Yuan over suggestions of his designed to assure strong central administration. The committee was set upon establishing a parliamentary system empowered to control the executive. The disputes so retarded deliberation that but one chapter had been completed before the President abruptly expelled the Kuomintang from the Assembly, thus terminating the committee's work. The completed chapter, which dealt with the executive branch, had been adopted by the Assembly. Under this chapter Yuan was elected "regular" President, as distinguished from his previous status of provisional President, on October 6, 1913. If this action by the Assembly appears inconsistent with the majority's distrust of Yuan it is explained by his recourse to bribery and intimidation.

Dissolution of the Assembly

On January 19, 1914, the President dissolved both houses of the Assembly, acting without warrant of law. Not until 1923 was the new document completed and enacted. And not until 1916, after Yuan's death, did the Assembly reconvene. Yuan also dissolved the provincial assemblies, completely stultifying the Republic. He was enabled to do this by his control of the army, which he had reorganized and which was loyal to him. Whether or not he would have acted so arbitrarily had the Kuomintang been willing to compromise it is impossible to say. China would have benefited had it been possible to agree upon a reasonable division of governmental powers. The country needed a strong executive. Yuan was experienced and capable, and he had the Western powers' confidence. He might not have attempted to re-establish the monarchy if he had been allowed the presidential powers he demanded. It seems unlikely that he would have respected any truly constitutional division of powers or any bill of rights. He is tarred in history as betrayer of the Republic.

The Dictatorship of Yuan Shih-k'ai

After dissolving the Assembly Yuan ruled as a dictator. He made a pretense of constitutional government by using pliable politicians in advisory councils and by promulgating bogus documents of a superficially constitutional nature. Yuan issued a "Constitutional Compact" on May 1, 1915, proclaiming it to be a merely amended provisional constitution. In fact it was a wholly new instrument which gave absolute power to the President. He also arranged for a new procedure to draft a "permanent" constitution. We would be pursuing a will-o'-the-wisp if we gave serious attention to these and other pretensions to liberalism by a man whose despotic and cruel acts led to his characterization as an animal "with the head of a tiger and the tail of a snake." It is anomalous that Professor John Goodnow, a distinguished American political scientist, later president of Johns Hopkins University, served as adviser to Yuan. A second more logical choice as adviser, in view of Yuan's political reactionism, was Professor N. Ariga, a Japanese legal authority. Ariga's influence is obvious when we compare the Constitutional Compact with the constitution of Japan. Yuan ignored a draft prepared for him by Goodnow which provided for a strong executive but also assured an independent parliament. Yuan substituted the imperial system of government for the provincial assemblies, but he also substituted military governors for the imperial viceroys, thus assuring loyalty to himself but preparing the way for the chaos that followed his death.

Failure of the Monarchy Plot

In the summer of 1915 a movement engineered by Yuan began with the objective of re-establishing the monarchy and making Yuan emperor. The prime movers of the agitation took as the basis of their argument a memorandum prepared for Yuan by Professor Goodnow. It dealt with the history of various republics, drawing conclusions upon the conditions requisite for republican government and applying these conclusions to the situation in China. The memorandum expressed the view that "a monarchy is better suited than a republic to China." But it laid down very explicitly three conditions to be satisfied, one of which was that provision be made for constitutionalism. Carefully disguised as a call from the citizenry, the return to monarchy under Yuan was proclaimed on December 12, 1915. Unfortunately for Yuan, the proclamation was met with strong objections from five powers — not including the United States — and several southern provinces. Throughout the country enthusiasm for a new monarchy was small. Fearing revolt and foreign displeasure, Yuan first postponed his enthronement, then canceled his decree of monarchy. He made various concessions designed to propitiate hostile sentiment, and prospects for constitutionalism were improving when, on June 16, 1916, he died of Bright's disease.

Peking versus Canton

The National Assembly returned to Peking and Vice-president Li Yuan-hung succeeded to the presidency. Li was honestly in favor of parliamentary government and encouraged the Assembly to continue its interrupted work on a "permanent" constitution. The Premier, General Tuan Ch'i-jui, disagreed with this program, became involved in disputes with the Assembly, and brought about its second dissolution in 1917. This action was no more legitimate than Yuan's treatment of the legislature in 1914. Both were acts of major force. Consequently the Assembly members did not consider that they had served their terms by mere lapse of time. They waited for a third opportunity to function, which did not come until 1922. In the meantime a considerable number of the members set themselves up at Canton. They lacked a majority of the houses but claimed to be the constitutional parliament. In 1921 this rump Assembly elected Sun Yat-sen President of China. He made vain efforts to force his way northward by military methods but was unable to organize sufficiently strong armies nor to maintain unity within them. After many vicissitudes Sun went to Peking in the hope of an alliance with the Manchurian warlord Chang Tso-lin that would restore him to power. He failed in this move and died in 1925.

From 1916 to 1928 the Peking regime was headed by generals. None of the six was comparable with Yuan Shih-k'ai in ability or in his hold upon the country. We need to say no more about them than to name them in the order of their presidencies: Li Yuan-hung, Feng Kuo-chang, Hsü Shih-chang, Li Yuan-hung again, T'sao K'un, Tuan Ch'i-jui, and Chang Tso-lin. Each attained the position by military-political maneuvers. None was elected constitutionally. For a few years a hand-picked assembly, the so-called Tuchün Parliament, (*tuchün* meaning "generals"), sat in Peking, obedient to the orders of its military masters. Some able and conscientious men served with corruptionists in the cabinet. But the government was in constant upheaval as the self-interested cliques conspired and fought for power. China was a Republic in name only.

Monarchy Again Rejected

The most bizarre incident of this period was the one-man attempt to re-establish the Manchu dynasty. This came about through the ineptitude of President Li Yuan-hung in calling the reactionary General Chang Hsün to aid him against his own former premier, General Tuan Ch'i-jui, whom he had dismissed for recalcitrance. Without consulting either President Li or the youthful ex-Emperor Hsuan Tung (Pu Yi), Chang Hsün broke out the dragon flags of the defunct dynasty and declared Hsuan Tung emperor. His *coup d'état* came to nought when it failed of support from the militarists opposed to Li. Tuan Ch'i-jui led an attack on the capital and drove Chang Hsün and his flags into hiding. The "Little Emperor" was allowed to remain in the section of the palace granted to him in 1912. Chang Hsün, like Yuan Shih-k'ai, had failed to take into account the jealousies of the dominant tuchün.

Whether because of their desire to present a democratic mask to the West or because of the traditional Chinese regard for a code of conduct, interest in finishing a constitution did not flag during the period of military government. During its brief existence in 1916–17, the Assembly worked upon the 1913 draft, though it accomplished little before the second dissolution. In several provinces constitutions modeled upon those of American states were drafted but none was carried into effect. Although these documents were drafted without authorization from Peking, thus reflecting the disunity into which the country had fallen, it was remarkable that the military governors approved the drafting and that men were available to do the work. These constitutions' existence contributed to the embodiment of the principle of federalism in the "permanent" constitution, which was completed in 1923 and promulgated on October 10 of that year. That constitution was drafted by members of the Old Parliament of 1913, who had returned to Peking from their exile in Canton. Not all still living were willing to return, but a quorum was present in each house. The two houses met in joint session to vote upon the document. Its adoption was made possible, indeed mandatory, by the attitude of the strong "Chihli Clique," headed by Marshal Wu Pei-fu, the ablest of the northern generals, with a reputation as a Confucian scholar.

A Glimpse of the "Old Parliament"

I attended a session of the House of Representatives in December, 1922. The following note may aid in understanding the nature of this experiment in parliamentarism. It was written upon my departure from the session:

I stand outside the House of Representatives to observe the scene as the members arrive. They alight from automobiles, carriages or rickshas. Their outer covering is monotonously uniform – a long, heavy ulster with a fur collar, and a fur cap. Each member has a small blue disk, identifying him as such, attached to his coat. They appear to be importantly conscious of their positions and walk rapidly into the drab building.

Passing into the lobby, my Chinese interpreter and I present our passes and are admitted to the section of the gallery reserved for foreign visitors. The gallery runs along three walls of the chamber, and is packed with visitors before the meeting is called to order. The chamber is decorated in pink and lavender; paper streamers of these colors stretch from the large brass chandelier to the corners of the chamber. Two flags are crossed over the chair of the Speaker. The seats of the members are arranged in a semicircle and are thinly upholstered in black leather. They face a high rostrum on which seats are provided for the Speaker, members of the cabinet, and the secretaries. In front of the Speaker's desk and a little below it is the tribune from which the more lengthy speeches are delivered.

The members drift in. Most of them are middle-aged. Their hands seek warmth up the sleeves of their long quilted black or dark blue gowns. At ten minutes before two o'clock a hand-bell is rung. Members then come in quickly to fill the empty seats, and a hum of conversation develops. The Speaker, a tall spare individual with a Teddy Rooseveltian moustache and teeth, takes the chair. Again the bell sounds and the doors are closed by police, who seem much too numerous. The roll is not called but is taken by tellers, who scurry up the aisles noting any vacant seats. Conversation continues as latecomers hurry in.

A clerk rises and begins to read a document. The matter seems to hold little interest for the members, who do not interrupt their chatting to listen. Absences are reported by the Speaker and are approved without formality. The business of the day is taken up as well as may be under the handicap of a constant and increasingly audible undertone of conversation. A member rises and without waiting to be recognized begins to speak. He asks why the salaries of members have not been paid. The Speaker tries to explain but the House goes into an uproar that completely drowns his words.

The matter of approving the appointment of the premier is brought before the House. A small but vocal minority insists upon discussing the matter at length. The majority objects. A rising vote is taken on a preliminary question. The tellers run up and down the aisles, counting the yeas and nays. The minority maintains its stand in spite of defeat on the vote. Speeches become more and more vehement, accompanied by much pounding of desks. In desperation, a minority member mounts the tribune to filibuster against the already-passed motion. Members of the majority cry him down and attempt to drag him from the tribune by pulling at his gown. His friends rush to his aid and grasp his gown from the opposite side. As he stands spread-eagled and in danger of having his clothes torn from him in the tug-of-war between opponents and supporters, a member hurls at him a heavy brass ink-box, which he catches and apostrophizes as the evil spirit of the majority. One of his friends begins to pummel the assailant and a general melee gets under way. The Speaker leaves the chair, declaring adjournment. The hands of the clock point to 2:35.

The "Permanent" Constitution

The constitution was a creditable instrument of thirteen chapters, written in direct and simple style. It vested sovereignty in the people and contained a long bill of rights. The powers of government were enumerated in three classes: national, provincial, and concurrent, thus carrying out the principle of federalism. National powers were divided among the usual three branches — executive, legislative, and judicial — no reference being made to Dr. Sun's five-fold system. The President was to be elected by the parliament for a five-year term and be eligible for a second term. The cabinet was responsible to the House of Representatives and upon vote of want of confidence in the cabinet the President was required either to dismiss the cabinet or dissolve the House of Representatives. In the latter event he was required to hold a new election of the House and to convoke continuance of the session within five months. Both houses were to be elected by the provincial assemblies and other electoral bodies. Proper provision was made for an independent judiciary. It is obvious that the "permanent" constitution was drawn up by able students of Western law.

It was legally in force from October 10, 1923, to November 24, 1924, when it was suspended, never to be re-instituted. Its early demise was an inevitable consequence of the country's chaotic condition. Its military sponsors, Generals Wu Pei-fu and Ts'ao K'un, controlled only three provinces near the capital. Their desire was to erect a platform to support Ts'ao K'un's election to the presidency. This they accomplished by bribery and intimidation of the parliament, but their day of triumph was short. They were ousted by a combination of two opposing cliques, the Fengtien and Anfu, led by the Manchurian general and dictator Chang Tso-lin. He made gestures toward constitutionalism but set himself up as President, retaining the post until 1928 when the forces of Chiang Kai-shek compelled him to flee. En route to Manchuria he was assassinated.

ERA OF THE WARLORDS

FROM the death of President Yuan Shih-k'ai in 1916 to the establishment of the National Government at Nanking in 1928 China was governed — misgoverned is more accurate — by militarists. We have already observed their emasculation of constitutionalism at Peking. It remains to explain their exercise of power in the provinces and to examine the economic and social effects of their rivalries. We are concerned not only with the structure of government, law, and theory, but also with political action — "behavior" is the contemporary term. We cannot apply all the techniques of behaviorism as it is being applied in the analysis of present-day politics, but it is possible to throw some light on contemporary societies by resort to historical data and personal observation of the recent past. Unless such sources are used, the new techniques drawn from psychology and mathematics must approach the present time under the serious handicap of a physician who attempts to prescribe for a patient without reference to his record of health and illness.

The period of 1916–1928 was not wholly one of confusion, corruption, and civil strife. It was also a time of literary creativeness and the beginnings of modern industrialism. These and other signs of a realization that China's survival depended upon her re-examining and re-appraising old ideas and methods will be dealt with after we have given charitable attention to the brambles and pitfalls of provincial politics — charitable because we remember the troubled history of America's march to unity.

Provincial Separatism
It is difficult today to believe that there was apprehension, during the chaotic period we are discussing, that China might break up into a number of provinces or groups of provinces, each proclaiming itself

a separate state. Yet such was the fact. Imperial China had never been closely unified, as we have seen. The imperial provinces had been administered by centrally-appointed officials, who took their cues from the class they belonged to, the gentry. The business of government was not extensive nor highly organized. Assured of the customary contributions of silver and grain, and unannoyed by petitions against injustice or failure to provide relief from famine or flood, the Court was not inclined to interfere with provincial administration. The Chinese state had been held together by a balance of forces of great age and universal acceptance: the monarchy, the mandarinate, and the Confucian moral code. This balance was destroyed by the Revolution. Yuan Shih-k'ai had failed to restore the balance and he had frustrated the Republican attempt to establish a new system. With his death Peking's personal control over provincial governors disappeared. Like a bottle thrown against a wall, the polity broke into many pieces. In each area the central figure was the tuchun, the military governor. He had been appointed by Yuan and had been loyal to him; he felt no such loyalty to Yuan's successors. Rather, he seized the opportunity afforded by Yuan's death to exalt himself. With a few exceptions the *tuchün* (plural of tuchun) were rapacious, corrupt men, utterly contemptuous of Republican ideals, motivated only by self-interest. Their selfishness was matched by their ignorance. Their power lay in their armies, recruited by conscription from the poverty-stricken peasantry and bandit hordes.

The tuchun was not often a trained military man. A writer of the period, J. O. P. Bland, describes him as "generally a sleek Confucianist scholar up to date, a slim and subtle intelligence, coldly calculating and quite ruthless, who uses men and money with consummate ability." His methods of political action were intrigue and bribery wherever possible, in preference to fighting. He denied the regularly apportioned share of provincial revenues to Peking, seized railway and salt funds, levied excessive taxes, requisitioned farm equipment, issued worthless currency, corrupted members of provincial assemblies, and devoted but little money to education and economic development. He lived recklessly and lavishly. Vice and the opium traffic found models in his conduct.

The period had its amusing side. It was filled with incidents that call for treatment in a Gilbert and Sullivan opera. Nondescript armies marched up and down the country, carrying umbrellas and teapots. Scarcely a month went by without reports of a clash in one area or another. These were seldom fought to a finish, and retreating troops scrounged upon the people as they fled. "Silver bullets" often decided the outcome of a battle. From a Tientsin newspaper I take the following jocular bit of doggerel, which contains more truth than caricature:

When the *Tuchun* Comes to Tea

Then said Copley of the Customs, "Kindly tell us
Tuchun dear, why you don't disband your *ping shih,* for,
From all we see and hear, SACK THE TROOPS is now the
Slogan, and on patriotic scores, don't you think you
Really ought to make a start at sacking yours?"

"But I have!" the *Tuchun* answered, "It was only yestermorn
I dismissed a hundred thousand, though my heart was fairly torn.
And to blunt the pang of losing them completely and for aye,
Sure, I kept them on the payroll, it's myself
That draws their pay."

"But we hear," observed the Salt-man, and support the
Doctor lent, and the Consul's trusty henchman and the
Banker bowed assent, "that the title of the *Tuchun* is
Abolished by decree of the Sovereign Folk of China.
Tell us, Sir, do you agree?"

"Do I not?" the *Tuchun* answered. "I suppressed it years ago.
Then became the Grand Panjandrum of the Province, don't you know;
Then the Super-High Factotum, then the Ultra-Noble Nob;
They can call me Bottle-Washer — if I only keep the job!"

Although in theory the army was a national force and the military governors national appointees, in fact there was no national army. Each province was in fact a separate unit with its own army. The armies varied in strength in 1925 between 22,000 and 275,000. The tuchün leagued together in cliques, pooling their forces to vie for control of the central government. Alliances were made and broken on bases of personal interest, and troops were lured away from one commander by another with a deeper war-chest.

Model Governor Yen

Among the tuchün one man stood out as a shining exception to the typical official bandit. He was Yen Hsi-san, tuchun of the western province of Shansi. While completing his military training in Japan, he had met the republican leaders and adopted their principles. When the revolution broke out he was appointed military governor of Shansi. He held himself free of obligation to any clique, though he was not always able to avoid collaboration. He recognized his legal relation to the central government and remitted to it what he regarded as its proper share of tax receipts. Within his own province he was called a model governor. The villagers hailed him as one to whom their welfare was his guiding principle. At a time when opium-growing was common and encouraged, Yen forbade it and provided facilities in hospitals for the cure of opium-smokers. He abolished foot-binding, and aided the improvement of agriculture, forestry, and roads. He suppressed banditry, encouraged new thought in education, and maintained law and order through the courts. When called upon to ally himself with the Kuomintang campaign to oust the tuchün he led his forces against the dictator Chang Tso-lin and drove him out of Peking.

Tuchunal government did not mean the abolition of the regular organs of administration, many of which had held over from imperial times. Each province had a civil governor, though this office was, in some provinces, combined with that of the tuchun. Associated with the civil governor were commissioners of finance, education, industry, and, in some provinces, foreign affairs. Assemblies elected by a dual process, in which male voters qualified by education or ownership of property chose an electoral body which in turn elected the assembly, existed in every province. Usually the members were amenable to executive orders, but in some provinces, as we noted earlier, genuine efforts were made by liberal legislators to set up constitutions that would assure the assembly's independence. In the districts the *hsien chang* was usually the counterpart of his traditional predecessors; in a few instances men trained in modern law and selected under the new civil service regulations held district magistracies. The towns and villages remained under the benign paternalism of the elders. The guilds continued to exercise their unofficial influence. Upon the humble rank and file the sun rose and set as usual. The *tipao* still struck the night hours on the gong hung outside the village hall. If, however, the localities were not greatly disrupted by the civil anarchy, neither were their people aided by its promoters to rise to higher standards of health, education, and economic welfare. They failed to reap the benefits which would naturally have been given primary consideration by an enlightened Republican administration.

The question often was raised: were the young Chinese who entered official careers endeavoring to practice the teachings of reform which they had received in their own and in missionary colleges, or were they falling into the old ways of nepotism, graft, and militarism? It was too early to discern a clear trend. Young China as yet held few important posts. It was still in a minority in even the lower ranks of the civil service. But it was rebellious against the militarists and their civilian co-conspirators, resorting at times to attacks upon cabinet offices. Students took an extraordinary interest in politics and felt a strong sense of responsibility. The great majority of them were supporters of Sun Yat-sen while he lived. It remained to be seen what would result when they were able to take over the conduct of affairs.

Foreign Aid to Tuchunism

Foreign governments and bankers fished in the troubled waters, seemingly unaware of the dangers this interference meant to the liberal movement. They maneuvered with the leaders of the reaction for railway, mining, industrial, and other concessions. The Germans encouraged General Chang Hsün in his attempted restoration of the Manchus. The Japanese loaned large sums to Peking. A consortium of American and European banking groups sought but failed to make loans under terms restrictive of Chinese sovereignty. Sun Yat-sen, on the other hand, was unable to get funds from foreign powers and his regime at Canton was regarded as an insurgency against the legitimate government at Peking. China entered World War I and aided in the allied victory. At the peace conference which followed, however, her claims for revision of the unequal treaties of the nineteenth century and the return of leased territories held by the powers were rejected. Germany had been forced to surrender her treaty position, but Russia, where czarism had fallen, was the only great power to make voluntary offers of equality. Not until World War II did China regain full standing in the international community.

Westernizers in the Business World

Timidly and spasmodically, two influences were being brought to bear upon China's political chaos. One was economic, the other educational. The voices of progressive Chinese businessmen were being raised against the interruption of transportation, the stalling of trade, the commandeering of farm products, the misuse of public funds, and the general demoralization of the country's political organization. These men had grasped the Western conceptions of quantity production, scientific research and methods, and strict business principles. They were slowly organizing a revolt of the bourgeoisie against militarism and officialism. They were organizing chambers of commerce in the principal cities, which addressed plain warnings to the tuchün. They had the power to refuse funds and to stop the wheels of industry. At the opposite end of the economic scale the lowly coolie was beginning to exhibit discontent with his desperate hand-to-mouth existence. The labor agitator was at work among the sailors and dockworkers, the ricksha men, and the factory hands. The Yangtze valley had become a prey to strikes which had regularly been won by the strikers. The government was frightened by the success of this procedure, so new to China, and attempted to crush it with gunfire. The over-supply of unskilled labor left small fighting margin to the workers unless new political leadership came to their support. Whether or not a combination of capital, proletariat, and peasantry would develop as an effective force for political reform would depend upon the foresight exercised in fostering the infant industrial revolution. It would be fortunate for China if this development was gradual. Otherwise the progress of industry might, one feared, by throwing great numbers of craftsmen out of work in their small shops and homes, cause them to combat the capitalist rather than combine with him to bring about political reform. The dissolution of the tuchunal armies which were giving a bare living to hundreds of thousands would throw the troops into the already-glutted labor market. On the other hand, Chinese workers were mobile and would go to new factory locations if properly directed and humanely treated. One business leader, H. Y. Moh, proudly boasted that he had never had a strike in his factories because he had always considered the interests of his men. An important field of research in industrial relations awaited the immediate attention of students and industrialists, one that demanded that the danger of social revolution latent in the situation be recognized. Unhappily, but not surprisingly, revolution outsped reform.

The Literary Renaissance

The era of military politics was discordant with the ideals of liberal leadership of the Republican movement. In harmony with those ideals was the contemporary literary, philosophical, and historical revolution, often described as a renaissance, "new thought movement," or "new culture movement." Its conscious purposes were, in the literary sphere, to do away with classical restrictions and to create a living vernacular literature; in other words, to encourage the writing of literature in the spoken language. In philosophy the movement centered in discussion of the relative values of science and metaphysics — whether man's actions were determined by forces outside himself or by his own will. In historical research the movement examined the classical writings: were they products of the imagination or were they based on evidence? Previously it had been accepted that Chinese history went back five thousand years; the critical work of the investigators reduced this to three thousand. Moreover, the writings accepted as historical by the investigators were treated not as sacred revelations but as the work of profound thinkers who, mere human beings, were not divinely inspired and not above criticism.

The recognized leader of the movement was Hu Shih, who had received his doctorate of philosophy at Columbia University and was a member of the faculty of Peking University. An early colleague in sparking reformist challenges was Ch'en Tu-hsiu, who had studied in France. Together they founded the magazine *La Jeunesse* which exercised tremendous influence upon Chinese students and upon the subsequent development of thought, literature, and politics. Thus did a distinguished body of intellectuals flourish in the midst of the period's semi-feudalism. We may regard them as the progenitors of a new China, the builders of the foundation of modernism according to a thoroughly scientific blueprint. Their work was not hindered by the warlords to whom their ideas seemed, apparently, neither practical nor ominous. But those ideas appealed to the people, who wanted to be able to read and to have their children educated. Though illiterate, the people were not uncultured. The reformist ideas also endangered the imperialistic position of the great powers, whose many sorts of control were attacked by the able protagonists of reform. Professional and business circles felt the influence of the movement and many of their members encouraged its leaders. Western educators felt warm sympathy for the movement and many took part in it as visiting professors and advisers.

In general, the leaders of this renaissance advocated democracy and urged that the democratic powers act upon their doctrine of self-determination of all peoples by releasing China from the unequal treaties and returning to her sovereignty areas held under lease as well as others that had been forcibly seized as foreign residential concessions. They insisted upon an end to foreign administration of the customs service, the salt gabelle, certain railways, and other public organs. Few of the intellectuals were attracted to communism, but a number of the ablest among them turned left when Communist Russia surrendered her treaty position. The majority of them were agnostic but not opposed to Christianity except as they criticized missionary schools for failing to provide up-to-date instruction in the physical sciences.

The period saw the simpler language of ordinary speech adopted by newspapers and magazines, and a considerable increase in the number of these vehicles of communication. A phonetic alphabet was devised and introduced into primary education. This did not displace the ideograms or characters to which the Chinese are devoted despite the huge obstacle they present to rapid extension of education. Undoubtedly the renaissance was more concerned to reach the middle classes than to hurry the progress of peasants' and laborers' education. An ancillary effort to choose about a thousand of the most frequently used characters, and to organize people's groups to teach them, had a limited success in a few localities. But China remains today hamstrung by her ponderous written language.

The Academia Sinica

A research institute, was established to work out methods of applying science to Chinese problems. Hitherto these problems, social and physical alike, had been approached by Western-educated teachers through Western books dealing with Western problems. With the support of funds provided out of Boxer Indemnity receipts, the institute flourished, with resulting benefit to the universities. Their students became as critical of the traditional education, and of their teachers, as they were of corrupt politics. Increasingly they sought further learning in the United States, France, Great Britain, and Germany, as well as in Japan. Soviet Russia established in Moscow the Sun Yat-sen University for Chinese students. It attracted many, as nationalism mounted and the West dallied in its recognition of the necessity of moving from promises to action.

Regrettably, the progressive industrialists and intellectuals had little effect upon the warlords' program of greed, graft, and gunnery. The greatest misfortune suffered by the central government was the deprivation of essential revenues. Year after year Peking received only a small fraction of the receipts from taxes on land, its principal potential source, and from duties on interior trade, wine, and tobacco. Its only sure sources of funds were the foreign-administered customs, salt, and railway services; but these funds could not be applied to normal purposes since they were pledged to payment of loan charges. Tuchün temporarily in control of the central treasury even demanded "loans" to sustain their armies. The government was bankrupt, its civil servants and teachers went unpaid. Only by incurring debt at Chinese banks, which demanded usurious interest, was it able to maintain itself.

REVIVAL OF THE KUOMINTANG

THE Kuomintang lost its fight to establish a parliamentary republic. But the party was not destroyed. New life was breathed into it by the university professors and students, by the progressive business leaders, and even by a few military governors, mainly from southern provinces which had been longer in touch with the West. Sun Yat-sen, up to the time of his death in 1925, kept the headship of the party and never ceased his efforts to rejuvenate it. A strong stimulant to its rebirth was China's unhappy experience in foreign relations. Both the Versailles Conference following World War I and the Washington Conference of 1921–1922 were deeply disappointing to China in that neither had seriously considered her demands that her unequal treaties be abrogated. Japan's aggressive program in Shantung province had been checked, but she was succeeding in Manchuria. The Chinese felt humiliated. The revival of the Kuomintang was, like its origin, a movement against bad internal administration and foreign controls. The Soviet Union took advantage of this opportunity to offer aid, and its offer was accepted. It is important to note that the Kuomintang owed much, in its reorganization and methods of operation, to the Comintern, the international arm of Russian communism.

The Program of Reform

The event which heralded revival was the Reorganization Conference, held at Canton in January, 1924. It was attended by delegates from all parts of the country, and was provided with agenda prepared by the party's central executive committee. Dr. Sun urged that factionalism be put aside and that the interests of the party be given prime consideration. A long statement of the party's program in domestic and foreign relations emanated from the conference. This program, essentially a formulation of Sun's Three Principles of the People and of his ideas on government, put forth as its only socialistic provision the requirement that monopolistic business enterprises be publicly owned. Otherwise it was a moderate program, embodying educational reform, protection of labor and the peasantry, civil rights, equality of the sexes, limitation of taxes, universal suffrage, development of natural resources, proper division of revenue between the central and local administrations, and other progressive measures.

In foreign affairs, the party stood for an end to unequal treaties, payment of loans other than those contracted for the self-enrichment of militarists, and most-favored-nation treatment for states willing to enter into new, equal treaties. No alliance with Russia was contemplated, although a loan of three million rubles was accepted to aid in establishing the Whampoa military academy. In 1923 Sun and a Soviet emissary, Alexander Joffe, had issued a joint statement of cooperation, and two Russian advisers, Michael Borodin and General Galen, had come to Canton, the former an expert propagandist, the latter a capable military instructor. These arrangements were not regarded by Kuomintang leaders as committing the party to communism, but as the only recourse open to them in their determination to free the country from the militarist leeches. The party leaders varied in their position along the political spectrum but none of them was a Communist and the majority were distinctly conservative. Although Chinese Communists were admitted into the Kuomintang, this was done on condition that they accepted the tenets of the Kuomintang. When they subsequently failed to respect this condition, they were expelled.

Party Reorganization

The Kuomintang was, however, reorganized along Soviet lines. Locals similar to Communist cells were set up by party organizers, and pamphlets advocating the desired reforms were distributed lavishly. The locals elected delegates to a national party congress, which elected a central committee empowered to act for the party. This committee chose a political council or politburo, the dominant policy group. The government set up at Canton in 1925 also followed the Soviet model. By then Sun Yat-sen was dead. His mantle of leadership was sought by a half-dozen men of long membership in the party: the principal contenders were Wang Ch'ing-wei, one of the earliest revolutionists, an orator and poet, and Chiang Kai-shek, head of the new army which had been trained at the Whampoa academy along Russian lines. Although Wang was the more radical, the Soviet adviser Borodin favored Chiang, who had visited Moscow to observe military training methods, because of his military ability. Even though a professed disciple of Sun Yat-sen, he was at heart a conservative who distrusted association with the Comintern but accepted it as the means of furthering the Kuomintang's program for regaining the central power. He became head of the party by virtue of his military command and Borodin's support. His sudden rise was resented by many Kuomintang leaders, because his position in earlier years had been unimportant, he was not well-liked, and he had no standing as a thinker or a politician. Had not the first business of the revised party been the undertaking of a military campaign it is quite unlikely that he would have gained party headship at the time.

The Kuomintang Takes to Arms

In July, 1926, the campaign northward got under way. It was aided greatly by the peasants' belief in the propaganda being spread by the army's stump speakers. This credulity assured the troops of food, information, conscripts, and equipment. The propaganda promised land and encouraged forcible seizure of land records, attacks on landowners, and the tearing up of boundary posts. Landowners fled for their lives and tenants took over their property. Foreign missionaries also were driven out and a few were killed. Obviously, these measures did not reflect the Kuomintang's policy, least of all the attitude of Chiang Kai-shek. They were, however, a part of the reckless nationalist reaction stimulated by Soviet propaganda and exhibited during the period in outbreaks at Shanghai, at Canton, and along the Yangtsze River, where foreign shipping was subjected to gunfire. At Nanking missionaries were hunted down, three were killed, and many foreigners were saved only by the presence of foreign gunboats which opened fire upon forces threatening a Standard Oil compound in which they had taken refuge.

The Hankow Junta

For the campaign the forces were divided. Those on the western flank took Hankow in October, 1926, and the Kuomintang moved its government from Canton to Hankow. The leaders there did not include Chiang Kai-shek, who was engaged in military operations in central and eastern portions of the Yangtsze valley. The Hankow group was a mixture of political attitudes but its general orientation was to the left of Chiang's ideas. Its preference was that Wang Ch'ing-wei should head the party and that the announced program of social reform should be pursued vigorously. When it attempted to read Chiang out of the party its rightist elements, who were militarily the stronger, forced the leftists out and sent Borodin back to Moscow. A test of strength between the remaining Hankow militarists and Chiang resulted in victory for Chiang. He was aided by three important groups: a strongly anti-Communist element composed of elderly scholars, a number of generals of semi-tuchunal character who had been associated with the revolution in its early stages, and a committee of bankers and businessmen of the large cities of central and south China. A less reputable group, the so-called Ningpo gang, contributed funds and triggermen in return for concessions to engage in vice, selling drugs, and other venal operations. Chiang also had the sympathy of foreign countries fearful of the Kuomintang's radical wing. He got British assistance in subduing the laborers of Shanghai after they had driven out the old regime there and turned over the city to Chiang. Foreign gunboats on the Yangtsze guaranteed Chiang's forces against attacks along the lower reaches of the river. Such attacks emanated from surviving elements of the warlord era, whose large armies were not fully overcome until 1929.

Rival Elements at Nanking

Not until April, 1929, was Chiang Kai-shek able to unhorse the Hankow military regime. In the meantime he set up a government at

Nanking which received foreign recognition as the national government of all China. Before briefly analyzing the new structure it is desirable to scan the composition of the party and to note major developments in the struggle for dominance and unity. In October, 1928, the membership in the Kuomintang was 425,000, a mere one thousandth of the estimated population. Only a small proportion of the membership took part in activities, and these were divided into three factions or blocs: the right, left, and extreme left. There was no center bloc. The ablest and largest faction was that of the right. It was headed by Chiang Kai-shek and included the distinguished legal scholar Wang Ch'ung-hui, the financier and Harvard graduate T. V. Soong, the wealthy banker H. H. Kung, the able diplomat C. T. Wang, and Sun Fo, son of Sun Yat-sen. The left bloc was headed by Wang Ch'ing-wei and his Cantonese followers. Madam Sun Yat-sen led the extreme left; it had been paralyzed by the expulsion of Communists from the party and had lost influence and could not function openly. There were also a number of small groupings attached loosely to the party or existing precariously outside it. A few of the original Hankow regime held offices, in both the party and its government, but the majority of offices were filled by the rightists.

Repudiation of Reformism

As early as April, 1927, the Kuomintang repudiated the social program announced in 1924. The party was alarmed by the direct action taken by the peasantry to get land, and had begun to realize that this was the result of the interpretation placed upon the Kuomintang's gradualist reformism by Communist members. In its manifesto of 1927 the party declared:

The Revolutionary Party wishes to assure every Chinese of entire liberty of thought and action. It will not, therefore, admit a supergovernment under Borodin. It only admits a government of a liberated China enjoying a full measure of freedom.

It continued:

The Revolutionary Party wishes to emancipate the Chinese people as a whole, that is to say, all classes, including farmers, workers, merchants and soldiers. It does not wish that any one class dominate the others and particularly it does not wish a dictatorship of the proletariat. . . . Dr. Sun admitted the Communists into the Party as collaborators, and the Russians as friends. If the Communists wish to dominate us, and the Russians to ill-treat us, that means the end of their activity.

The confiscated properties were restored to their owners. In December, 1927, the Kuomintang expelled its Communist members.

Early in 1928 the party discarded its whole Soviet-inspired doctrine and methods of operation. It dissolved the local cells and its farmers', youths', and merchants' organizations. All the fiery slogans were prohibited, as were unauthorized mass meetings. Financial support was withdrawn from agricultural, educational, and industrial bodies, and measures for social reform were postponed. Emphasis was moved from social reform to social order and constitutionalism. By this abrupt shift the Kuomintang risked losing the mass support which had enabled it to win control of south and central China, the industrial heart of the country, with a population of some two hundred million. Madam Sun Yat-sen expressed her opinion that the party had repudiated Sun's ideas. She asked whether the revolution was to be merely political, declaring that the principle of the people's livelihood was being forgotten and that the laboring and peasant classes, the new pillars of a free China, were not being considered. She urged that party policies not be so changed as to turn from revolution to the support of the social structure which the party was formed to alter. She denied that the peasant and labor movement was a new product, alien to China, and she affirmed that Dr. Sun had held the uplifting of the masses to be the basis for social and economic transformation. To repudiate this ideal was to become the tool of the militarists. She warned the party that its future success depended upon its keeping to the revolutionary path. Her prophetic words went unheeded.

Chiang's Rise to Supremacy

Chiang Kai-shek was occupied after 1927 in consolidating his grip on the party and the country. In the former effort he was faced with dissent not only from Wang Ch'ing-wei and his radical but non-

Communist colleagues but from liberally-minded men in the conservative wing of the Kuomintang—such men as the eminent scholars
T'sai Yuan-p'ei and Wang Ch'ung-hui—who wished to proceed
along a truly constitutional path. Chiang professed to be a faithful
disciple of Sun Yat-sen but he was unacquainted with democracy,
primarily a soldier, and supremely self-confident. He did not hesitate
to criticize Wang for opposing party centralism nor to imprison Hu
Han-min, one of the most respected elders of the party. He took all
party and government posts of controlling importance for himself
and selected a majority of delegates to party congresses. The result
was that the Kuomintang became, in practice, an extremely conservative party in which Chiang and members willing to bow to his will
dictated policy and program.

Chiang's program gave high priority to disbanding the tuchunal
armies. This was unquestionably essential to the unification of the
country. But Chiang failed to discriminate among tuchün. He meas-
ured generals as he did politicians, by their degree of submissiveness
to his plans. Chiang owed the capture of Peking to the model governor, Yen Hsi-san of Shansi, whose forces drove out Chang Tso-lin in
1928. Another tuchun, Feng Yu-hsiang, the so-called Christian general, had aided also in suppressing warlordism in north China. Both
men were strong enough to insist on retaining their armies and their
provincial bailiwicks, but were not opposed to a Kuomintang central
regime. Both were older than Chiang and naturally resented his insistence upon the immediate disbanding of their armies. The upshot
was an alliance between them, and armed conflict. Chiang won, as he
won other contests with warlords reluctant to surrender their rich
provincial areas. But in doing so he expended great sums and neg-
lected to inaugurate measures of badly-needed reform. With less
haste he might have made more speed. While the maneuvering for
power continued, peasant forces were gathering to form the armies of
Mao Tse-tung. Japan was preparing to seize Manchuria. Precious
time was lost, to the ultimate humiliation of Chiang and the Kuomintang.

Could they have saved themselves by adopting other policies: land
and labor reform to assure popular allegiance; gradualism in the

treatment of the more liberal warlords? We cannot be certain of the answer. It is clear, however, that reliance upon force alone proved mistaken, since in politics the measure of correctness is success. One who argues that the Kuomintang dug its own grave can be charged with affecting wisdom after the event. But it would seem that the party threw away a great opportunity. It had envisaged that opportunity in 1924. Why did it lose the vision? "Where there is no vision, the people perish." So also do political parties and leaders.

Ironically, the Kuomintang was saved temporarily by the progressive son of a former bandit, Chang Tso-lin. General Chang Hsueh-liang, who succeeded his father as tuchun in Manchuria, declared himself opposed to the Yen Hsi-san–Feng Yu-hsiang clique, which had ventured to set up a rival government at Peking and had been joined by Wang Ch'ing-wei. The younger Chang marched his army to Peking, driving its ambitious pretenders out. Thus ended the fighting in north China. Chang pledged support to Chiang, bringing Peking into the orbit of the Kuomintang government. Chang Hsueh-liang remained the actual ruler of Manchuria but his collaboration with Chiang's government was given official color by his accepting the titles of chief administrator and defense commissioner of the area. Chang ran up the Nationalist flag there despite Japanese objections. He also was brought into the Nationalist Government as a member of the State Council.

The End of an Era

In late 1931 it could be said that the era of the warlords was over. Throughout all China the National Government at Nanking was recognized as the central power. The military cliques no longer threatened that power. It could not be said, however, that the country was unified in the sense that the authority of the central government was exercisable purely as a matter of law. Nanking could not appoint provincial governors solely on the basis of constitutional right. The political influence and the military forces of military holdovers had to be taken into account. In the southwestern provinces of Szechuan, Kweichow, and Yunnan, as in Manchuria, the mandate of Nanking did not run unless their governors — all military men — were in agreement with it. The central government's revenues were withheld unless the provincial governors were satisfied with the attitude of Nanking toward them, evidenced tangibly by non-interference in provincial matters and by grants of funds. The actual relationship was confederationist, not unitary. Only by the most careful attention to the sensibilities of its loosely affiliated allies could the new regime hope to survive. This situation in part explains the government's neglect of social reform and Chiang Kai-shek's show of favoritism in appointments toward sycophants he believed he could rely upon. It helps to explain his absorption of high offices himself and his adoption of a more and more dictatorial posture.

On October 4, 1928, a revised organic law, drawn up in accordance with the recommendations of Sun Yat-sen, was promulgated, and the 1927 regime was thus legalized by the Central Executive Committee of the Kuomintang. Nanking was chosen as the capital in preference to Peking as being further inland and less vulnerable to attack. Peking was renamed Peiping, meaning "northern peace." (Peking signifies "northern capital," Nanking "southern capital.") The rightist bloc dominated the Kuomintang machine, with Chiang Kai-shek at the controls. Yet the antagonism to him within the party was so strong that on the eve of the Japanese invasion of Manchuria he faced a military coalition of southern governors. The attack by Japan, in September, 1931, prompted the holding of a party conference in October, at which it was agreed that the powers of the President would be curtailed and the holder of the presidency would be barred from holding any concurrent posts. It was further agreed that Wang Ch'ing-wei should be premier and should exercise the executive power. Wang then came to Nanking. In a pretense of self-denial Chiang resigned from the presidency, a move designed to demonstrate that the government could not function without him. A new agency, the National Military Council, was established, with Chiang Kai-shek as chairman. With this post in Chiang's grasp both the presidency and the premiership were inferior offices. Wang Ch'ing-wei felt himself betrayed and resigned the premiership after a few months.

THE RISE OF COMMUNISM IN CHINA

COMMUNISM arose in China as a result of the success of the Bolshevist Revolution of 1917 in Russia. Before that success Chinese thinkers who were critical of Confucian and other classical doctrines had put their faith in Western democracy and science. The foremost among these intellectuals were Hu Shih, Li Ta-chao, and Ch'en Tu-hsiu, respectively professors of philosophy, history, and literature at the University of Peking, China's leading institution of learning. Originally their interest in communism was academic; Professor Li founded the Society for the Study of Marxism in 1918. Professor Hu Shih did not agree with his colleagues but remained a strong exponent of Western democratic ideals. Li and Ch'en did not lead the nationalist outburst against internal militarism, corruption, and great-power imperialism. This outburst began with student demonstrations on May 4, 1919. Li and Ch'en were drawn into the nationalist movement by the students, and were themselves led to consider communism as a recourse by the treatment of China's claims to revision of the unequal treaties at the Versailles and subsequent international conferences. Moreover, whereas Marx had advanced his historical materialism to attack capitalism in the West, Lenin added his thesis of the responsibility of finance capitalism for the sorry plight of China and other non-Western peoples. Many Chinese intellectuals came to believe that the democratic route to independence and modernism was too gradual, that the Communist way was preferable because it was faster. Like Sun Yat-sen in his advocacy of a republic they overlooked the history of democracy and the obstacles to be overcome at the grass roots. Thus it was that they adopted the Leninist expansion of Marxism. We may note here that the young Mao Tse-tung was an assistant to Professor Li and a member of the Society for the Study of Marxism.

Organization of the Party

In 1921 the Chinese Communist party was organized in Shanghai, and in 1922 it was formally inaugurated at Canton. Propaganda was directed first at the coolies in cities. Many young Chinese students went to Moscow, where, as we have seen, a school had been established for them named the Sun Yat-sen University. They returned to China to play a leading role in the propaganda campaign which so notably aided the military campaign of 1926–1927. From Moscow came Alexander Joffe to confer with Sun Yat-sen, who had not joined the new party but, as we have noted earlier, had become discouraged that the Republic could succeed without help which the democracies had refused. Joffe and Sun issued the following statement in 1923:

Dr. Sun Yat-sen holds that Communism or even the Soviet system cannot actually be introduced into China, because there do not exist here the conditions for the successful establishment of either Communism or Sovietism. This view is entirely shared by M. Joffe, who is further of the opinion that China's paramount and most pressing problem is to achieve national unification and attain national independence; regarding this great task he has assured Dr. Sun that China has the warmest sympathy of Russia.

This statement was the basis of an entente between the Comintern — the Communist International — and the Kuomintang. Though not a joint manifesto with the Chinese Communist party, it had the effect of an alliance with that party after the Kuomintang accepted Chinese Communists to membership. Under it Russia sent Borodin and Galen to Canton and provided aid in funds and arms.

From Reformism to Communism

Ch'en Tu-hsiu became chairman of the Chinese Communist party. Students formed the active element in it. They devoted themselves to organizing labor unions and to promoting the choice of converts to communism as union leaders. At this early stage Ch'en and his colleagues were primarily interested in basic social betterment in a country where men, women, and children worked long hours at low wages and under conditions not fit for cattle. They were not yet embarked upon the totalitarian path; indeed they appeared not to be animated by the Leninist concept of the necessity of absolute obedience to party directives and of iron discipline in the ranks. Although they had disowned Confucius, their thinking was similar to his central thesis — that society would be rectified through virtuous leadership. They were urged by Lenin and other Comintern leaders in Moscow to affiliate with the Kuomintang and its bourgeois capitalist supporters, lest the young movement be crushed at birth. To many Chinese Communists this proposal seemed a repudiation of the doctrine of the identification of the Communist party with the proletariat. This it certainly was. The thought behind it in Moscow was that ends justify means, that theory must yield temporarily to hard facts, and that there was reason to hope that the Communists eventually might take over the Kuomintang. As we already know, the Chinese Communists did enter the Kuomintang as individuals but retained their own party, called in Chinese the *Kungch'antang*. The affiliation was profoundly influential but brief, coming to an end in 1927. We have already (pp. 62–64) traced the major aspects of the military campaign of 1926–1927 and the consequent establishment of the National Government at Nanking. With this success the Kuomintang reverted to its strong anti-Communist stand.

The Agrarian Factor

We need not here attempt to go into the controversies of the collaborationist period among the Chinese Communist leaders on the one hand and between them and Moscow on the other. These controversies are as clearly sketched as our sources permit by Benjamin Schwartz in his *Chinese Communism and the Rise of Mao*, Chapter IV. We should note, however, that it was during this period that Mao Tse-tung diverged from the party line of emphasis upon the organization of the urban laborers to emphasis upon the organization of the peasantry. It is important to realize that the Chinese peasants' discontent antedated the Russian revolution by many years. It is erroneous to maintain, as so many casual observers have, that the Chinese peasantry was stirred to revolt by the Bolshevists. The peasants' feeling was the powder in the high explosive shell, to which Communist agitation and the Kuomintang's promises added the firing mechanism, the detonator. Mao's home province, Hunan, in central China, has had a long record of peppery resistance to oppression. We have seen how violently its peasant associations and those of neighboring provinces responded to the propaganda for land reform. Their interest was personal, not nationalist or Communist. Mao, himself the son of a peasant, saw in the peasantry a tremendous potential for realizing the aim of the revolution: the overthrow of landlordism and militarism. In March, 1927, he called vigorously for the inclusion of this force among the revolutionary weapons. At that time he did not suggest the formation of peasant armies but underscored the economic power available in the peasants' attitude. Mao's urging that the peasantry be made the vanguard of the revolution fell on deaf ears both in Moscow and in the centers of Kuomintang control. But it was destined for acceptance after the Kuomintang expelled its Communist members, and when Mao's influence in the Chinese Communist party had increased. With his rise to greater prestige and the shift to the military struggle against the Kuomintang and the National Government began the third phase of the Chinese Communist movement. This phase continued for some ten years, from 1927 to 1937, and resulted in the establishment of a Communist regime at Yenan in the northwestern province of Shensi. It was modified, but not altered in its ultimate objective, by a period of quasi-collaboration with the National Government against the Japanese invaders. The final phase followed World War II and culminated in the transfer of the Communist capital to Peking in 1949.

Moscow's Mistake

It is apparent that in assuming the probability that a handful of Communists could take control of the extremely conservative Kuomintang, with its junta of seasoned politicians, its business and landed allies, its large army, and its collaborators in the foreign residential areas, Moscow exhibited either incredible ignorance of the Chinese complex of factors or comparative indifference to the fate of Chinese who undertook to carry through an impossible enterprise by methods of persuasion and economic reorganization. It is possible that if Sun Yat-sen had lived he might have been able to reconcile the two major elements and to have brought about a moderate reform program in which the Chinese Communist leaders would have accepted a place in a liberalized Kuomintang such as he had hoped to develop. This is unlikely but deserves consideration. Before the split in 1927 the Chinese Communists were seeking much the same ends as the more liberal wing of the Kuomintang: social and economic reform, abolition of political corruption and regional militarism, and termination of alien controls. It appeared possible that they might have repudiated the Soviet alliance, which had proved disastrous to them, in return for Sun's social program, which savored of socialism and contemplated a period of political tutelage, but which was aimed toward eventual democracy. For such a reasonable outcome, however, leadership was lacking. China was doomed to a generation of civil strife culminating in totalitarian communism.

Kuomintang Terrorism

Western peoples have been well provided with the record of terrorism of the Communists. We know far less of the brutalities, the massacres, and the imprisonments perpetrated by the Kuomintang and its former opponents, the tuchün, during the years that followed the breakdown of the Kuomintang-Communist collaborative campaign. No reliable figures are available but it is estimated that between 1928 and 1932 more than a million revolutionaries were killed.[1] Indescribable methods of torture were used to elicit information. Young people who had taken part in the propaganda work sanctioned by the Kuomintang were hunted down and butchered, often without trial. Many who sought asylum in the International Settlement and the French Concession of Shanghai were handed over to Chiang Kai-shek for execution. According to the *China Forum*:

The Terror extended to every village, town, city and industrial district. The gates of towns and cities were closed and soldiers turned loose on the population. The soldiers looted, raped, left the streets littered with corpses and the wells clogged with the bodies of outraged girls and women. . . . In Canton, on December 11, 1927,

[1] Figures given were published in *Five Years of Kuomintang Reaction*, reprinted in May, 1932, from the *China Forum*, a newspaper in Shanghai, edited by an American, Harold R. Isaacs.

workers, peasants and revolutionary intellectuals made a desperate attempt to save the revolution and call a halt to the savagery. With comparatively little bloodshed they captured power and established the Canton Commune. Two days later the victory of the White troops, said to have been aided by foreign gunboats, turned Canton into a slaughter pen. In one day alone 3000 men and women were mown down by machine guns, and altogether 5700 workers, soldiers and citizens killed by methods not only of shooting but by being hacked to pieces, disembowelled, burning to death. . . . During this period the British police of Hong Kong searched all ships of refugees from Canton, arrested and deported to certain butchery hundreds of workers and peasants.

Urban Workers Subdued

The tactics of terror succeeded in the cities. The workers turned away from Communist leadership and returned to their more moderate program of reforming working conditions, hours, and wages. This shift did not save them from further persecution as strikes continued and unionism progressed, but it deprived the Communist leaders of mass action in urban centers. Moscow, now dominated by Stalin, was slow to accept the idea that its doctrine of the necessity of urban proletarian leadership to the success of a Communist revolt might not apply in China. It continued to discount the peasantry as a suitable advance force for the struggle. Stalin laid the collapse of the alliance with the Kuomintang at the door of Ch'en Tu-hsiu, and maneuvered to replace him with others, of whom the major figures were another intellectual, Ch'u Ch'iu-pai, and a Moscow-trained labor organizer, Li Li-san. Chou En-lai, a likable publicist destined to rise to the premiership, worked closely with Li Li-san. But these three failed to stimulate the urban unions to venture again to pit their weakness in arms against the Kuomintang armies. With their failure the weight of the revolutionary task fell upon the peasantry, under the leadership of Mao Tse-tung. In 1927 Mao was thirty-four years old.

Mao Tse-tung Takes Over

During the period 1927–1931 Chiang Kai-shek was occupied with consolidating the Kuomintang regime at Nanking. These same years were utilized by Mao Tse-tung and other Communist advocates of

reliance upon the peasantry to organize soviets in a half dozen provinces of central and southern China. Late in 1931 a provisional central junta set itself up at Juikin in southern Kiangsi. These units were
under constant attack but were aided by the mountainous terrain.
The nucleus of their military strength was composed of elements of
the Nationalist armies which separated from them when Chiang
broke with the Kungch'antang, the Chinese Communist party. Peasant recruits swelled the forces to a hundred thousand men. They were
attracted to join by gifts of land confiscated from large estates. Their
prospects of success in their program of outright determination to
displace the National Government seemed forlorn, since they faced
a combination of military power, wealth, warlord control of provinces not yet brought within the Nationalist orbit, and foreign apprehension. Their sole reliance was the peasantry. Yet from the outset
of Chiang's military effort to destroy them, their tactics of guerilla —
hit-and-run — fighting, coupled with a desperate disregard for personal safety that was new among Chinese soldiers, frustrated Chiang's commanders. Not until he brought airplanes into his campaigns
were the Communists forced to flee from Kiangsi. In October, 1934,
they began their Long March westward and northward, fighting their
way for six thousand miles through twelve provinces and over eighteen mountain ranges. In October, 1935, the remnant reached Yenan
in the province of Shensi. Of the ninety thousand who had begun the
trek only twenty thousand reached Yenan.

There they found an autonomous regime which had arisen out of
the warlord era and was in control of a border region comprising
parts of the three provinces of Shensi, Kansu, and Ninghsia. Its ruling
members included landlords, scholars, small farmers, and Communists. The last-named were a minority of the regional council and administrative staff. This regime recognized the Nanking government
as the central authority but asserted autonomy within the border region. With the arrival of Mao Tse-tung, chairmanship of the regional
organization passed to him. Nanking refused to recognize the area as
autonomous, but Mao's authority gradually expanded over other
north China regions in which guerrilla regimes had been established.
Eventually this trend of expansion extended to central and south

China, and armies were recruited under regional commanders who looked to Yenan for directives. An estimated population of eighty-six million thus came to fall within the Communist sphere of control, though nominally subject to Nanking. Obviously this nibbling at the central power could hardly have occurred but for the war with Japan. The Communist forces played a strenuous part in resisting the Japanese but gained assurance thereby and were able to win popular support throughout north China. At the end of the war they were in a position to challenge the National Government. Out of that challenge civil war erupted, with consequences that surprised and shocked the Western world.

Dialectic Defeated

To recapitulate: Chinese communism, like Chinese democracy, was an offshoot of nationalism, which had originally been stimulated by Woodrow Wilson's eloquent support of the principle of the self-determination of nations. Communism was, like democracy, a concept imported from the West. It was resorted to after the failure of the first Republic, which was also based upon Western ideals, and after the failure of the second Republic to carry into effect its promised program of economic and social reforms. The intellectuals who envisaged Marxism as a persuasive ingredient capable of vitalizing Chinese reformism by the strength of its dialectic failed, as had Sun Yat-sen, to appreciate the residual vigor of conservative forces. In the beginning the Communist movement resembled early republicanism. Both movements, as intellectual ideologies, sought to move too rapidly into a new era of political independence and social dignity. Both sought to achieve in decades what Western democracies have struggled for centuries to attain. Not until military power was allied with ideology in sufficient strength to overwhelm existent opposition to revolutionary change did it become possible for communism to reach its first plateau. We have now to consider the struggle between the Nationalists and the Communists and the evidence as to the sincerity of Communist promises to the people of China.

THE NATIONAL GOVERNMENT OF
THE KUOMINTANG

THE National Government installed at Nanking in 1927 provided itself with an Organic Law or constitution in 1928. Between that date and 1949, when the Communist triumph forced the Nationalists' evacuation to Taiwan (Formosa), some eleven revisions of the basic law were promulgated. These were of minor significance until the revision of 1936, which was an essentially new document. The constitution of 1936, in revised form, was promulgated in late 1947, though completed in 1946 (see appendix). Thus it may be said that the system formalized in 1928 was in legal operation for some twenty years. We turn our attention now to that system.

The National Government was modeled upon the Soviet system. Like that system it was organized for control by a single political party, though in political and economic ideology the Kuomintang was at the opposite pole from the Communist party of the U.S.S.R. The National Government differed from the Soviet system in that it embodied the principle of five powers or branches advocated by Sun Yat-sen. No pretense was made to parliamentarism, which was believed unsuited to China. Yet the Nanking structure included a legislative branch; it did not, in form, provide for rule by executive decree. Although often criticized as a Kuomintang dictatorship, and called by other disparaging titles, it was in legal form equipped to check executive arbitrariness. In theory it was an elite leadership for a period of tutelage, during which the people would be instructed in knowledge vital to responsible citizenship, as Sun Yat-sen had laid down.

Organization of the Kuomintang

The central components of the Kuomintang, the party organization, were a national congress, a central executive committee, and a central supervisory committee. For each province, district (*hsien*), and locality (*chü*), there were corresponding congresses and committees, as in the U.S.S.R. By its constitution the party designated the national congress its supreme body while in session. When the congress was not in session the supreme power rested in the central executive committee. The central supervisory committee was authorized to audit party finances and to censure misconduct. Both national committees were elected by the national congress. Within the C.E.C. a standing committee exercised its functions when so authorized. In practice the standing committee or politburo ruled the party except when the party Leader bypassed it.

The position of party Leader (Tsung t'sai) was not provided for at the inception of the National Government. Dr. Sun Yat-sen had held a similar position and he continued to be regarded as Leader after his death. His title as Leader was Tsung li, which title is still dedicated to him. Not until 1938 was the variant Tsung ts'ai accorded to Chiang Kai-shek. By amending the party constitution to confer this title the party also altered the power status of the C.E.C. and the politburo. This was the consequence of the fact that the Leader was empowered to make final decisions, and even to ignore the decisions of the national congress of the party. Whether or not this arrangement carried with it the establishment of a one-man dictatorship depended upon the continuance of the power of the congress to determine the future status of the Leader. Presumably the congress could do so, yet the Leader's power to suspend the congress's decisions, coupled with the fact that it has not attempted to exercise such power, leaves the issue in doubt. In practice Chiang's attitude toward the position and his possession of military command have made the issue academic. In practice he has been a dictator of party policy. Since Kuomintang policy has been government policy, he has also been a dictator in government.

Democratic Centralism

The party constitution embodied the democratic principle of election of the national congress by the provincial congresses and of provincial and district congresses by the congresses of the next lower echelon; the local congresses were to be elected by members of the party in their respective localities. In each echelon elections were to be held at stated intervals, and elected members were to be free to express their opinions and to select their committees. Under the adopted Soviet principle of democratic centralism the views of the lower-echelon bodies passed upward to the national congress which made the final decisions. Once these were made known they were not subject to question. In practice the C.E.C., the politburo, and the Leader did not fully respect the constitutional provisions. In their anxiety to control decisions, they manipulated the selection of provincial committees and their selection of members of the national congress. As Professor Ch'ien Tuan-sheng phrases the resultant system in his outstanding book *The Government and Politics of China*, "There has been plenty of centralism but little democracy" (p. 123).

The "supreme power" of the national congress of the Kuomintang amounted in fact to little more than the right to discuss matters brought before it. It was a body of several hundred members which met but six times in twenty years though constitutionally entitled to convene biennially. Its membership was at times appointed, at other times elected under the direction of the C.E.C. Its influence was negligible. The effect of this emasculation was to dampen the interest and faith of the most capable element in the party membership, the young college graduates. Failure to maintain the enthusiasm of this element, which played so important a part in the revival of the Kuomintang, greatly weakened the party. It tended to turn these able young people into malcontents who sought other outlets for their reformist ambition and their political careers.

Party Administration

The major agencies for administration of the party's work as a party were the organization department and the training commission. The former was charged with recruiting members, maintaining membership files in which members' records were meticulously kept with the aid of a secret service, and organizing party branches. Applications for membership were carefully scrutinized and expulsions were numerous. In comparison with the population, Kuomintang membership was not large, never exceeding four million. The organization department was headed by two extremely conservative politicians, the brothers Ch'en Li-fu and Ch'en Kuo-fu, whose screening methods kept out progressive youth. The training commission was intended as a tutelage agency in party procedures and popular participation in politics. Had this agency carried out Sun Yat-sen's program of teaching the people the essentials of democracy it might have justified itself and its superiors. We must grant that this program was highly idealistic in view of general illiteracy. But in fact the commission was hamstrung by the indifference of the Leader and the C.E.C. to its work and their concentration upon furthering their own monopoly of power.

Between the agencies of the Kuomintang and the organs of the National Government was the central political council or C.P.C. Apparently this body was intended by Dr. Sun as a counseling board, independent of both the party and the government and responsible only to himself. In its development it became a committee of the central executive committee, and a channel to convey C.E.C. decisions to the government. The majority of its membership, which varied from time to time, were also members of the C.E.C. It afforded opportunity to give positions to persons not otherwise honored. During World War II it was replaced by a supreme defense council but subsequently it was reinstituted.

Favoritism by the Leader

We must take notice of the existence of three groups composed of persons who enjoyed the special favor of Chiang Kai-shek on the basis of his confidence in their unswerving devotion to him. These were the misnamed political study group, the army group, and the organization group. The least powerful of these factions, all of which were composed of Kuomintang members, was the political study group. Its members were not scholars but businessmen, whose interest and influence were largely in provincial and local opportunities for control. The army faction dominated the party's agencies and members in the military services. Its members regarded themselves as the true representatives of party objectives. Favoritism toward them tended to weaken the army by putting incompetents in the higher offices. The organization faction, as already noted, monopolized control of civilian membership and organization. The factions did not recognize each other's sphere of influence but were in constant strife to extend their activities into any situation. Chiang Kai-shek played them against one another to his own advantage.

In the hope of cleansing the Kuomintang of corruption and inertia Chiang Kai-shek established a youth corps. Unfortunately, this excellent idea was not given the support required for its successful implementation. Instead of upholding leadership by educators, and encouraging youthful members in their natural critical liberalism, Chiang permitted the control of the youth corps to fall into the hands of the army group above-mentioned. Result: the corps lost its creative members and became a copy of the decadent Kuomintang.

The Conduct of Government

We turn now to the structure and operation of the National Government. Although there was much interference with governmental organs by organs of the Kuomintang, which parallel the pyramid of government, the government existed under its own organic laws. Our treatment presents it as it operated during most of the period from 1928 to 1948, omitting minor and temporary departures from the normal situation.

At the apex of the governmental pyramid was the State Council, elected by the C.E.C. of the Kuomintang, which also designated its chairman. The chairman was not president of China — there was no president of China — but was termed president of the National Government. All members of the Council were members of the Kuomintang. In theory, the Council was the supreme organ, determining policy, approving legislation, determining the budget, making appointments to major offices, and controlling even the armed forces. The president had no independent powers but exercised influence as chairman of the Council. But in practice, save during periods when Chiang Kai-shek occupied the presidency, the Council was principally an honorary body of negligible significance. During such periods it largely reflected the desires of the president, the Leader of the

Kuomintang. However, an elderly gentleman named Lin Sen, who was President from 1931 to 1943, was highly respected and sagacious. He kept the Council in good countenance despite its lack of authority.

The Five Yuan

Under the Council were five *yuan* or branches of government: executive, legislative, judicial, examination, and control. Of these the executive yuan was the most powerful, though it was often subjected to interference by the high organs of the Kuomintang. In nature it was a cabinet. Its president, like the presidents of the other yuan, was chosen by the C.E.C. He appointed and dismissed the ministers and commission heads, subject to party approval. With the president of the yuan these officers composed a council for discussion and the formulation of policy. The ministers and commissioners were subordinate to the president of the yuan; their positions were secretarial rather than political. Individual ministers varied in influence according to their standing in the Kuomintang. In relation to the formally superior State Council, the executive yuan enjoyed greater authority except when Chiang Kai-shek was chairman of the State Council. When he occupied the presidency of the executive yuan it was dominated by him. It is important to note that while in theory both the Kuomintang and the governmental system were designed to prevent dictatorship by any individual through the placement of power in committees and councils rather than in a president, premier, or department heads, in practice this design was defeated. Through his several political assets — the command of the military forces, the backing of men of wealth, the confidence of Western governments, and his personal qualities — Chiang Kai-shek became the man of the hour. He liked the title of Generalissimo, though he did not assume it formally. China needed a strong man. She had found him in Chiang Kai-shek. But China needed also a man who would apply his strength not to personal advancement but to the amelioration of her people's distress. That Chiang was a patriot, that he coveted for China her due place among the nations, cannot be questioned. That he faced tremendous obstacles must be recognized. But his relish for power blinded him to opportunities to use able and honest men, and to conditions that could not be remedied unless such men were permitted to share power with him.

Kuomintang Control of Policy

As in Western governments, the administrative departments carried out the policies of the Leader and the ruling authorities in the party committees and the executive yuan. There were nine ministries: foreign affairs, military affairs, navy, interior, education, communications, railways, finance, and industries. Among nine commissions one dealt with Mongolian and Tibetan affairs, another with famine relief. Outside the executive yuan was the economic council, established to awaken interest in a variety of desirable projects. Also outside of it was the Academia Sinica (p. 59), in which excellent scholarly investigations were conducted. Ministers and heads of other administrative agencies controlled decisions insofar as they were not themselves controlled by the president of the yuan. As members of the yuan council, they attended meetings of that body and their signatures were required upon its published decisions.

The Military Commission

Before describing the other yuan it is essential that we note the true nature of control over military affairs. This control lay in the military commission, outside the executive yuan; it was headed by none other than Chiang Kai-shek. This agency somewhat resembled the combination of offices in Japan during the same period, termed collectively the supreme command. It afforded Chiang another official hat which he could put on in case ill winds should blow others from his head. It placed the ministries of military affairs and the navy in the confusing position of having two masters, and its huge complex of subordinate agencies was an expensive and wasteful duplication of many party and civilian services. It became, during the war with Japan, the real center of governmental authority, ruling out any semblance of civilian control. The effects of this departure from well-tried principles were diversion of funds from economic and social programs, jealousies among military factions, and inefficient administration by poorly qualified personnel. These fundamental errors were to result in the loss of popular confidence and support.

The Legislative Yuan

The legislative yuan was not a law-making body. Its members, normally eighty in number, were appointive, not elective, assuring their deference to the C.E.C. They were subordinate to the president of the yuan, and their accomplishments varied with the initiative and determination of the president. While the yuan was empowered to propose law bills, so were the other yuan and the central political council. In practice most legislation was initiated, as to substance, by that council, which sent its proposals to the legislative yuan for drafting. Thus the legislative process was, in the main, one in which the political council, itself a committee of the C.E.C. of the Kuomintang, decided the principles to be enacted, leaving to the legislative yuan deliberation upon phraseology and engrossment. Although the yuan was, under the organic law, competent to reject a measure, it seldom ventured to do so, and such rejections could be nullified if the political council chose to resubmit the bill. The yuan also was frustrated by the ordinance power of the executive, which often moved into the legislative sphere. The yuan is entitled to credit for improvement of the technique of drafting legislation. But its lack of independence was an insuperable bar to the exercise of legislative power.

The People's Political Council

The futility of the legislative yuan in the face of the government's difficulties prompted demands for a consultative assembly. The demands did not envisage a true parliament. What was sought was a body representative of the country, which might assist the government in its time of crisis. After years of procrastination the People's Political Council was brought into being in 1938. It endured for ten years, during which it was convened four times. Membership varied from 200 in the first session to 362 in the final one. The Council was discontinued when the constitution of 1947 was adopted, providing for a national assembly.

Representation was wide, including Outer Mongolia and Tibet and overseas Chinese as well as the provinces, and distinguished leaders in the professions and in business. Members were elected through a double process of nomination and selection in which the Kuomintang's C.E.C. played a determining role. Superficially, the rules governing elections barred Kuomintang control of the Council by prohibiting election to it of members of the high committees of the party, the C.E.C. and the C.S.C., but presiding officers were selected by the C.E.C., and Kuomintang control over elections assured large representation of the party. However, it could not be said that the Council was a mere platform for persuasive rhetoric about governmental policies. Many of its members were highly critical and not a few were competent in expression. The ministers and other government officials were brought under heavy fire and numerous critical proposals were made. Since the Council had only advisory powers it could not legislate nor bring down the executive. It is impossible to estimate the significance of the Council's work. The opinions of Chinese political scientists vary. Undoubtedly it operated toward stimulation of administrative responsibility and the continued ideal of constitutional government. It afforded an opportunity for opposition parties to be heard. The government gained in knowledge of conditions and attitudes in remote areas, and the citizenry was encouraged to believe that its views were being considered. But for the Japanese attack and the subsequent breach between the government and the Communists, the Council might well have become a significant participant in policy-making.

The Judicial Yuan

The judicial yuan was of minor importance, its functions confined to supervision of the supreme court, the administrative court, and the disciplinary commission. At intervals the ministry of justice was placed within the judicial yuan but it normally was within the executive yuan. The latter thus had charge of the administration of justice in the courts below the supreme court, acting through the ministry of justice. The ministry of justice appointed the judges and procurators (prosecuting attorneys) of the provincial or high courts. Judges of the *hsien* (district) courts were appointed by the provincial governments.

As the supervisory functions of the judicial yuan were limited to the proposal of laws relating to its own organization, and to providing a frame for the judicial agencies within the yuan, our interest in it may be confined to those agencies.

The Courts

The supreme court was the highest court of appeal for both civil and criminal cases. China had comparatively few men well educated in her codes, which were based largely on up-to-date German codes, but there were enough such men to provide a competent supreme court. In addition to its exclusively appellate jurisdiction the supreme court was entrusted with standardizing the interpretation of laws and with advising the government on the exercise of the pardoning power. The high courts in the provinces heard major cases originally and minor cases on appeal from the district courts. As in imperial times much "peace-talking" was done outside the courts, usually by the elders in the villages and towns. To a considerable extent the district magistrates functioned as judges but in some of the *hsien* there were separate judges more or less qualified in the modern codes. The development of the courts was slow, as it depended upon the growth of a legal profession. On the whole, however, judicial administration improved during the period.

The administrative court was similar in jurisdiction to the administrative court of European states deriving their systems from Roman law. In China there were provincial as well as national courts for cases involving suits by private persons against officials. Cases could be brought in the event that petitioners felt that their complaints had received unsatisfactory treatment by administrative officials. The commission of disciplinary action dealt with impeachments of nonpolitical officials by the control yuan. Political officials were disciplined either by a committee of the National Government or by the C.E.C. of the Kuomintang following impeachment by the party supervisory committee. These hearings did not extend to criminal matters, which were heard in the ordinary courts. The record of the disciplinary agencies was far from impressive. With a single political party monopolizing power in any country, the misconduct of its leaders and civil servants is not likely to be advertised by disciplinary action.

The Control Yuan

The control yuan, organized along the same lines as the other four, was the agency of censorship of official conduct. Deriving its reason for being from the imperial censorate, it was an anachronism in a theoretically republican democracy. With the aid of regional commissions of control the yuan made a show of periodic inspections of administrative operations. It also investigated complaints by citizens against individual officials. Numerous complaints were received and a considerable proportion of them were investigated. However, neither the yuan members nor the regional commissioners were technically qualified for this difficult task. If impeachment was decided upon, the yuan had no power to mandamus the person impeached or to remove him. It was limited to bringing charges to the judicial yuan and to notifying the official's superior officer that charges were pending. It might, and often did, publicize the charges, a procedure as likely to ruin an innocent man as to force a guilty man's resignation. Fundamental among the weaknesses of the control process was the absence of any clear definition of impeachable offenses. Too often, in consequence, charges were ill founded. Personal dislike or rumors might prompt unjustifiable allegations. Confidence in the yuan was undermined, and the disciplinary commission in the judicial yuan often was impelled to discharge a complaint on grounds of insufficient evidence. On the basis of data now available, which are inadequate for a definitive judgment, it appears that the control yuan, though in general deserving of credit for a serious effort to ferret out illegal and neglectful administration, succeeded only in minor degree.

Within the control yuan was the ministry of audit. It was well staffed by competent, responsible officials. Their function was to audit government accounts, in which they were aided by provincial branches and others attached to public corporations. Their work was hampered by the absence of annual budgets and the exclusion of military expenditures from their purview, which included inspection of accounts and properties at any time.

The Examination Yuan

The examination yuan performed the functions of a civil service commission. Its equality with the other yuan, which differentiated it from the civil service commission in the United States, derived from the imperial system. It differed from the old system, however, in that it embodied in one yuan both the power of examination and the power to recommend candidates for office. These functions were performed by separate departments within the yuan: the examination commission and the personnel ministry. The former supervised the many boards of examiners set up throughout the country, appointed by the president of the yuan from among scholars, officials, and professional men. The latter dealt with appointing officers in the central and provincial governments, the districts, and the localities. Since, as in all the yuan, the president of the yuan held the power of decision, he controlled the determination of the subjects, questions and grading of examinations, the membership of examining boards, and the certification of successful candidates. He also controlled the appointments to the personnel ministry and the functioning of the ministry.

Examinations were required by law for candidates to both elective and appointive office. For the former they were made use of to verify such qualifications as age, residence, and freedom from liability to legal action. For appointive positions they were given on three levels — high, ordinary, and special. They closely resembled corresponding levels of university and school examinations. For examinees who passed a period of in-service training followed. Unfortunately this time was not served in a government department but in an institute of indoctrination for youth interested in party work. Able men were resentful of such treatment, while mediocre candidates found it helpful toward ingratiating themselves with Kuomintang leaders. Undoubtedly it was a major factor in discouraging university graduates from candidacy. The number of candidates was surprisingly inadequate, with the result that appointments were made much more extensively from the ranks of the untested than from successful examinees. This deficiency was offset to a notable degree by the traditional desire for education and respect for scholarship, which helped to stiffen the backbone of the National Government's bureaucracy.

Provincial Administration

We noted earlier that the Kuomintang, while reserving power for itself, attempted, with little success, to keep power out of the grasp of individuals by placing it formally in committees, councils, and yuan. The same principle was applied in the effort to reorganize provincial government. At the inception of the Nanking regime China's Middle Kingdom of eighteen provinces had increased to twenty-eight. The added ten were the three in Manchuria, Sinkiang, and the six new provinces which formed a cordon between the original Middle Kingdom and the territories of Outer Mongolia and Tibet. These six were Ninghsia, Sikang, Ch'inghai, Chahar, Suiyuan, and Jehol. The amount of central control varied but in theory China was a unitary state, not a federal system. The law called for "governments" of commission form, with seven to eleven members, appointed by the central government, which also designated which member should be chairman. The legal prohibition against military officers' holding the chairmanship was usually ignored in practice. In some provinces quasi-independent military men appointed the commission and took the chairmanship themselves. Normally there were four administrative departments: civil affairs, finance, education, and reconstruction. Provinces might also establish departments of industry and of agriculture. Each department was headed by a member of the commission. In addition the administrative structure included a police agency headed by the chairman of the commission. In practice this agency was staffed from the armed forces. Close liaison was maintained with provincial organs of the Kuomintang wherever local autonomy did not work to prevent it. The powers of the province were comprehensive but were exercised under the supervision of the central yuan. In provinces not controlled by the national authorities a semblance of unity was sought by the payment of subsidies.

Neglect of Tutelage

No provincial assemblies were set up during the two decades between 1928 and 1948. Executive ordinances took the place of legislative acts. This was an unfortunate discrepancy for a period of tutelage, when experience in political action should have been helpful.

The absence of assemblies reflected the Kuomintang's concept of their proper role, a major weakness which Sun Yat-sen had not fully understood. The provincial congresses of the party attempted to supervise the commissions, an attitude resented by the latter and in many provinces frustrated by the political and military dominance of the chairman of the commission. Even in provinces where Nanking's authority was recognized the provincial chairman's power was likely to resemble that of the former governors. The change was in form, not in fact. The provinces were essentially autonomous, as they had been under the empire.

Local Administration

Among the ten kinds of locality the district (*hsien*) continued to be the most important. In the main, it was subject in administration to the provincial government, but it also acted as a direct agent of the central government in performing certain functions, among them collecting taxes. The dominant official continued to be the district magistrate, who was aided by section and bureau chiefs in the performance of his manifold duties. In a few districts assemblies, elective by popular vote, were inaugurated but the development of assemblies was hindered by bureaucratic opposition and popular ignorance and indifference. Generally speaking the districts, like the provinces, remained mere administrative divisions, ruled by appointed officials. The same may be said of the cities, towns, and other localities. The situation could hardly have been otherwise in view of the people's lack of preparation for the political rights of citizenship.

Manchuria, Outer Mongolia, and Tibet

We need not study the government of Manchuria during its occupation by Japanese troops from late 1931 to 1945. Manchukuo, as this great area was named during the period, somewhat resembled Texas in the sense that it tended to exhibit a consciousness of itself. But the propaganda of the Japanese to the effect that it was because of this attitude autonomous was without substantial justification. The area gained greatly in economic development under the Japanese but its people remained loyal to China.

Over Mongolia the Manchu dynasty had exercised suzerainty, and the first Republic succeeded to the imperial relationship to the territory. Four provinces were created out of inner Mongolia: Chahar, Suiyuan, Ch'inghai, and Jehol. With Russian support, Outer Mongolia resisted integration into China and established a Republic under Russian protection in 1924. In all but name it became part of the Soviet state.

Tibet had also been under imperial Chinese suzerainty for many centuries when the Manchus were overthrown, and had accepted this status. But it resisted the effort of the first Republic to reduce it to the status of a province. With British support Tibet was able to maintain its autonomy until overwhelmed by Chinese Communist forces in 1951.

WAR-TIME PROBLEMS AND POLICY

THE National Government was engaged in controversies with Japan even before it was firmly in power at Nanking. Throughout its existence, civil and foreign war, at times hot, at other times cold, was endemic. If its record of economic, social, and political progress was not brilliant one must, in fairness, ask that judgment take account of war-time impediments to accomplishment. The period of twenty years — 1927–1947 — between the inauguration of the government and its establishment of formal constitutionalism may usefully be dealt with in two parts of ten years each. Our concern is not with the causes and course of the wars but with the problems engendered by them, the policies formulated, the progress made, and the ultimate demoralization of the Kuomintang and its political system.

Toward National Unity

Political unification was the watchword of Leader Chiang Kai-shek following the installation of the National Government. To a considerable degree this had been attained by 1930, as we have noted earlier. But to assure control of the country economic measures were called for. Basic was the need for railways and telecommunications lines. In 1927 China had but eight thousand miles of trunk railways, most of them in north China and Manchuria. During the first decade of the new administration the railway from Canton to Wuchang was completed, affording a rail route from the former city to Peking via ferry from Wuchang to Hankow. Another important line was built, with Dutch assistance, from Haichow on the east coast into the western province of Shensi. Fifty thousand miles of motor highways and a nation-wide network of telegraph and telephone lines were constructed before work was halted by the Japanese invasion in 1937. With German aid the principal cities were linked by airlines.

The development of heavy industries as government enterprises was begun, and private manufacturers of textiles, operators of silk filatures, and other industrialists were aided with higher tariffs, lower taxes, and scientific investigation of processes and markets. These constructive measures could not be carried to any significant point because of the sad state of the treasury. In 1934–1935, for example, tax revenues amounted to but $650,000,000 (Chinese currency). Between 1927 and 1933 internal borrowings, at high interest, exceeded $1,200,000,000. The situation was worsened by the necessity of devoting some three-fourths of national revenues to modernizing the army. This was seriously undertaken, with German, Italian, and American military officers as advisers.

The New Life Movement

The peasantry, urban workers, and the schools had to be content with propaganda urging them to devote themselves more vigorously to national reconstruction and the defeat of imperialism. We find much of this exhortation in *China's Destiny,* not written by Chiang Kai-shek but published under his name. Although Chiang sought to present his ideas as a disciple of Sun Yat-sen, to whose books he frequently referred, he also exalted traditional doctrine, quoting Confucius, Mencius, and others. Like the classical writers, and unlike Sun Yat-sen, Chiang did not dwell upon the wide gap that separated doctrine from practice, in regard to governmental obligations to cherish the people's welfare. We need not here repeat earlier references to the extremities to which the warlord era had driven the masses. Unhappily, conditions did not improve under the Kuomintang. Rather they became worse, as taxes fell more heavily upon the people and military conscription called away their youth. In place of the economic reforms promised in 1924 Chiang espoused the so-called New Life Movement. The people were enjoined to work harder and spend less, to refrain from spitting, to keep their shirts buttoned, and to respect the ethical tenets of their great sages. These injunctions fell as bitter irony upon people who were mixing willow bark with millet porridge to encourage their stomachs to feel fed. For them there was no meaning in Chiang's well-intended but unrealistic preaching, from which a few sentences may be cited. They are characteristic of his Jovian utterances:

The New Life Movement is the basic movement for social reconstruction, and its object is to modernize the Chinese people. . . . The most important items in its program are training for local self-government and planning for the people's recreation and education. . . .

In regard to local self-government . . . although the form of the Chinese state was monarchical, the spirit of government of and by the people prevailed. . . . Since the latter part of the Ch'ing dynasty, all thought has been based on foreign theories, and the fact that the rural districts and villages constitute the foundation of the state has been forgotten. . . . Success in reconstructing the rural districts and towns will ensure a healthy development of self-government. When local self-government is healthy it will serve as the basis for realizing the principles of democracy and the people's livelihood.[1]

After thus disparaging, by inference, the first Republic's effort to apply Western experience, and expressing the view that the way to self-government was, for China, the revival of ancient customs, Chiang appears not to believe that responsibility for social reform rests upon the central government. He writes:

It is clear that the responsibility for social reconstruction rests primarily upon the local authorities in the rural districts. . . . It is to be hoped that all those who are interested in building up the state will recognize that all forms of service to the state should include a period of service with such local authorities. . . . Do not linger in the metropolitan areas, and do not be lured by empty fame; live a simple and frugal life and engage in the basic work of national reconstruction.

Chiang's Point of View

No one is opposed to respect for the virtues of Chinese civilization. Chiang was justifiably proud of them and wise in recalling them, if indeed the people needed his reminders. But he erred in distorting their values for contemporary China and in urging reliance upon them. The people had progressed beyond accepting such an opiate,

[1] *China's Destiny*, pp. 166–168.

as Chiang's mentor Sun Yat-sen had pointed out, and as the liberal wing of the Kuomintang realized. Although Chiang had had no contact with Western institutions abroad, other than a brief experience in the Soviet Union, he had had the benefit of Sun's teachings and of friendships with Christian missionaries. At one stage, indeed, he professed to have become a Christian. It is therefore difficult to comprehend his emphasis upon traditional thought and his apparent dislike, amounting almost to contempt, for Western ideals and institutions. We find this attitude throughout his writing. One may surmise that he was unable to throw off his natural resentment, so vigorously enunciated, toward the effects, as he saw them, of nineteenth-century imperialism upon China's world stature, her economy, and the attitude of her people. In addition, however, he was obsessed with a desire for power which led him to depend upon himself. This desire grew with feeding, causing him to reject progressive counsel. Whether or not he would have changed, had not civil and foreign war jeopardized the state, cannot be proved. Such evidence as exists points against a change. In many respects Chiang resembled Yuan Shih-k'ai. Like Yuan he retarded political and social change.

Exponents of Liberalism

It is indicative of Chiang's distaste for liberalism that he and his conservative colleagues at Nanking would not let minor political parties take part in the period of tutelage. Of the several such parties, the largest, called the National Salvation Association, was a loosely-knit combination of splinter elements which worked strenuously for social betterment and was closest in its program to the Communists. On the conservative side were the National Socialists, a group of intellectuals, who were sincere gradualists, favorable to democracy. Their subsequent change of party name to Social Democratic more accurately defined their platform. Further to the right was the Young China party, very strongly critical of a united front with the Communists. Favoring such a front was the Third party, supporting agrarian reform. The Rural Reconstructionists, not claiming to be a political party, centered their efforts upon teaching the villagers a limited number of ideographs. Somewhat similar in aim was the Vocational Education group. Eventually, a federation of democratic elements, calling itself the Democratic League, emerged in Hong Kong, fearful of the Kuomintang's displeasure if it were organized within Kuomintang jurisdiction. Some of its leaders had held high office in that party. It gained representation in the People's Political Council, but its calls for ending one-party government, repression of free speech, the secret police, and other evils were ineffective. The League viewed itself as a bridge between the Kuomintang and the Communists in a coalition government.

Attitude of the Kuomintang

Toward none of the minor parties did the Kuomintang show a desire to cooperate. On the contrary, it became more hostile toward them, suppressing writers and teachers resident within its area of control. This attitude drove many able men toward the Communists, not on ideological grounds but in the hope that collaboration would defeat the Japanese. This trend was taken by the Kuomintang as an omen of its displacement. Self-preservation seemed, to Chiang and his conservative colleagues, the route to national salvation, to be assured only if cooperation could be obtained on their terms, the core of which was the continued supremacy of the Kuomintang.

Chiang Kai-shek Kidnaped

For the decade 1927–1937 the Nationalist policy was to exterminate the Communist regime centered at Yenan in Shensi province. Not only was this policy fruitless, it awakened strong opposition among Chiang's allied generals as the failure to resist Japan in Manchuria and north China foretold further encroachment. Eventually Chiang Kai-shek was kidnaped by General Yang Hu-cheng in Shensi, who was exasperated at the wastage of effort. Yang was joined by the "Young Marshal" Chang Hsueh-liang, whom the Japanese had driven out of Manchuria, and who had been ordered by Chiang Kai-shek to campaign against the Communists. With Mao Tse-tung's cooperation the kidnapers prevailed upon Chiang to stop his anti-Communist drive and to postpone the settlement of issues upon which Nanking was at odds with Yenan. Chiang was accepted as commander-in-chief by the Communists, with the approval of Moscow, while the Communists continued to command their forces and to rule the area they had occupied. Uneasy cooperation continued into 1941. It had significant consequences: the expansion of Communist contacts with the peasantry and town workers from Shansi to Shantung, and the resultant spirit of sacrificial resistance to the Japanese invaders, who began an all-out war in the summer of 1937. Mao Tse-tung and his toughened guerrilla troops won popular confidence through their success in hampering the Japanese advance, though they could not stop it. Mao took the opportunity also to inaugurate reforms which contributed to confidence: elective councils, lowering of tax and interest rates, the gift of land to tenants of allegedly traitorous landlords, free schools, and so on. Men and women of all economic classes were offered the new experience of voting, office-holding, and free discussion. Given something to fight for, thousands of youths joined the Communist army; other thousands were given arms, and aided the troops by providing information, food, and vehicles; destroying railway and telegraph lines; and harassing the enemy so effectively that small detachments dared not venture out of blockhouses. In consequence, the Japanese failed to subdue the countryside. Their conquest was confined to the urban centers, and their forces were severely drained. Ironically, it was the struggle with the Japanese, who had claimed that their invasion was necessary to save a neighbor from communism, that made possible the triumph of communism in China.

Quarantining the Communists

While the military activities in north China greatly aided the resistance effort of the government forces, the social and economic developments there were deeply disturbing to Chiang Kai-shek, for obvious reasons. He had accepted the united front program out of dire necessity. But it had entailed the recognition of an *imperium in imperio* which might not be terminable when the war ended. It might be preferable to restrict Communists' resistance by denying them arms, ammunition, money, and medical supplies. It might also be desirable to wink at the Japanese use of puppet Chinese troops against the Communist armies. It was deemed necessary to quarantine the Red forces by ringing them round with a cordon of two hundred thousand of Chiang's best troops. Measures of this sort eventually provoked a clash between Chiang and General Stilwell, sent by the United States to aid in the conduct of the war. When skirmishes between the government's regulars and their Communist allies culminated in a bloody battle, the short period of cooperation ended, early in 1941. The bitterness engendered was an ill omen of subsequent relations.

All-Out War with Japan

We come now to the problems and policies of the second part of the period of Kuomintang government, the years 1937 to 1949. Some reference to this part was unavoidable in surveying the previous decade. But the two parts are distinguishable, since not until 1937 was the egregious plan of Japan's militarists to reduce great China to the status of a satellite made clear to the world. The details of the plan are now well known and repetition would not be relevant here. It will be recalled that from Japan's seizure of the Liu Ch'iu (Ryu Kyu) Islands in 1879 she had chipped away at Chinese territory and sovereignty. At long last Chinese nationalism had been aroused to make a stand to the death against further encroachment.[2] In a statement issued in November, 1937, at the time of its transfer to Hankow, the Government said: "For the sake of our national existence, of the status of our race, of international justice and world peace, China finds no ground for submission. All those who have blood and breath in them must feel that they wish to be broken as jade rather than to remain whole as tile." In 1938 the Szechuan city of Chungking became the national capital. It remained the capital until the end of World War II, when the Government returned to Nanking.

Space Exchanged for Time

No praise can be too extravagant for the Chinese resistance. It was conducted from an area not yet industrialized nor equipped with railways. Public finances were attenuated by the loss of revenues from

[2] For a succinct treatment of the relations between China and other states, see H. S. Quigley and G. H. Blakeslee, *The Far East, An International Survey*, Boston, 1938, and H. S. Quigley, *Far Eastern War, 1937–1941*, Boston, 1942, both published by the World Peace Foundation.

the occupied eastern section of the country. The choice of Nanking as the capital in 1927, determined by apprehension of war with Japan, had been proved wise. Peking (renamed Peiping), fell quickly under the enemy's attack, and was forced to accept a puppet junta of amenable Chinese elders. The National army was able to slow Japanese progress toward Nanking until a considerable amount of industrial machinery could be transported to the interior. New factories were also set up to produce essentials of army and household equipment. New arsenals turned out small arms and ammunition. New highways were built toward unoccupied provinces, enabling the import of machinery and munitions. Various minerals were exported in payment for imports. This Herculean effort had important consequences in tying western provinces more closely to the central authorities and in the modernization of their economies.

Puppetry at Nanking

In 1940 the Japanese persuaded Wang Ch'ing-wei to become president of a so-called Reorganized National Government at Nanking. Wang had left the Kuomintang fold in 1938, unwilling to endure the dictatorial rule of the Leader-Generalissimo. Since Wang had been an ardent revolutionist from the outset of the Republican movement, it is difficult to regard him as a traitor, difficult also to believe that one of his intelligence was deceived by the Japanese. A more reasonable interpretation of his behavior is the one he gave: that China could not expect to win the war, and that a policy of compromise might work out to be her salvation. He was able to recruit a few members of the puppet regime at Peking and to have his regime modeled upon that of the Kuomintang. Although neither Wang nor the Japanese could have been in doubt as to the real locus of control, it is not impossible to believe that history may reveal that rumors of secret collaboration between Chiang and Wang were founded in fact.[3] An intriguing speculation might be indulged in upon the outcome of the struggle with communism had China accepted Japan's assertions of well-meant cooperation. Would Wang have sought to revive the

[3] See Don Bate, *Wang Ch'ing-wei: Puppet or Patriot*, Chicago, 1941, and Graham Peck, *Two Kinds of Time*, Boston, 1950.

united front policy? Had he done so would the Communists and the Japanese have accepted such a policy? In view of her defeat Japan would have had no choice in the matter. Communist conditions for a post-war coalition, after so prolonged a struggle with the Kuomintang, might well have been unacceptable to any Kuomintang leadership, as they were to Chiang Kai-shek. Whatever one may think about such possibilities, Japan foreclosed their consideration by resorting to war to compel obedience to her program.

Japan's "Cooperation" Policy

Japan's economic policy during her occupation was far-reaching. It included the creation of holding companies to "cooperate" with Chinese owners of industrial and commercial enterprises, transportation and communications lines, banks — indeed all concerns deemed capable of contributing to the success of Japan's master plan of hegemony. Though this policy entailed the diversion of resources, products, revenues, and profits, it also had permanent advantages for China. It saved her factories, and added to the technical know-how of Chinese participants. Invested Japanese capital eventually was lost to Chinese entrepreneurs and the government when Japan lost the war. On balance, China may have gained more than she lost.

Wartime Education

Educational institutions suffered severely during the war. But the government aided university students and faculties to move westward, and even established new technical and normal colleges in Free China. Large numbers of teachers and students found their way to these schools. Cultural progress was accelerated in Yunnan, Szechuan, Kweichow, and other interior provinces. In occupied cities, since cultural infiltration was a major feature of Japan's co-prosperity propaganda, Chinese universities were administered by a mingling of Japanese and Chinese instructors. For the edification of the masses, the Japanese offered membership in a New People's Association, the main tenets of which resembled very closely those of the Kuomintang's New Life Movement: rejection of democracy and communism and return to Confucianism. Like the latter, this society awakened little interest. The brutality of the Japanese soldiery was an even more effective deterrent to popular respect than the indifference of the Kuomintang to the people's welfare.

A New Constitution

As in 1923, so in 1946, the Kuomintang adopted a "permanent" constitution. Like its ill-fated predecessor the document embodied liberal principles. It provided for a national assembly, to be elected by the people, both men and women, twenty or over. It was to meet every three years. Its functions included election of the president, impeachment, and amendment of the constitution. It was not empowered to pass laws. The legislative yuan was promoted to parliamentary powers. In addition to legislative power it was allotted the right to approve or disapprove the president's appointee to the chairmanship of the executive yuan, or cabinet. The five yuan were retained. The president was to be not merely the chairman of a state council but president of the country. A complete, unqualified bill of rights guaranteed personal liberty and equality for all citizens. Relations between the central and provincial governments were modeled upon the American federal system, and the respective spheres of authority were defined. Provincial governors and legislatures were to be elected by the people. The constitution also listed the powers of the districts and provided that district magistrates and assemblies also should be elected. Liberal "fundamentals" of policy were laid down in the fields of economics, social welfare, and education. Thus ended the period of tutelage.

Emergency Powers of the Leader

During 1946 supplementary laws were promulgated, and in March, 1947, the National Assembly convened. It was a huge body of more than twenty-eight hundred members, some five hundred of whom were from minor parties. The expected dominance of Kuomintang members was present but an impressive number of those members had won election against machine-sponsored candidates of their party. Inevitably Chiang Kai-shek was elected President. His charismatic hold on the members was stronger than ever, now that the war was won. Even those of the Kuomintang who opposed machine control of the party insisted upon his accepting the presidency. On other matters the Assembly was highly argumentative. Its resemblance to democratic models was slight. It assumed powers constitutionally belonging to the legislative yuan, also an elective body. At Chiang's demand it amended the constitution in fact though not in form by passing "Temporary Provisions" which authorized the President to take any emergency measures needed, leaving to him the decision as to what constituted an emergency. Even though the conflict with the Communists may have warranted this action, the President's constitutional powers were so large that Chiang's wiser gesture would have been to rely upon them, trusting to his colleagues to support him. As throughout his career, Chiang failed to trust any institution or any person but himself. Panoplied as he was with the devotion of his party, he had, but missed, the opportunity of clothing the skeleton of constitutionalism with the flesh of liberalism. Particularly tragic was the fact that his failure persisted in spite of the warnings of his own supporters and the danger that persistence in his course would ensure prolonged civil war.

An Academic Worm Turns

In January, 1946, a professor of political science at the Southeast Federated University in Kunming, Yunnan province, gave a courageous lecture to his students. Professor Chang Hsi-jo was then a member of the Kuomintang. From his lecture four brief paragraphs may be in point here. He said:

The political malady that China suffers from today is that the political power is monopolized by an extremely reactionary and despotic political faction dominated by a group of ignoramuses, most stupid and most corrupt. This conglomeration is the Kuomintang. Today this faction exists for its own interests. All the high-sounding slogans, such as "for the nation" and "for the people," are mere words, tricks to fool the people. This group professes to "bring happiness to the nation and well-being to the people." In reality it plunges the nation to ruin and the people to misery. Legally the Kuomintang is said to be a government. Morally it is simply a bandit.

Professor Chang continued:

Everywhere you find the promise: "limitation of capital; equalization of land ownership." What are the results? Where did they limit
capital? Ask the war profiteers. How are they going to equalize ownership of land? Equalize perhaps until farmers can no longer afford
to plant the fields, owing to heavy government taxation of the land.
Not only have they done nothing about it. They admit that they don't
even have a plan.

On the subject of political tutelage he said:

These several years of Kuomintang rule are said to be a period of
tutelage. But where? Who has come to train you to exercise political
rights? The real intent of the so-called tutelage is merely to postpone
constitutionalism indefinitely.

Professor Chang's criticism extended to Chiang Kai-shek:

Wherein lie the causes of these happenings? It is because the political power these years is entirely in the hands of one man. It is a personal edict system. The moment the personal edict is issued none can
refuse to carry it out, even though some of the enlightened subordinates are fully aware that they should refuse. So even though they are
ministers by name, they are merely big or small houseboys. It is the
boss who hires a number of houseboys. . . . From the standpoint of
those who shout "Long live the Leader" and worship and treat him
as an emperor, we ought to kowtow to this virtuous and wise Son of
Heaven. But from the viewpoint of those who will not be corrupted
by them I may borrow other men's words: "You have all the good
words and done not one good deed." [4]

Criticisms by Americans

Despatches from American representatives in China bore out the
validity of Professor Chang's criticism. From many such despatches
the following excerpt may be quoted as typical:

The Kuomintang is losing the respect and support of the people by
its selfish policies and its refusal to heed progressive criticism. It seems
unable to revivify itself with fresh blood, and its unchanging leadership shows a growing ossification and the loss of a sense of reality. To
combat the dissensions and cliquism within the Party, which grows

[4] From an unpublished paper in the author's possession. Professor Chang
later turned to communism and is now a member of the foreign ministry at
Peking.

more rather than less acute, the leadership is turning toward the reactionary and unpopular Ch'en brothers clique.

The Generalissimo shows a similar loss of realistic flexibility and a hardening of narrowly conservative views. His growing megalomania and his unfortunate attempts to be "sage" as well as leader — shown, for instance, by "China's Destiny" and his book on economics — have forfeited the respect of many intellectuals, who enjoy in China a position of unique influence. Criticism of his dictatorship is becoming outspoken.[5]

What Will History Say?

The Kuomintang's time in power was a period of ordeal by battle. Centralization of political power is always and in all states attendant upon such periods. In mature democracies political parties de-emphasize their differences and draw together in support of the administration. The party in power makes use of the national resources in every field regardless of party politics. China was not a mature democracy. Moreover, the cleavage of economic and social policy between the two dominant parties was too deep for confident cooperation. Also, China was far from unity, quite apart from the Kuomintang-Communist rivalry. These circumstances argue that the final verdict of history will be less critical of the Kuomintang and its Leader than the quoted comments, which were typical of liberal opinion as World War II ended. However, it may hardly be questioned that the dominant elements in the Kuomintang rejected the counsel of their own liberal supporters, counsels made worthy of consideration by the experience of Republican China and by many historical examples of the consequences of autocratic rule and loss of the mandate of Heaven, evidenced to the Chinese people by economic distress and political corruption.

[5] Department of State, *United States Relations with China*, 1949, p. 568.

THE PEOPLE'S GOVERNMENT AT
AT PEKING

BETWEEN the end of the Pacific phase of World War II in 1945 and the establishment of the Communist government at Peking (Peiping) in 1949 serious efforts were made to reconcile the opposing ideas of the Kuomintang and Communist leaders regarding bases of a political and economic order that might make possible the creation of a coalition government. Mao Tse-tung, guaranteed American protection, went to confer with Chiang Kai-shek at Chungking in the autumn of 1945. Mao's terms called for the recognition of Communist autonomy in China's five northern provinces. He asked for a country-wide plebiscite to test popular reaction to this proposal; he wanted a federal system, with a central government elected by the people, and with provincial authority over provincial affairs. His terms were rejected and civil war was resumed. But the effort to work out a compromise continued, mediated by General George Marshall, America's great soldier-statesman. His mission failed because neither side trusted the other. Chiang insisted that the Communists acknowledge his headship of the state and permit their troops to be integrated with the National army. He declared his willingness to appoint Communist leaders to national offices, to recognize local Communist officials, and to proceed with measures of social reform. Mao and his colleagues, on the other hand, were unwilling to surrender their military forces, regarding them as their only guarantee of influence.

Why Communism Won

The crevasse between the two positions could not be bridged. The Communist forces were stronger than before the war. Although the National troops were better armed they suffered from poor leadership and reckless strategy. Large numbers deserted to the Communists, and great quantities of military matériel furnished to the Nationalists by the United States were captured by the enemy. Just as in the Nationalist campaign of 1926–1927 the peasantry had aided the Kuomintang forces, and for similar reasons, so they now aided the Communist troops. Within four years the Nationalists were driven back to the Yangtze. There the Generalissimo gave up the struggle and fled with the bulk of his army to Taiwan (Formosa). The Communists crossed the Yangtze and overran south China. Their attack on the islands Quemoy and Matsu failed, and they did not attack Taiwan nor the British colony of Hong Kong.

Peking Turns Red

The "People's Government" was inaugurated on October 1, 1949, at Peiping, to which the old name Peking was restored. To prepare for the new régime a consultative conference had been held in September, attended by 662 delegates selected by Mao and his associates. Represented in the conference were the peasants, urban labor, and middle-class sectors believed amenable to Communist leadership. Other political parties were represented in negligible numbers. The conference quickly accepted the organic law presented to it, a law replaced in 1954 by the present constitution.

The constitution (pp. 222–235) is composed of a hundred and six articles, divided into four chapters. Its preamble blandly asserts that the People's Republic is a "democratic dictatorship." It states that "from the founding of the People's Republic of China to the attainment of a socialist society is a period of transition. During the transition the fundamental task of the state is, step by step, to accomplish the socialist transformation of agriculture, handicrafts, and capitalist industry and commerce." It further declares that "the people of our country forged a broad people's democratic united front, composed of all democratic classes, democratic parties and groups, and popular organizations, led by the Communist party of China." It expresses the state's intent to concern itself with the needs of the different nationalities of the country, and "in the matter of socialist transformation, to pay full attention to the special characteristics in the development of each." While affirming "indestructible friendship" with the Soviet Union and the "people's" democracies, it asserts that "China's policy of establishing and extending diplomatic relations with all countries on the principles of equality, mutual benefit and mutual respect for each other's sovereignty and territorial integrity . . . will continue to be carried out." The preamble concludes: "In international affairs our firm and consistent policy is to strive for the noble cause of world peace and the progress of humanity."

Democratic Dictatorship

Chapter I, entitled "General Principles," proclaims that the People's Republic is a democratic state led by the working class and based on the alliance of workers and peasants, thereby deferring to Marx and Lenin despite Mao's earlier insistence that primacy of leadership should be accorded to the peasantry. The Principles state further that all power belongs to the people and is exercised through national and local congresses, which practice "democratic centralism." The rights of nationalities within China are declared to be equal, and to include the right of nationalities to foster their own cultures. Compact nationalities are free to enjoy autonomy — so says the constitution — but they are inalienable from the Republic. Capitalist and individual ownership are countenanced, subject to step-by-step nationalization. All natural resources belong to the "whole people." The state "deprives feudal landlords and bureaucratic capitalists of political rights for a specific period of time according to law; at the same time it provides them with a way to earn a living, in order to enable them to reform through work and to become citizens who earn their livelihood by their own labor." It may be noted that the great number of landlords killed during the purge of 1951–1953 were deprived of the promised opportunity to reform themselves.

The National Congress

The lengthy second chapter defines the "State Structure." It provides for a National Congress, a Chairman of the Republic, a State Council, a National Defense Council, provincial and local congresses and administrative councils, a hierarchy of courts and prosecutors, and a national capital, emblem, and flag. The National Congress is declared the highest organ of state power and the only legislative authority in the land. Thus China is a unitary, not a federal, state.

The National Congress is a single chamber of 1,226 members elected (the present one in 1958) by the provincial congresses, autonomous regions, the two largest municipalities—Peking and Shanghai—which are subject to the central government (Tientsin is no longer in the same class), the armed forces, and Chinese resident abroad. Its term is four years and it meets annually for short periods. The Congress has the power to amend the constitution; to pass laws; to decide economic policy and questions of war, peace, and amnesty; and to approve the budget and other proposals laid before it by the Chairman of the Republic and the premier. The Congress elects the Chairman of the Republic, who is not only the chief executive officer of the state but also Chairman of the praesidium which presides over the sessions of the Congress. There are two vice chairmen, one of whom is Madam Sun Yat-sen. The Congress also elects the president of the Supreme Court and the chief procurator, who is the equivalent of the attorney general of the United States. It may remove officers elected by it and others appointed by the Chairman of the Republic with congressional approval. It also elects all members of the praesidium and a number of committees, the most powerful of which is the Standing Committee. This body exercises the powers of the Congress between sessions. It has fifteen vice chairmen and sixty-two other members. Its chairman is the Chairman of the Republic. Since the National Congress is a huge body, meeting so briefly — from one to two weeks — once a year, its supremacy in law has a hollow ring in practice. It is in fact a massive rubber stamp for executive decisions. At best its importance lies in providing some opportunity for its members to gain experience in the form and to some extent in the methods of representative government.

The Chairman

The Chairman of the Republic has, constitutionally, the usual powers of a president in a republic. These include appointment of superior officers, conduct of foreign relations, and military command. He ratifies treaties, declares war and peace upon decision of the Congress, and convenes "supreme state conferences." This last-named power appears to run counter to congressional supremacy, since such conferences are essentially meetings of Communist party leaders — which means that the Chairman's authority to convene a conference at his discretion cannot be exercised without the approval of the Chairman of the party. As we shall later see, however, no power is exercisable otherwise. Added to the duties of the Chairman of the Republic is his chairmanship of the National Defense Council, which has thirteen vice chairmen and ninety-nine other members. Noteworthy is the preference for group rather than individual headship of important executive organs.

The State Council

The State Council combines the functions of a privy council and a cabinet. It is a rather large agency, composed of a premier, sixteen vice premiers, six directors of general coordinating offices, thirty-three ministers each heading an administrative department, and eight commissioners, whose functions also are administrative. Members of the State Council are appointed by the Chairman of the Republic and may be removed by him, yet they are presumed to be responsible to the National Congress. Nineteen of the ministries are concerned with one or another field of economic administration. Two ministries, those of Defense and National Security, carry out military policy under the National Defense Council and the General Staff, headed by a chief of staff. The National Defense Council necessarily operates under the supervision of the Military Committee of the Communist party.

Mao and the Military

When Mao Tse-tung turned over the chairmanship of the Republic to Liu Shao-ch'i in 1958 he retained his headship of both the Central Committee and the Military Committee of the party. Communist China's army consists of 2,500,000 first-line regulars, between 1,500,000 and 2,000,000 regional district troops, and a public security gendarmerie of between 500,000 and 1,000,000 men. In 1958, coincident with the inauguration of communes, the policy of "every man a soldier" was proclaimed. If carried out, this program would provide a militia of some 200,000,000 men. About 500,000 regulars were discharged in 1958 to be utilized in training the militia.

From the 1920's to the present Mao Tse-tung's military doctrine has been that China should be prepared for "imperialist" attack, not for offensive war outside her boundaries. To that end she should, he holds, depend upon an army of the whole people with high morale, not upon nuclear armaments. Although his view is regarded as out-dated in Moscow and by some of his ablest generals, Mao's recent writings suggest that he continues to put his faith in the guerrilla methods that brought him to power. But Mao undoubtedly sees the mass militia as an instrument of national unification and a fertile field for indoctrination in nationalistic communism. Peking's intervention in Korea and its threats of intervention in southeast Asia in the event of Western military support of rightist regimes demonstrate that the Communist leader regards such measures as defensive. Mao's indif-ference to nuclear arms may well reflect China's present incompe-tence to arm herself with them.

The Communist air force is modern, equipped with three thousand planes. The navy is small, composed principally of frigates and sub-marines.

The Conduct of Foreign Relations

For the conduct of foreign relations there are three central agen-cies: the coordinating Office in Charge of Foreign Affairs, the For-eign Ministry, and an "unofficial" foreign ministry which deals with states having no regular diplomatic relations with Peking. The Min-ister of Foreign Affairs also heads the Office, which has four deputy directors. In the Foreign Ministry are five vice ministers and four assistant ministers, all well-educated and experienced in foreign af-fairs. The Ministry also includes six geographic and six functional divisions. Official tenure is well protected and Communist party membership is not a primary factor in appointments below that of minister. As of mid-1960 the foreign service was staffing thirty-two embassies, two offices of chargés d'affaires and one legation, plus a number of consulates. These agencies are staffed by cultural and military attachés as well as by diplomats and consuls. In a strenuous effort to prepare foreign-service officers the government has established five institutes, and the universities have expanded their curriculums in foreign languages and the social sciences.[1]

The Judiciary

The constitution gives little attention to the judicial system. It provides for a supreme court; provincial, local and special courts; and for a corresponding hierarchy of procurators. While declaring that the courts are independent, it states contradictorily that they are responsible to the congresses of their respective jurisdictions. It authorizes the procuratorate to ensure observance of the law by administrative officers. In Chinese Communist theory, the courts, like the executive branch, are not independent in our sense. Except for the president of the supreme court all judges are elective. They serve for four years unless re-elected, not for life or during good conduct.

Powerful Procurators

Communist theory has no place for the principle of habeas corpus, but entrusts protection of the individual to the procurators and the congresses. The procurators are extremely powerful, more so than the judges. They are expected to see to it that all agencies of the state, including the courts, observe the law. The congresses elect and may remove judges; they also elect lay assessors, who sit with the judges to observe and report upon their work. There is no provision for trial by jury. The congresses do not elect the procurators; they are appointed by and are under the direction of the chief procurator.

Communist China has abolished the codes of law formerly in force and is developing new codes. Mass trials were held for seven years, but today a man receives a judicial trial and is entitled to defend himself if he can find a lawyer. Theoretically the procurators are, except in political cases, defenders as well as prosecutors of the defendants.

[1] D. W. Klein, "Peking's Evolving Ministry of Foreign Affairs," *The China Quarterly*, October–December, 1960, pp. 28–39.

Decision is comparatively swift as but one appeal is allowed. Arrests must be reported to the local procurator within twenty-four hours. The length of detention before trial depends upon the procurator. Justice is said to be "even" except in political cases. Persons sentenced to prison are re-educated in factories of many types.[2]

Provincial and Local Government

Provincial and local political organs participate in government under the principle — "doctrine" would be a more appropriate term — of democratic centralism. This implies that such functions as they perform are carried on under the direction and subject to the authority of the central government. In the twenty-five provinces,[3] the so-called autonomous regions, and the cities, counties, districts, and towns, there are elected congresses and administrative councils, patterned after the National Congress and the State Council. Except in the smaller cities, districts, and towns, where election of the congresses is directly by the citizenry, the congresses are elected by the congress of the next lower level. The councils are elected by the congresses on the same levels. Democratic centralism calls for the supervision of congresses and councils by the corresponding bodies on the next higher level. Supervision includes the power to revise or annul decisions. The decisions that may be taken at each level are not of great significance since there is no division of authority, which resides in Peking. But the provincial and local bodies frame their budgets, maintain public order, and draft plans for public works and for economic and cultural improvements. In 1958, with the beginning of the organization of communes, the local government of towns and villages was absorbed by them.

Political Tutelage

Because of the high illiteracy and the people's lack of experience with elections it was found necessary to send teams of educated young

[2] A brief description of the judicial system is given by Justice Agarwala of India in his *Government and Politics of China.*

[3] The Communist official list of provinces includes Taiwan as a twenty-sixth province. The former provinces of Ninghsia, Suiyuan, and Chahar are now combined under the title the Inner Mongolian Autonomous Region. Otherwise

people into towns and villages to stimulate interest and to instruct the people in election procedure. Volunteers from the cities were re-cruited for work on the farms to enable farmers and their wives to devote time to learning the new procedures. The registration of voters was conducted by members of election committees, who went into the fields and homes of the peasantry. Discussions were carried on concerning the qualifications that should be sought in candidates and persons who were regarded as possessing the desirable qualities. Within each electoral district one list of candidates only was sub-mitted to the voters, the list containing the same number of names as there were places to be filled. Voters were, however, permitted to write in other names, an ironic provision since few voters were able to write. In many localities voting is, for that reason, by acclamation or show of hands.

Private Rights

The political and civil rights of citizens are defined in the nine-teen articles of Chapter III of the constitution. Equality before the law is guaranteed. Women are legally equal with men. The age quali-fication for voters is eighteen. Civil rights include freedom of speech, press, assembly, association, procession, and demonstration. No right of private property is listed in the bill of rights. All citizens have the right to work, to be implemented through "planned employment." They also have the right to leisure; to state aid during illness, disa-bility, and old age; and to education, research and cultural pursuits. They are obligated to protect public property, pay taxes, and per-form military service.

The Autonomous Nationalities

Available data upon the rights enjoyed by the "autonomous na-tionalities" indicate that their autonomy is largely fictitious. China embraces numerous minority peoples, and to appear to be imple-menting the constitutional provisions for their cultural autonomy the government has recognized so-called autonomous areas of varying

the old pre-Communist provincial names and boundaries exist today, the ex-periment with regional groups of provinces having been found contributory to separatism.

size. Figures given on the number of such areas range from seventy to more than a hundred. Inner Mongolia is the largest of such areas; the Turkish people of the large province of Sinkiang are invested with "autonomy." The Chinese-Tibetan agreement of May, 1951, provided that Tibet would become a quasi-autonomous region. Often the areas are not, in fact, racially homogeneous. Some of them have a majority of the dominant Han Chinese. The minorities are under continuous pressure to conform to Communist patterns of thought and action. Even their languages are being supplanted and their cultural heritage contemned as inferior to the Chinese. Their opposition to de-culturation has resulted in harsh measures against "insurgent nationalism," but their comparative weakness obviates revolts that would threaten the totalitarian regime.

Similarity to the Soviet System

Obviously, Communist China's government is modeled closely upon that of the U.S.S.R. It bears no resemblance to the system of the first republic, it partially resembles the Kuomintang structure, and it is but slightly similar to Western democratic governments. It provides for three-fold division of functions but not for parallel division of powers. Its difference from Russia's Soviet system lies partly in the relative superiority of the Chairman of the Republic to the premier, partly in the Chinese introduction of communes.

Where Power Resides

To comprehend the reality of power it is necessary to examine more closely the position of the Communist party in relation to the formal structure of government. The leadership of "the broad people's united front" constitutionally attributed to the Communist party has from the outset been domination, though other parties, groups, and individuals are tolerated provided that they fellow-travel along the lines laid down by *the* party. Political power rests in the Central Committee of the party, which is elected by the national congress of the party, a different body from the National People's Congress. The Central Committee is composed of the principal party leaders. Its present Chairman is Mao Tse-tung, who at sixty-eight is physically and mentally vigorous and who undoubtedly will remain Chairman so long as he desires to. Within the Central Committee, which averages a regular and alternate membership of 165 persons, is a seasoned elite called the Political Bureau or more briefly the Politburo, which has 19 regular members inclusive of the Chairman and 6 alternate members. Within the Politburo is a standing committee of 7 to 10 members headed by Mao Tse-tung.

The Dictators

Although no dictatorship can ignore its less influential colleagues, if we are to identify the dominant agency of party and government we find it in the standing committee of the Politburo. Among its veteran members those best known outside as well as inside China are Mao, Liu Shao-ch'i, Chou En-lai, and Chu Teh. Liu is second only to Mao as a theorist, Chou is Peking's foremost diplomat, Chu Teh its leading elder statesman. Within the government Mao no longer holds office, Liu is Chairman of the Republic, Chou is premier, Chu is a vice-president and adviser to the Ministry of War.

Secretariat and Party Congress

Associated with the Central Committee of the party is the highly influential central secretariat. The national party congress is elective but if circumstances should require suspension of the electoral process the Central Committee has authority to select the members. The party congress meets annually but it is little more than an instrument of the Politburo. Its stated functions: "to hear, receive, discuss and ratify reports submitted by the Central Committee and other central organs, to decide upon and amend the party program and the constitution of the party, and to elect the Central Committee," may have potential significance but at present they merely symbolize the asserted role of the party's rank and file.

Provincial and Local Organs

Under the central agencies of the party are provincial, autonomous area, county, municipal and inferior agencies organized similarly. "Democratic centralism" requires that these submit to those on the next higher level and that all submit to the Central Committee. At the base of the party pyramid are branches and fractions, the latter composed of three or more members. These basic groups exist in factories, mines, villages, business concerns, streets, military units, offices, and schools. Their principal duty is to recruit members by carrying propaganda slogans down from Peking to fellow workers. Of special interest is the responsibility placed upon fractions and branches in the military units posted throughout the country. Indoctrination of the troops is very thorough and accompanied by the attempt to inculcate a high sense of the duty of treating the people kindly in order to turn their traditional distrust of the soldiery to respect and confidence.

Administration to the nth Power

It is noteworthy that the three hierarchies of political action — those of party, army, and government — exist constitutionally side by side, not one above the other. Party control is accomplished by political means rather than by law. Yet it is more absolute than law could make it because the party controls the army. Party control is manipulated through the monopoly of important positions in all three hierarchies by party leaders. The same men — or others of long experience, proved devotion to the party, ability, and integrity — appear in high posts in the party, the army, and the government. They also head the numerous auxiliary propaganda and mass support organizations. The staffing and cost of the enormous bureaucracy impose a tremendous burden upon available personnel and public funds.

Party Membership

In 1954 the membership of the party was reported officially to be 6,500,000 men and women. In 1957 it had risen to 13,000,000, with an additional 23,000,000 in the Young Communist League. Any person eighteen or over may become a member if properly recommended, but persons not regarded as workers are not likely to be accepted. Peasant members outnumber urban workers. The party's interest in raising women to full equality with men has made for particularly enthusiastic female members.

The Trend toward Unity

In view of the vast extent and huge population of China one cannot but marvel that it is possible to keep the numerous agencies of the Communist political machine in motion from the central control tower in Peking. What Sun Yat-sen termed "a sheet of loose sand" may be less unified than it appears to be. There is still opposition to the regime, and revolts have broken out in some areas. But the cement of Communist control unquestionably has stiffened the political structure, and the grains of sand are, apparently, drawing together to form a firm fabric. Serious students of Chinese politics agree that this trend is explained by the facts that Mao and his colleagues had had thirty years of experience before the Peking government was inaugurated, that they used that period to plan their system, and that they have worked tirelessly, ruthlessly, and honestly to make it succeed. The people have given it a chance to prove itself. Whether or not it does so will depend upon how acceptably its policies, programs, and performance redound to their social, economic, and political advancement.

THE IDEOLOGY OF MAO TSE-TUNG

MAO TSE-TUNG was born in the central province of Hunan, which has produced more than its share of radical thinkers, in 1893. His father, a peasant who had served in the imperial army, was, as owner of four acres of land, classified as a well-to-do farmer. At the age of eight, Mao entered school, where, like his mates, he was initiated into the classics: Confucius, Mencius, Laotze, and others — heavy fare for children. He found them uninteresting (he preferred romances and stories of rebellion), but useful in enabling him to remind his harsh father that a filial son deserved a kinder parent. At thirteen he was taken out of school and put to work on the farm. But he continued his reading and gradually became aware that the old romances never had peasant heroes but always glorified emperors and soldiers. And real-life incidents such as the beheading of famine-stricken peasants for protesting against the government's failure to aid them aroused his concern.

Returning to school, he studied the works of the reformers K'ang Yu-wei and Liang Ch'i-ch'ao, learning of their efforts for constitutional government. He read also of Sun Yat-sen and his first political party, the T'ungmenghui. At eighteen he joined the army of the Republican Revolution but was not called upon to fight. Then for a period he attended middle school, finding it dull. He spent his time in the library at Changsha, Hunan, where he read, in translation, Adam Smith, Mill, Darwin, Montesquieu, and other liberal thinkers. Among Chinese writers who influenced him at this period were the renaissance leaders Hu Shih and Li Ta-chao. In 1918 he took a job in the library of the University of Peking. This brought him into contact with Professor Li, the university librarian, whose thinking was pro-Communist. A few years later, at the age of twenty-six, he became a writer and teacher and was politically active in the New People's Society. He took part, during the era of the militarists, in the movement to set up representative government in Hunan, but became convinced by the oppressive attitude of Governor Chao Heng-ti that reforms could be wrought only through mass action, backed by force. In that year, he married a brilliant girl, Yang K'ai-hui, who was killed in 1930 by the militarist Ho Chien. Mao has had four wives, one who was forced upon him by his father and with whom he never lived. His present wife is Nan P'ing, a motion picture actress.

Mao's Rise to Leadership

Mao Tse-tung was a secondary figure at the Shanghai conference of 1921, called to found the Chinese Communist party. But by 1924 his knowledge of how to deal with the peasantry brought him to notice. He was appointed a member of the executive staff of the Kuomintang, after its decision to admit individual Communists. Promptly he collided with senior Communist leaders over the issue of peasant versus proletarian headship of their movement. The Russian advisers insisted that the urban workers should be the mainstay of the party; Mao believed that the peasantry were stronger and more reliable. Eventually, Mao won his point, but he and his co-believers were impeded rather than aided by the Comintern's opposition in the early stage. Later Stalin aided them by turning over captured Japanese arms to their army in Manchuria. But in the main the Chinese Communists had to rely upon themselves.

Chu Teh

It will be helpful, before turning to Mao's ideology, to look briefly into the backgrounds of his principal colleagues: Chu Teh, Chou En-lai, and Liu Shao-ch'i. Chu Teh, a vice-chairman of the Republic and formerly head of the army, was born in Szechuan province in 1886, the son of a landlord. Educated for an army career, he backed the opposition to Yuan Shih-k'ai in 1916. After a period as a corrupt, opium-smoking official, he became interested in social reform through his un-tuchunlike interest in reading. He rid himself of the opium habit, pensioned off his concubines, and, in 1922, joined the Kuomintang. At thirty-eight he traveled and studied in Germany. He joined the Communist party, visited Paris and Moscow, and in the latter city studied under Chinese instructors. He returned to China in 1925 and donated the bulk of his fortune to the Communist party. He preceded Mao in the organization of peasant armies after 1927, but accepted Mao's leadership and has fought by his side ever since.

Chou En-lai

Chou En-lai was born in Kiangsu province in 1898. His grandfather was a wealthy official, his father a teacher, his mother a well-educated lover of literature. Chou was a brilliant student at an American missionary university, Nankai, in Tientsin. He joined Sun Yat-sen's revolutionary movement and was imprisoned for a year by Yuan Shih-k'ai. He went to France after his release, and studied there for two years. After a third year of study in Germany, he returned to China a Communist. He joined the Kuomintang, serving as secretary of its new military academy in Whampoa, near Canton. Thereafter he became an agitator among the workers at Shanghai. When Chiang Kai-shek carried on a pogrom against them, killing thousands, Chou was outraged. He joined Mao and Chu Teh, remained with them, and rose to become foreign minister, later premier, at Peking. He is recognized internationally as an extraordinarily able diplomat.

Liu Shao-ch'i

Liu Shao-ch'i was born in Hunan in 1898. The only one of the four Communist oligarchs who ranks as a scholar by old as well as contemporary Chinese standards, he knows Confucius and Marx equally well, and uses his knowledge to draw persuasive parallels between their ideas. Now Chairman of the Republic, he comes close to rivaling Mao in influence. His writings vie with Mao's in quantity and quality.

Mao's Versatility

Mao Tse-tung's photographs give one the impression that he would feel more at home in a rice paddy than in a study or an imperial palace. His face is round, his body pudgy, his garb drab and undecorated. Appearance is deceptive. He has found time between battles and political activities to set down his thought in numerous essays, speeches, and monographs, and much of his writing has been translated into English and other languages. His five-volume *Selected Works* have been published in London. His critics contend that he lacks originality, that he parrots Marx and Lenin; they devote more attention to his strategy than to his theory. It is true that Maoism defers to the earlier apostles of communism and he makes no attempt to conceal his dependence upon them. But it is also true that he has ideas of his own and that he has not hesitated to distinguish between conditions in the industrialized West and conditions in China and other parts of Asia which call for separate consideration of the applicability of Marxism to Asia. Our treatment here makes no pretense of being more than an introduction to Mao's ideology.

In his *New Democracy* he affirms that the truth is the revolutionary practice of the people. The aim of Chinese Communists is to build a new culture; since economics and politics are the primary determinants of culture, economics and culture must be changed, a change that is to come in stages.

Three Revolutionary Stages

The first stage is to bring about the united front of all revolutionary classes, which he terms the "new bourgeois-democratic" stage. The second stage is to be democratic socialism. He includes within the united front the proletariat, the peasantry, the intellectuals, and the petty bourgeoisie. He regards this front as "the new historical peculiarity of the Chinese Revolution." He differentiates the Chinese lesser bourgeoisie from the Russian, pointing out that Russia had not experienced quasi-colonialism. He lumps the rich bourgeoisie with the landlords and the pro-capitalist elements of the bureaucracy as outside the united front.

Mao characterizes the Kuomintang as revolutionary in its attitude toward imperialism but dictatorial in its treatment of the people. It used the term "citizen" to conceal the fact of bourgeois rule, the rule of wealthy landlords, businessmen, and officials; and it compromised, he avers, with internal feudalism and foreign imperialistic capitalism.

He believes it essential that the people rule; that the government be elected by the people, from the villages to the capital; that the suffrage be equal, irrespective of differences in sex, belief, property, or education. In the economic field, writes Mao, the state must own all big banks, big industries, and big commercial concerns. The large landholdings must be broken up and distributed among the cultivators. But for the present, private capital and land-ownership should be permitted, since China is not ready for full-scale socialism — that is, communism — which is the third stage.

Mao's View of Sun Yat-sen

Evidently hoping to profit by associating the revered father of the Republic with himself, Mao holds Sun Yat-sen in great respect, speaking of him as willing to adjust his own thinking to Communist ideology, though falling short of evolving a socialist interpretation of history. Mao holds that Sun's Three Principles of the People were pro-Communist. Sun's thinking, according to Mao, lacked "revolutionary thoroughness" in that it was a historical view of livelihood rather than one founded in dialectical and historical materialism. It was in process of transformation through alliance with the Communist doctrine of the Soviet Union and collaboration with workers and peasants.

The "People's" Culture

The "new culture" that will rest upon political and economic change will differ from the old, which Mao describes as a combination of feudalism and imperialism, the former inherited from classical doctrine, the latter imported from the West. It will be a "people's culture" in which foreign ideas will be made use of. The Chinese classics also will not be ignored, but all ideas will be adapted "under the guidance of proletarian thought." In a striking passage which suggests that in 1940 Mao was either sincerely taking an independent line or wishing to appear independent, he says: "The thesis of wholesale Westernization is a mistaken viewpoint. To import things foreign [has] done China much harm. The same attitude is necessary for the Chinese Communists in the application of Marxism to China. Marxism should not be applied subjectively and dogmatically. Such Marxism is useless. The point is to grasp the general truths of Marxism and apply them to the concrete practice of the Chinese Revolution, i.e. first to achieve the Sinization [Chinification] of Marxism. Subjective and dogmatic Marxism is a caricature of Marxism as applied to the Chinese Revolution. Chinese culture must have its own form, that is a national form. A national form and a new democratic content, that is our new culture of today."

Evidence of Independence

Mao's early alliance with the Soviet Union by treaty in 1950, and his subsequent reiteration of unfaltering loyalty to the mother-state of communism, has been accompanied by evidence that alliance does not entail subordination. On January 16, 1957, a joint statement of his government and Poland's reaffirms Mao's attitude toward independent interpretation and application of Marxism. In part the statement reads:

The delegations of both countries state that the common idea of building socialism is linking the socialist countries. Mutual relations between them should be shaped by the principles of proletarian internationalism and based on a community of ideology and aims. At the same time, relations between socialist countries as independent and sovereign states should be based on the principles of respect for their sovereignty, non-interference with their internal affairs, equality and mutual benefits.[1]

"Freedom" via Communism

Mao appeared to have given another proof of independent thinking in his address of February 27, 1957, on "The Correct Handling of Contradictions among the People." Apparently the speech was prompted by the Hungarian uprising which was so brutally crushed by Soviet tanks and troops. Undoubtedly Mao wanted to forestall a similar revolt by expounding his view that contradictions should be expected, even welcomed, in a Communist country, and that they should be dealt with by persuasion, not by force. This thesis runs counter to Lenin and Stalin, and was declared by Khrushchev to be

[1] *New York Times*, January 17, 1957.

mistaken. Mao did not, however, withdraw it. He had said that by "people" he meant only those who support the Communist revolution. Their contradictions, i.e., their criticisms of the government, differ from those of opponents of socialism; the proper way to deal with supporters is that of democratic socialism, which combines discipline and guidance with freedom. Said Mao:

Under this system the people enjoy a wide measure of freedom and democracy, but at the same time they have to keep themselves within the bounds of socialist discipline. . . . In settling matters of an ideological or controversial nature among the people we can only use democratic methods, methods of discussion, of criticism or persuasion, and education, not coercive, high-handed methods. In order to carry on their production and studies effectively and to order their lives properly, the people want their government, the leaders of productive work, and of educational and cultural bodies to issue suitable orders of a compulsory nature. It is common sense that the maintenance of law and order would be impossible without administrative orders. Administrative orders and the method of persuasion and education complement each other in solving contradictions among the people. . . . In many cases administrative orders alone will not work.

Who May Contradict?

Mao relates in his address that the concept of "unity-criticism-unity" was worked out in 1942 to resolve the antagonism between those party leaders who insisted on "ruthless struggle and merciless blows," whom he calls "left doctrinaires," and those who stood for attaining and preserving unity through criticism, whom he terms true Marxists. He refers to his own frequent affirmations of this latter concept, and to the successes it has had in practice, crediting it with the success of the revolution. He admits that on occasion members of "the people" have been wrongly treated, having been mistaken for counter-revolutionaries. He says that many party functionaries continue to confuse contradictions among the people with contradictions between the revolution and its enemies, and therefore continue to treat friends who express criticism as though they were enemies. He condemns this practice as likely to disrupt the party. At this point he refers to Marx and Lenin, saying:

Marxist philosophy holds that the law of the unity of opposites is a fundamental law of the universe. This law operates everywhere, in the natural world, in human society, and in man's thinking. Opposites in contradiction unite as well as struggle with each other, and thus impel all things to move and change. Contradictions exist everywhere, but as things differ in nature so do contradictions. In any given phenomenon or thing, the unity of opposites is conditional, temporary, and transitory, and hence relative, whereas struggle between opposites is absolute.

Mao then lays down the dictum, also of Marxist origin, that

Contradictions in capitalist society . . . cannot be resolved by the capitalist system itself, but can only be resolved by socialist revolution. . . . The basic contradictions in socialist society are still those between the relations of production and the productive forces, and between the superstructure and the economic base. . . . When we say that socialist relations of production are better suited . . . to the development of the productive forces we mean that [they] permit the productive forces to develop at a speed unparalleled in the old society, so that production can expand steadily and the constantly growing needs of the people can be met, step by step.[2]

Unwatered Blossoms

Mao does not argue empirically, since he gives no comparative data on productivity in capitalist and socialist countries. His treatment is purely dialectic, in the manner of Marx.

He concedes that Marxism has not yet won a majority of the people and that the middle class of China still oppose it, while its intellectual followers are few. He accepts these facts as logical but believes that time and study will remold all classes. He sums up his strategy for bringing this to pass with the slogans: "Let a hundred flowers blossom," and "Let a hundred schools of thought contend." Art and science, says he, can progress only if different schools of thought are allowed to contend freely. This statement sounds liberal in the true sense of objectivity, of willingness to hear all points of view. But Mao makes it clear that this is not his thought; that contending ideas must have as their aim the improvement of the socialist system, not the substitution of another system for it. He asks: "What

[2] *New York Times,* June 19, 1957.

should be our policy toward non-Marxist ideas?" He answers: "So far as unmistakable counter-revolutionaries and wreckers of the socialist cause are concerned, we simply deprive them of their freedom of speech." (Mao admits that between 1949 and 1954 some eight hundred thousand "unmistakable counter-revolutionaries" had been killed; this pogrom surely was effective in depriving them of all freedoms.) Obviously it requires exceptional courage to express criticism when a critic cannot be sure that he will not be treated as a counter-revolutionary. This is especially true in view of Mao's condemnation of "revisionism" as more dangerous than "doctrinairism." Yet there were brave men who chose to criticize, with dire results for themselves. In consequence Mao's rhetorical "hundred flowers" and "hundred schools of thought" turned out to be empty phrases. This might have been expected, since he had set forth six criteria by which ideas relating to politics, art, and science might be distinguished as "blossoms" rather than "poisonous weeds." His criteria were:

1. That they help to unite China's nationalities.
2. That they help to consolidate the people's democratic dictatorship.
3. That they are beneficial to socialist transformation and construction.
4. That they help to consolidate democratic centralism.
5. That they tend to strengthen the leadership of the Communist party.
6. That they are beneficial to international socialist solidarity and the solidarity of the peace-loving peoples of the world.

After stating that his criteria contemplate co-existence between the Communist and other democratic parties, Mao says clearly that the other parties will be required to meet his criteria and to remold their ideologies accordingly.

Mao a Realist

Mao Tse-tung's ideology is essentially pragmatic. It is concerned primarily with the application of Marxism to Chinese conditions. His writings reveal that he has read widely and thought out his own interpretations of what he has read. His own thinking is clear, more so than that of Sun Yat-sen. If it is not profound, if it adds little to Marx and Lenin, it is also not slavishly controlled by them. There is no comfort in his writings for those who seek evidence of any tendency away from communism toward democracy. Mao is a dyed-in-the-wool Communist. He is also a convinced proponent of international communism. His concessions to small-scale capitalism and to reluctant democrats are for temporary purposes. He is not, however, a Soviet stooge. He is a nationalist first, an ally of Russia second, an internationalist third. His internationalism is not accommodative of co-existence with other than his own concept of democracy, but is limited to collaboration with other inflexible advocates of world-wide communism.

Are we to conclude that Mao is incapable of changing his theories? If so, is he also incapable of changing his strategy for their application within China and in international relations? How important are these questions? Mao at sixty-eight may not long continue to dominate the thinking and policies of his party. While he does so it is unlikely that his ideology will be modified importantly. But he is eminently practical as a strategist and tactician. His capacity for maintaining his leadership without invoking the purges of colleagues that have left a bloody trail in the Soviet Union suggest that he would prefer to advance the national interest by peaceful means rather than by war, that his international policy and program would be more considerate of co-existence than his writings and propaganda imply.

COMMUNIST SOCIAL POLICY

COMMUNIST social policy in China, as elsewhere, professes to aim for the uplift of the masses and the removal of privilege and of control of the masses by the privileged classes. It professes to proceed on the assumption that the people in general have been taught that their place is to work, not to think; to accept a secondary status, and to leave the direction of their lives to their betters — the landlords, the intellectuals, and the capitalists. The Communists regard it as their first objective to bring home to the people the idea of their own importance. This involves eradication of the older concepts. It calls for methods of education not dependent upon literacy; for direct, compulsory participation by the unlettered as well as the literate, in a vast enterprise of learning. In order not to defeat itself by appearing to substitute a new patronage for the older one, it must convince the people that they are self-propelled, not forced, that the new idea is their own. The process is one of conversion. Critics call it brainwashing; the Communists call it study. It is primarily persuasive, not intellectual, since it is designed to indoctrinate, not to stimulate thought. Its textbooks are handed down from above. The conclusions to be reached are not left to the "students" but laid down as revealed truth. The reward of acceptance is not heaven but paradise on earth, sometime.

The Pattern

Social policy becomes a pattern of social control in the presence of this primary objective. This need not mean, and it does not mean in China, that the totalitarian regime is insincere in its promises to raise the people to a deserved place of dignity. It does mean that for an indefinite period social planning will focus on control of thought and action, and that the advancement of the people's welfare will be a secondary objective. It means also that control objectives may often be disguised as welfare objectives. The term "study" connotes welfare, but whether or not study really conduces to welfare depends upon what is studied and how study is carried on. The Communist requirement that every individual belong to a small group of seven to thirteen members, led by a cadre (leader) who is a devoted apostle of the Marxian faith as interpreted by Mao Tse-tung, is well-conceived to accomplish its purposes. The group is the right size for discussion, in which every member is expected to take part. Members know each other intimately. The leader has no difficulty in identifying members plagued by doubts — "deviants." Members criticize each other vigorously and engage in self-criticism. They are urged to join in games, dancing, and other relaxing activities between discussion meetings. That "all work and no play" makes not only Jack a dull boy but his society a dull environment is the theme of this aspect of the program. The people are to be inspirited with respect for and pride in their country. It will be recalled that Sun Yat-sen pointed out that self-respect and national loyalty were lacking in China, and that he had hoped to instill them through tutelage. The Kuomintang had adopted his program but had not carried it into effect. The Communists are profiting by the Kuomintang's mistakes. They are not only tutoring the masses but enlisting them as panel members of the process of tutelage.

For many Chinese the process is mentally painful. They find bewildering the topics introduced for discussion: revolution and counter-revolution, imperialism, bureaucracy, capitalism, socialism, and so on. For literate men and women the acceptance of indoctrination in place of education is embarrassing, often impossible. For the overtly unaccommodating the prospects for a career are poor; the possibility of imprisonment is always present. For the intellectual who conforms outwardly, driven to do so by harsh necessity to feed and house his family, there is leniency, since the Communists realize their need of him. But leniency has limits. Its price is high. Sons of distinguished scholars — of such great minds as Hu Shih and Liang Ch'i-ch'ao — have been required to denounce their fathers, the most heinous crime in the catalog of the family system. Similarly, men and women of Western education must publish statements that label their teachers imperialists, under whose seductive instruction they were led to admire democracy. Were these denunciations sincere? From those who have fled in thousands we know that theirs were not. From those who remained in China we have no answer, but are justified in doubt.

Terror Tactics

Fear supports persuasion in the Communist arsenal. Although the bloody terrorism of 1951–1953, which wiped out the landlords, was put in storage thereafter, the memory of the pogrom remains, and the ever-present threat of its return is embodied in the civilian cadres, the police and the army units which pockmark the countryside. Fear motivated the peasants' acceptance of collectivization of the land, and the compulsion of office-workers to go into the fields. But the city man is less amenable than the farmer, and more ingenious in resistance. An official directive in November, 1956, issued by security officers in Shanghai, called for "mobilization of all organs . . . to counteract sabotage activities of spies and counter-revolutionaries, the distribution of reactionary handbills and placards in government departments, schools and factories, and disturbance by employees because of dissatisfaction with wages, amenities and the distribution of necessities." The third-degree methods used day after day and night after night upon recalcitrants in brain-washing are terrifying and benumbing to the senses. Only the strongest can keep their minds clear under such pressure.

Education

For examples of the content of social policy which these methods of control are designed to effectuate we turn to education, the arts, religion, and the position of women. Education is directed toward sloughing off the old reliance upon traditional culture and replacing it with scientific and practical knowledge. The Communists gave serious consideration to abolishing the ideographs and substituting roman letters, the alphabet used in the United States and most European countries. Apparently their decision was for gradual romanization. Meanwhile they are attempting, so far with small success, to teach illiterate adults the most frequently used ideographs, which number between a thousand and two thousand. The study of Russian has been introduced in special schools and by radio. Russian books have been translated by the hundreds and published by the million. Just as many English, Dutch, and other foreign words have been added to the language, either in their native form or in translation, so Russian words are being added, particularly those related to science, technology, and Communist ideology.

Elementary education, through middle (i.e., high) school, covers eleven years. Workers and peasants are admitted to middle schools for spare-time study. Public education is free. If official figures may be trusted, enrollment in elementary and higher education increased by one hundred per cent between 1949 and 1954; the spare-time enrollment of peasants and urban workers in 1953 was nearly fifteen million. From four per cent in 1949 the national educational outlay increased to approximately fifteen per cent in 1954.[1] All but a very few of the universities have been transformed into scientific and technical schools. University administration and curriculums are patterned upon those of Soviet Russia. In some universities small study groups not only go to class together and study and discuss together, but wash and eat together.

The Fine Arts

Mao Tse-tung is something of a poet. During the Long March from Kiangsi to Yenan he wrote a short poem commemorating the army's crossing of a mountain pass:

Loushan Pass

Cold is the west wind;
Far in the frosty air the wild geese call
    in the morning moonlight.
In the morning moonlight
The clatter of horses' hooves rings sharp,
And the bugle's not is muted.

Do not say that the strong pass is guarded with iron.
This very day in one step we shall pass its summit.

[1] Agarwala, *op. cit.*, pp. 85–87.

We shall pass its summit
And then the blue hills will be like the sea,
And the dying sun will be like blood.

It might be expected that a dictator who writes with imagination would wish to encourage imaginative writing. Mao's order that all the arts — literature, painting, music, and the rest — shall "serve the interests of the workers, peasants and soldiers, use their language, and go into their midst," does not inhibit creativeness but does restrict creative minds by requiring that all the arts must be employed as Communist tools, and that writers and artists must follow party directives. Western music is denounced as being devoted to technique, and as insensitive to social problems. Painters, writers, and composers not only must confine themselves to subjects of social significance; they must present them in a spirit of adulation of communism or of Mao or of some "labor hero," and express contempt for other social systems. To a degree it may be said that Chinese creative work is merely catching up with Western ideas of what the arts may properly portray. In the United States, for example, the poems of Walt Whitman and Gertrude Stein, the novels of Steinbeck and Sinclair Lewis and many others, and the paintings of Grant Wood, Curry, and Blume, are charged with concern for human welfare. When the Communists deprecate Western art forms as "bourgeois imaginative thinking," they are either exposing their own ignorance or concealing their knowledge. Here again we detect the compulsion of fear. We feel it when a dramatist with the superior talent of Tsao Tu disparages technique while questioning mildly that the technique of Shakespeare, as well as the beauty of his poetry and the frankness of his moral lessons to monarchs and noblemen, has assured the undying and universal recognition of his greatness. Fortunately, Chinese art and literature, though limited in scope, have kept vigor and, in many examples, lyrical beauty. If it be true, as James Cameron says in his *Mandarin Red,* that a poem of 237 lines, entitled "The Seventh All-China Congress of Trade Unions," is a catalog of delegates "in verse as blank as a factory door," the short poems of a Shanghai workingman and a Shensi peasant breathe strength and confidence. The former, entitled "Workers," runs:

We stamp our feet, and the earth trembles;
We blow a breath, and the roaring river makes way;
We lift our hands, and mighty mountains shiver;
We stride forward, and none dare block our path.
We are the workers — our strength is invincible.

The peasant's poem is entitled "Irrigation":

A three-pound pickax of steel
With one stroke cracks the crystal palace.
The Dragon King trembles
And bows, promising fearfully:
"I'll give water, I'll give water,
I'll do anything you say." [2]

Maoist Double Talk

Mao Tse-tung should either revise his guidebook, *China's New Literature and Art,* or admit to hypocrisy in his "Hundred Flowers" statement on the subject in February, 1957. In his guidebook he says: "Our literature must give expression to the thoughts and emotions of the workers. . . . We must stress their fighting will, their unbounded loyalty to the well-being of the whole." His later statement reads: "We think it is harmful to the growth of art and science if administrative measures are used to impose one particular style of art or school of thought, and to ban another. Questions of right and wrong in the arts and sciences should be settled through free discussion in artistic and scientific circles, and in the course of practical work in the arts and sciences. They should not be settled in summary fashion."

Religion a State Tool

The policy of Communist Peking toward religion is pragmatic: use religion to support communism. Denominations that will accept the government's policies, methods, and censorship are permitted to hold services. They are not required to preach Marxism or Maoism. They may even challenge the dogma of materialism. But they may not question any statement or action of the officials. They must employ complaisant pastors, run up the national flag, and become apologists for the government. Except for those who are in prison on

[2] *Atlantic*, December, 1959, p. 94.

espionage charges, under house arrest, or ministering to diplomatic missions, all clergymen from the United States and western Europe have left. In a subtle way the churches are allies of the government.

It is something of a paradox that the huge Buddhist temple, the Lama Temple, in Peking, has been restored from the dilapidated condition it had fallen into, while the nearby Confucian temple remains in poor repair. Buddhism is a genuine religion, Confucianism a body of ethical doctrine. The explanation may be that Lamaism is the Tibetan form of Buddhism, treated gently to win Tibetan confidence. Confucianism represents the old virtues of ancestor worship, filial piety, and political paternalism. Confucius's assumption of the god-given right of absolute monarchy is quite in line with authoritarian communism. But his requirement that rulers be lenient with the people if they hope to retain the mandate of Heaven suggests obligations embarrassing to a dictatorship. The Confucian temples may stand; they too have political value. But to repair and repaint them would be to condone the whole body of Confucian doctrine, to invite rather than merely tolerate their use by worshipers. Except for Christianity, which has a very small following in comparison with native faiths, the religions of China are not evangelistic. The government need not fear that native religions will oppose it. As for the people, religion is largely a matter of ceremonial. They find their ethical code in Confucianism, their rites for births, marriages, and funerals in Buddhism or Taoism. They are not ardent about doctrine, church attendance, or other aspects so important in Western religion. They are eclectic, content to accept rituals that seem suited to particular needs. The great uneducated mass is animistic, believing in the good spirits, and building spirit-walls in front of their doors to keep out the evil spirits, which cannot turn corners. If asked about the immortality of the soul they would probably reply as did Confucius: "The soul can no more exist without the body than sharpness without the knife."

A New Deal for Women

The Chinese Communists have made a special point of enlisting the enthusiastic support of women by providing for their legal equality with men. The marriage law of 1950 replaces parental choice of a mate with free personal choice. It abolishes bigamy, concubinage, and the exaction of money or other gifts in connection with marriage. Widows are permitted to remarry without stigma. Each partner to a marriage may inherit the other's property. Children born out of wedlock have the same rights as those born in wedlock. Under the law "it is strictly forbidden to drown new-born babies." Premarital sex relations and prostitution are forbidden to women.

Life for women is much freer than hitherto, though they have long been permitted to engage in professions and occupations outside the home. Like everyone else, they are organized to exhaustion and they are expected to dress in drab, bag-like uniforms. They have responded cordially to their new deal and have become Mao's most energetic allies. Since their influence upon children in the home is likely to be greater than their husbands', it would seem that Mao has killed two very large birds with one stone. But he met his match when it was decreed that children were to be brought up in nurseries and boarding schools so that their mothers would be relieved of household chores, to work for the state. To this type of freedom the women said NO. The government had to withdraw the decree. Family life is subject to interruption as husbands are moved en masse to temporary work on irrigation, construction, and other projects. But the women have kept the children at home.

As would be expected, legal rights running counter to custom have been misunderstood. Many women have misinterpreted the marriage law as encouragement to marry and divorce as recklessly as their sisters in Hollywood. Communist cadres — group leaders — have taken advantage of their positions to play at marriage. The number of children born out of wedlock has increased. In 1953 it was officially estimated that more than a million divorce cases were in process. Another estimate gave the divorce figure as two million annually. Infanticide and the abandoning of children also have increased. While poverty underlies these figures, they are related also to the "depth and complexity of the moral and spiritual crisis" of contemporary family life in China." [3]

[3] S. L. Fu, "The New Marriage Law," *Contemporary China*, Hong Kong, 1956, pp. 134–135.

On Balance: Improvement

To summarize: Chinese Communist social policy embodies good and bad features. No person of democratic point of view in the tradition of Western democracy would accept as good its crass subordination of the individual to the state, its methods of stultifying the human mind, its straitjacketing of education, its narrowing of freedom in the arts, or its subjection of religion to its own purposes. On the other hand, it has improved the lot of the common man and woman and their children. Educational opportunities have been expanded. Women have become first-class citizens. The cities have been cleaned up, so that life for the worker is healthier, probably happier. Foreign visitors comment upon the absence of beggars from the streets, the look of redemption upon the faces of the people.

What Westerners must bear in mind is the importance to the Chinese laborer of a full rice-bowl, clothing, and fuel sufficient to warm his simple cottage and to heat water for his tea. He is far less concerned with liberty than with subsistence. Only as he rises in the economic scale will he question his masters' manipulation of the intricate machinery of power. He will question it — he always has — if his living conditions worsen. The key problem of the Communists is to balance the burden of industrialization against the minimal requirements of the people's livelihood.

This does not mean that the people have accepted the suffocating dogma of communism or its brutal, hypocritical, and joyless methodology. They revealed their distaste for them in the criticisms which poured forth when, in early 1957, Chairman Mao experimentally lowered the bars. The Chinese remain the urbane, humor-loving, intelligent, and proud heirs of a unique civilization. They are an eternal people. They will decide their future in their own way.

COMMUNIST ECONOMIC POLICY

COMMUNIST economic policy in China has given first place to the development of heavy industry, secondary emphasis to light industry. We noted earlier the unusual number of ministries in the economic field. Many Russian economic advisers have been brought in, and industrial development has been hastened to ensure a solid foundation for a modern economy and for military power. In accordance with socialist principles large-scale industries are state-owned and state-operated except where it has been found necessary temporarily to permit continuance of some private concerns under strict regulation and control. Combinations of state and private operation also continue to exist. Privately-run small handicrafts have not been eliminated. Railways, telecommunications, and other enterprises of a naturally monopolistic or strategic nature are state-owned, as are banks, insurance companies, and other commercial interests.

The government has encouraged the growth of cooperatives, inclusive of credit and marketing, mutual aid societies of urban labor, and similar organizations connected with agriculture. These are aided but are also supervised by the state in the purchase of raw materials and technical equipment and in sales and administration. Trade unions exist but their officers are treated as government personnel. Workers are educated along technical, industrial, and commercial lines. At the outset of the regime it was promised that private ownership was to continue in agriculture except for large estates, which were to be confiscated and portioned out to tenants; subsequently this promise was repudiated.

Restriction of Private Enterprise

The accompanying table of percentages, published with due caution by the United States Consulate General at Hong Kong on the

basis of Chinese Communist releases, suggests the trend from private
to public industrial production during the period 1949 to 1955.

	1949	1952	1955
State firms	26.3%	41.5%	51.3%
Cooperatives	0.4	3.2	6.3
State-private firms	1.6	4.0	13.1
Private firms	48.7	30.7	13.2
Private handicrafts	23.0	20.6	16.1
Total	100.0%	100.0%	100.0%

These figures indicate that in 1955 approximately a fourth of mainland China's industrial output was in private hands.

The First Five Years

Dr. Sidney Klein, a reputable economist, made this comment
upon accomplishments during the period 1949–1955: "from a purely
economic point of view we can say that much has been accomplished
. . . Agricultural and industrial output has been increased sharply,
transportation and communications facilities have been improved,
the productive power of the armed forces and of women has been increased, educational opportunities for all segments of society have
been enlarged, etc.[1] Dr. Ronald Hsia says that "mainland China's
gross industrial value output, expressed in 'constant 1952 prices,' increased 132.4% in 1957 over 1952. In capital goods the increase
was 204.2%, in consumption goods, 85.1%." [2]

Regional Development Plan

The Communist plan has been to combine emphasis on heavy industry with regional development conducive to military strength. In
accordance with this plan three regions are receiving attention: north
China and the Manchurian provinces, the five northwestern provinces, and three southwestern provinces. Plans for the first region
center on iron and coal mining, production of iron and steel, and
ship-building; for the second region on iron-mining, steel production,

[1] "Economic Development in Communist China," *Journal of International
Affairs*, XI, 2, 1957, pp. 111–121.
[2] "China's Industrial Growth, 1953–1957," *Annals of the American Academy of Political and Social Science*, January, 1959, pp. 73, 77.

exploitation of petroleum deposits, and the generation of electric power; for the third region on the mining of tin and copper. In order to connect these regions with the more industrialized East and South, railway construction on a huge scale is essential. The government cannot hope to borrow funds adequate to the fulfillment of this ambitious program within a short period. Dependence for capital must rest on income from exports, chiefly consumption goods badly needed at home. Another necessity is the use of manpower instead of machines, which requires strict regimentation of the labor force.

The Great Leap Forward

The second five-year plan, for the period 1958–1962, was heralded as "a great leap forward." Cost and quality were subordinated to volume and speed. Production increased, stimulated by better food and by assurances that communism would pay off for everyone who devoted himself to its success. Apparently the latter appeal had considerable effect, though anyone who has lived even briefly in pre-Communist China finds it difficult to believe that it is possible for the workers to toil more continuously and strenuously than they customarily have. We may cite the opinion of a Japanese economist who wrote, after a recent visit to China: "I believe that, rather than Communist China's organizational revolution, more importance should be attached to the spiritual revolution of the Han race which it made possible, and to which Communist China's successes are, to a far greater degree, due." [3] In the face of conflicting statements of fact and interpretation, and without adequate published data, it is impossible to estimate accurately the degree of accomplishment under the second five-year plan. Peking has admitted that in some fields of effort early reports were unreliable. In other fields accomplishment appears to have gone beyond prediction.

Industrialization Emphasized

Major effort under the plan has been expended upon heavy and light industry, transportation, water power, mining, agriculture, land

[3] T. Kamekichi, "Communist China as I Saw It," *Japan Quarterly*, January–March, 1960, p. 30.

reclamation and foreign trade. Sample targets for 1962 include for steel production ten and a half million to twelve million tons, for cement approximately the same tonnage, for coal nineteen million to twenty-one million tons, for aluminum ingots a hundred thousand to a hundred and twenty thousand tons, for crude oil five to six million tons, for electricity forty billion kilowatt hours, and for timber thirty-one to thirty-four million cubic meters. Progress toward realization of projected industrial production has, on the whole, been prognostic of success.[4] But the steel from hundreds of thousands of tiny furnaces set up in peasants' backyards was of inferior quality. And diverting labor from the coal mines for other projects resulted in a shortage of coking coal. Production of chemicals increased but at a slower pace than had been foreseen.

Among the 1962 targets in light industry are, for sugar 2,500,000 tons, for salt 11,000,000 tons, for edible vegetable oils 3,200,000 tons, for cotton yarn 8 to 9,000,000 bales, and for cotton piece goods 235 to 260,000,000 bolts.[5] Attainment of these targets is being pushed by the extensive improvement of existing factories, mines, filatures, and refineries; the construction of new mills; the opening of new mines; afforestation; and exploration.

Labor's Role

Some attention is being given to labor's role in the management of industry. Both state and state-private enterprises are managed by joint committees which include workers elected by labor unions. State-private concerns operate under committees representing the government, private capital, and labor. Management of enterprises is in some instances under central supervision, in others under local direction. The committees discuss and vote upon matters of policy and operation. The manager of the concern, however, who acts as chairman, is empowered to over-rule committees' decisions. There are also Communist party secretaries attached to each enterprise who are superior in authority to the manager. Another recent innovation, reminiscent of Soviet Russian Stakhanovism, is the establishment of

[4] Target figures published in the *Asian Annual* (London), 1960, p. 33.
[5] Communist figures of industrial production value in 1958 were 117 billion yuan ($48,750,000,000), Union Research Institute, *Communist China*, p. 50.

"production committees" composed wholly of technicians and workers. These committees, inaugurated in industrial concerns in 1958, purport to encourage an "outstanding workers' movement." The plan offers special incentives in the form of bonuses and privileges to workers whose output exceeds normal. Attention is drawn to such workers by the posting of their names on honors lists and by press notices of their achievements. They are expected to exhort fellow-workers to work harder and relied on for suggestions of improved methods and tools. Better quality as well as larger quantity are the goals of this procedure.[6]

Transportation

Under the first five-year plan some thirty-one hundred miles of new railways were opened to traffic. Further progress is being recorded under the second five-year plan. At the end of 1958 nearly twenty thousand miles of line were in use and other projects were under way. While the mileage of railway is small for so vast a country it is to be compared with the eleven thousand miles operative in 1930, inclusive of the Russian- and Japanese-built lines in Manchuria, which totaled about two-thirds of the whole. Peking now is linked to Canton by rail, after construction of a lengthy bridge over the Yangtze River between Hankow and Wuchang.

The mileage of new and more modernized older highways had been raised to two hundred eighty thousand by the end of 1959. It was claimed that six times as many miles of new roads were built in 1958 as in 1957. Though durable surfacing was laid on extensive portions of the roads, about half were so hastily built as to be impassable in rainy weather. Improvement of rivers, canals, and harbors made headway. New airlines were opened within China and connecting the country with south Asian centers and with Moscow.[7]

Land to the Landless

Turning now to agriculture: We noted earlier that the Communists won the support of the peasantry by promising them land. This prom-

[6] D. Sun, *Eastern World*, July, 1959, pp. 24, 26.
[7] Union Research Institute (Hong Kong), *Communist China, 1958*, 1959.

ise ran counter to the Communist theory that all means of production belong to the state, but until Mao Tse-tung and his comrades were confident that they had firm control of the country they did not feel strong enough to repudiate their promise. They had vivid memories of the Soviet failure to collectivize the Russian land quickly, and of the disaster that befell the Kuomintang when it reneged, in 1927, on its 1924 program of land-redistribution. To the Chinese peasant the good earth is security from famine, the symbol of respectability, and the burial place of his ancestors. From 1949 to 1954, therefore, land policy consisted in the confiscation of large estates and the distribution of confiscated land to the landless. Communist figures on land ownership before confiscation began showed ten per cent of the people owning sixty-eight per cent of the land; Kuomintang figures showed ten per cent owning fifty-four per cent. Within three years 118,000,000 acres were redistributed. The Communists claimed that only three per cent of the land then remained in landlord hands, only eight per cent in the hands of "rich" peasants, while former tenants or farm laborers owned sixty-three per cent of the cultivated land. With the land there were also confiscated buildings, animals, implements, and foodstuffs, all of which were redistributed. A new day seemed to have dawned for poverty-stricken peasants.

The landlords resisted this sweeping deprivation: many killed or starved their livestock, burned buildings, destroyed implements, and ploughed up crops and irrigation ditches. These futile moves played into the hands of the government, which used them as justification for massacre of the landlords, whom it termed "bandits." Mao Tse-tung admitted the killing of eight hundred thousand; other Communist officials placed the figure at two million. In effect the landlord class was wiped out as a political factor. But all too soon the peasants learned that their new day was a mirage. They were not permitted to manage their tiny farms to suit themselves, but were subjected to directives of the ministry of agriculture about ploughing, planting, harvesting, and other procedures. Their taxes were increased, and only such parts of their crops as remained after compulsory deliveries to the government were left to them. They resented these strictures, but crops were good, peace was assuring more help on the farms, and incomes were higher. Mao, the son of a peasant, seemed to have peasants' interests at heart.

The Beginnings of Collectivization

Events were soon to demonstrate that those interests were secondary in Communist plans for industrial development which would ultimately provide modern farm machinery. For mechanized farming it was believed necessary to join together the millions of small farms into larger acreages. Social considerations gave way to economic long before the needed machines became available. The process of change began in 1954 with the establishment of cooperatives. In that year the crops were poor and the government declared that the cooperatives were out-producing the small farms. It also charged the peasants with exhibiting a capitalist point of view. Although there was some opposition within the government, Chairman Mao insisted upon going ahead with the organization of cooperative farming. By the end of 1956 his cadres of henchmen had set up five hundred thousand cooperatives. Thereupon began the second phase: the collectivization of the cooperatives and the remaining small farms. Within 1957 this phase was completed; all the land except garden plots was collectivized. The collectives were composed of a number of villages, with from five hundred to a thousand households in each collective. From being owners the peasants were reduced to being wage-earners.

The failure of the peasants to rebel against this betrayal has been explained variously. It has been pointed out that they lacked leadership, and that they were intimidated by troops and police. Another view is that physical conditions improved, infusing the people with a new spirit. Though revolt did not break out, resistance took other forms. Some peasants left the countryside. Those who remained were intensely resentful of the arbitrary methods of the local managers and party cadres. They found the new order of things complicated, destructive of community ties, and contemptuous of their status as individuals, of which they have always been very proud. Their time was so controlled by officials that they were restricted in the practice of household handicrafts, with consequent lowering of money income. Their complaints led Mao to criticize his functionaries sharply and to step up the propaganda line: "to work for the group that includes oneself is to one's own benefit." Free markets for surplus products were re-established but the peasants interpreted "surplus" so liberally that restrictions were reimposed.

The Communes

In 1958 the third phase of the collectivization program was inaugurated. The collectives were amalgamated into communes. In moving so far and so fast the Chinese outdid the Russians and did so without their blessing. The process was completed within the year but not without difficulty. In the course of operating the communes changes have been made which reflect the realization that the original plan for them was overly ambitious. It required that all land, implements, farm animals, buildings, fertilizer, seed — all means of production — and also the funds of collectives composing a commune, should become the property of the commune. Even the garden plots were taken over. Production was to be managed and produce distributed by the commune. Moreover, the communes became units of government, displacing the older local units within the area of each commune. Thus the means of production and the produce became state property. Progress toward full-scale communism was evidenced further by the provision that each member of a commune was to get an equal share of the produce whether or not the member had contributed equally with other members to the total production. Members were not individuals but the former collectives which had been amalgamated into a commune. The member collectives were administrative units within the commune. The managers of the collectives distributed the produce to individuals in the form of food and other necessities. Wages were paid partly in kind, partly in cash. When it was found that the cash payments were too small to provide incentive they were increased; this change entailed early departure from the original plan of equal income to every worker. It was found necessary also to alter the plan of equal payments by the communes to their member collectives, since some collectives had more productive soil than others and were more densely populated.

Reform of the Communes

Within less than a year of experimentation, important additional changes were decided upon. Ownership of the means of production and of agricultural produce was restored to the collectives. Garden plots, houses, chattels, small animals, bank deposits, and tools were restored to individuals. The communes were left with only administrative supervision, so far as agriculture was concerned, but continued to hold ownership in industry and commerce. The originally planned creation of urban communes was postponed. Military administration in communes was separated from civil. Developing factories, procuring farm equipment, and assisting the member collectives to market produce remained under communal management. The result closely resembles the situation in Russia.

Popular Antagonism

The peasants reacted vigorously against the discrimination shown in the limitation of the communal organization to rural areas. Large numbers moved into the uncommunized towns and cities. Those who remained on the land were antagonized by the local cadres – the Communist party overseers – who treated them abominably, ordering them about and penalizing opposition by stopping meal service at the communal mess halls. In retaliation the peasants wasted food grains and poultry, harvested crops carelessly, and even poisoned fish ponds. Though no comprehensive report is yet available it is evident that should the peasants' sentiment not be appeased by more considerate administration the comment of an unnamed observer in 1959 may be proved warranted. He wrote: "it is very unlikely, if not entirely impossible, that the Chinese Communists can consolidate the rural communes and use them as means of transition from socialism to communism. It seems likely, instead, that the crisis of the communes would lead to a total collapse of the Peking regime." [8]

Productive Programs

Communist agricultural policy has sought to bring more land under cultivation, extend irrigation facilities, introduce new crops, provide

[8] *Ibid.*, p. 218.

implements and animals, and develop research on insecticides, plant-breeding, diseases of cattle, and so on. Public investment in these projects has been as considerable as the priority of emphasis upon industrialization permits. Agricultural production, during years of good weather, is increasing. The original indifference to population control has been replaced by an educational program designed to demonstrate the necessity of limiting the birth rate. Methods of contraception are taught and the people are aided in getting medical assistance in using them. Reliable Western opinion agrees that the masses are relatively better off than hitherto, though still at a low level of livelihood.

An Over-worked Peasantry

The target for agricultural production under the second five-year plan is the doubling of 1957 output by 1962. This optimistic program faces many handicaps, among them a shortage of draft animals, the slow progress of mechanization, the diversion of manpower from the farms to such enterprises as the building of dams and public buildings, and the small-scale production of steel. The scarcity of chemical fertilizers has not yet been overcome. The peasants' morale has declined under the communal system, and the overexertion required by political task-masters is affecting their vigor. In recent years the harvests have been poor and recourse to such coarser foods as corn, sorghum, millet, and potatoes in place of the preferred rice and wheat has been necessary. None of these conditions, including areas of famine, is new to China. But their continuance over extended periods often has led to riots and rebellion. The present regime's awareness of the danger latent in them was evidenced in 1961 by its contracts for the purchase of large quantities of Burmese rice and Australian, Canadian, and French wheat.[9]

Fiscal Policy

Leaving the treatment of commercial policy to be dealt with in the next chapter as an aspect of foreign policy, we conclude here with

[9] *New York Times*, February 7, June 8, June 9, June 10, 1961.

a brief examination of fiscal policy. The national budget is prepared by the ministry of finance, which submits it to the State Council. That body considers the draft budget in relation to general lines of policy laid down by the Central Committee of the Communist party. The State Council revises the draft and sends it up to the Standing Committee of the National Congress for final consideration and action. Provincial and local budgets are prepared similarly, each subject to approval by the party and governmental echelons immediately above the drafting level.

In the national budget for 1955, submitted in June, 1954, expenditures were estimated at approximately the equivalent of $10,000,-000,000 (U.S.). Of this sum 45 per cent was allocated for economic construction (i.e., capital investment); 21 per cent for defense; 15 per cent for educational, cultural, scientific, and health work; 13 per cent for administration; and 6 per cent for reserve. On the revenue side 45.05 per cent was to be obtained from taxes on industry and trade, 13.43 per cent from taxes on agriculture, 35.94 per cent from state enterprises, 3.52 per cent from the sale of bonds, and 2.06 per cent from miscellaneous sources.[10]

Government figures on the national budget of 1958 place total revenue at the equivalent of $17,439,000,000 (U.S.); total expenditures at $17,066,600,000 (U.S.). Revenue from taxes was approximately $7,864,000,000; from state enterprises $9,175,000,000; from bonds $330,000,000; and from other sources $130,000,000. Expenditures were as follows: for economic construction, $10,945,800,000; for social, cultural, and scientific services, $1,812,500,000; for defense, $2,083,300,000; for administration, $945,000,000; for interest on loans and for foreign aid, $450,000,000; for credits to banks, $687,500,000; and for other purposes, $142,000,000.[11]

The principal taxes are on income from agriculture, trade, industry, urban realty, investments (now almost negligible), and various transactions on which stamp duties are paid. So far as is known there are no taxes on salaries and wages, and no inheritance taxes. Taxes

[10] E. S. Kirby, ed., *Contemporary China* I, Hong Kong, 1956, pp. 66–83.
[11] Union Research Institute, *Communist China*, 1958, pp. 30–37.

on the surviving private enterprises are heavy, not only because revenue is needed but to further the process of their extinction. The prices fixed by the government on the portion of agricultural produce which must be sold to it are low, amounting to heavy taxes on the farm population. It is estimated that national, provincial, and local levies amount to half the total national income.

COMMUNIST FOREIGN POLICY

THE two main pillars of Communist China's foreign policy are the attainment of national equality and territorial entity on the one hand and the maintenance of solidarity with other Communist states on the other. These two pillars stand out more clearly today than they did in 1949, when Mao Tse-tung, at the inception of the Peking Communist government, stated that China "must incline" toward Soviet Russia. When, in 1950, Mao went to Moscow and signed a treaty of alliance with the Soviet Union, the general tendency of Western observers to label China a satellite of the Russian state was confirmed. Subsequent developments, particularly Peking's support of Poland in 1956, when President Gomulka expressed the Polish people's demand for independence from Russian dominance, called for revision of this interpretation of China's relation to her mentor. Although Chinese denunciations of American policy in the Far East grew more and more virulent from year to year, it became evident in June, 1960, that Peking was not truckling to Moscow, when its leaders condemned "revisionism" as "whitewash" after Khrushchev had declared that war with capitalism was not inevitable. To students of the Chinese consciousness of culture the earlier assumption that any government of China would accept satellite status was unhistorical. The Russians themselves did not credit it, as they revealed in their cautious treatment of China as an equal, a very different attitude than they took toward European satellites. They not only understood Chinese psychology; they also recognized that the Chinese Communists had won power mainly through their own efforts, and that the most populous nation in the world was emerging from the age of imperialism.

Communist Solidarity

The second pillar of foreign policy — solidarity with other Communist states — was highlighted by Peking's reaction to the crisis in Hungary, which also arose in 1956. In that situation there was a prime factor which was not present in Poland: the determination of the Hungarian revolutionists to have free elections and freedom to withdraw from the Warsaw Pact, the Communist alliance against NATO. Like the Russians, Mao saw in this attitude the danger that communism would be displaced in Hungary and that the solidarity among Communist states might be weakened. Although Mao subsequently criticized the severe methods of repression employed by the Russians he supported their policy toward the revolution as essential to the preservation of international communism. Comparing his views of the two crises, one may conclude that he stood for national independence but not for freedom to reject communism.

International Relations

Since a political edifice — like a temple, a bank, or a milking stool — cannot stand on but two pillars, the Communists set up a third: that of diplomatic relations and trade with all states. They invited recognition as soon as their regime was established. Today between thirty and forty states have extended recognition. Among them are the United Kingdom, India, Pakistan, Burma, Indonesia, Syria, Egypt, Israel, The Netherlands, Sweden, Switzerland, Denmark, and Norway, as well as the Communist states of Europe. In 1950 the Secretary-General of the United Nations suggested that Communist China should be admitted to that body. Early in that year the United States appeared to be giving serious consideration to following the British lead, when criticism was raised in the Congress over incidents involving American consular officers in Mukden and American embassy premises in Peking. This mounted to fever heat when Chinese troops entered the Korean war. Subsequently objections were multiplied by the so-called China Lobby, a mixture of elements, some of them supporters of Chiang Kai-shek as a former ally, others opposed to any dealing with a Communist state. An organization named "The Committee of One Million" took a moral stand, likening Mao to Hitler.

Politicians used the issue as a stick with which to beat the Democratic administration for allowing the Communists to defeat the Kuomintang. American policy inhibited Canada and Latin American states from granting recognition and from voting for China's admission to the United Nations. From year to year, however, the pressure of governments which had recognized Peking for its admission to that body increased as the unlikelihood of Nationalist return to the mainland, unless as a result of another world war, became apparent.

Peking and Moscow

A tremendous power potential within 650,000,000 Chinese and 200,000,000 Russians was represented in the treaty of alliance signed at Moscow in February, 1950.[1] Ostensibly directed against a possibly resurgent Japan, the treaty actually mirrored the attitude of the signatories toward the United States, though expressed, as are all such treaties, as a defensive pact. Supplementary agreements assured return of properties taken by Stalin at the end of World War II. They further provided for the creation of joint companies for economic development in Manchuria and Sinkiang, for trade, and for Soviet credits to China of $300,000,000. The Soviet government returned the Manchurian railway network to China. In 1953 Peking reported that the Soviets had promised aid in setting up or renovating 141 large-scale enterprises. The following year, after a visit in China by Khrushchev and Bulganin, then the Soviet premier, Russia agreed to withdraw from the naval base at Port Arthur, sell her interest in the joint-stock enterprises in Manchuria, exchange scientific and technical data, and collaborate in building a railway from Lanchow in Kansu province via Urumchi in Sinkiang, to Alma Ata in Russian Turkestan. The Soviets also promised additional equipment, more aid to enterprises, and further credits of $130,000,000. In early 1956 a railway was opened between north China and Siberia, through Outer Mongolia. In that year the number of Russian-aided industrial establishments in China totaled 256, total credits amounted to $625,-000,000. Payment was made by exporting to Russia the bulk of China's surplus agricultural and mineral products. China exports

[1] See appendix.

grain, soybeans, oil seeds, tea, meat and egg products, wool, hides, tin, antimony, and tungsten. She imports from Russia such products as machinery, tools, military equipment, and petroleum. When it is recalled that before World War II China was, on balance, an importer of food, it is apparent that in lean crop years domestic consumers must suffer under the necessities imposed by export policy.

Concern beyond Asia

Premier Chou En-lai visited Warsaw and Budapest as well as Moscow in 1956, concerned to exercise what influence he could to maintain the bonds among Communist countries. His visits were helpful to Khrushchev, whose views of the way to deal with contradictions among Communists, while not identical with those of Mao Tse-tung, were closer to them than the more arbitrary ideas of Molotov and other extremist members of the Soviet oligarchy. Mao thus placed Khrushchev under some obligation to him, and grew in stature among Communist leaders. Chou's visit also revealed that China was not indifferent to events in Europe and did not intend to take an isolated role in world affairs. Subsequent developments confirmed this conclusion. More and more it became clear that the Kremlin could not exclude Peking from its decisions in dealings with Europe and the United States.

Memories That Abide

What, one may ask, has happened to China's long-held fears of Russian imperialism, which cost her more territory than her wars with Japan? Have these fears and resentments been dismissed as relics of the past? Is Peking fully confident that Moscow can be trusted not to revert to earlier adventurism at her expense? One must doubt that Chinese leaders are fully confident about a close relation with Russia. It is more to be suspected, in the light of history, that they would prefer to be less dependent upon her for capital, military equipment, technical aid, and machinery. They will desire Russian support of Chinese foreign policy but will be chary of involvements which would overtax their immature industrialism. They will be on guard against Soviet moves in Asia and Africa which challenge China's new pretensions to cultural mentorship of Asians and Africans. For her part, Russia will not favor joining in a war over Taiwan. Nor will Soviet ideologists yield to Chinese in the interpretation of the prophets of communism. Obviously the Sino-Russian alliance has in it elements of weakness.

Communist China and Japan

Peking and Tokyo are at opposite poles of political doctrine. But both would like to expand trade with each other. The pre-war significance of their trade relations is evidenced by the averages for 1934–1936: China's exports to Japan $102,400,000 — more than ten per cent of Japan's imports; China's imports from Japan $170,000,-000 — 18.2 per cent of Japan's exports. In 1954, after nine years of peace, Communist China's exports to Japan amounted to but $40,-770,000; her imports from Japan were but $19,106,000. In 1955 Taiwan's total trade with Japan was greater than Communist China's total. The effort to increase trade has, in the absence of diplomatic relations, been carried on by unofficial trade organizations. Agreements reached in 1952, 1953, and 1955 brought total trade in 1956 up to $162,000,000, with a balance in China's favor. With the purpose of adjusting the balance, the Japanese government, in 1957, removed 272 items from an embargo list which had been in effect since the war in Korea. However, a fourth unofficial trade agreement has not been implemented, owing to Peking's unwillingness to continue trading unless political recognition and attendant diplomatic relations are established. Today only a trickle of trade is moving in each direction.

Mao Tse-tung and his confreres sought to stimulate the sensitive nerve of Japanese nationalism by accusing the Japanese government of kowtowing to the United States. Prime Minister Kishi had some difficulty with leaders of his Liberal-Democratic party in holding to the line of non-recognition. He took the position that Japan's foreign policy was its own, but stated somewhat contradictorily that Japan would not act to recognize Peking except in and through the United Nations. Japanese businessmen want to maintain their very profitable cooperation with the United States but they also want the China trade. It may be surmised that Premier Ikeda, a less conservative leader than Kishi, will seek accommodation with Peking. But the frantic Communist and left-wing Socialist demonstrations of 1960 against the revised treaty of alliance with the United States strengthened the Japanese conservatives by arousing popular fears of civil strife. Measures likely to be taken in the future by any Liberal-Democratic administration in Japan to suppress resistance may so antagonize Peking as to render impossible the arrival at regular diplomatic relations. The split of 1959 in the Socialist party of Japan inhibits any prospect of a Socialist government for the foreseeable future.

China and Other States of Asia

Communist China has been recognized by most of the states of Asia. None of these states except Mongolia, North Korea and North Vietnam has a Communist government. Although the Maoist interpretation of Marxism is accepted by Communist parties in Asian countries, those parties are weak except in the three states mentioned and in Laos, which is neutralist. The Chinese learned at the Bandung Conference of 1955 that Communist imperialism was as hateful as the old colonialism to all the participating governments — twenty-nine from Asia and Africa. Chou En-lai, representing China, made a considerable impression upon members by adopting a conciliatory line, going so far as to say that his government hoped for a peaceful settlement of the Taiwan question. Chou's prestige had been increased by the influential part he played at the Geneva Conference of 1954 in bringing the war in Vietnam to a conclusion. Save in Korea and Vietnam the Chinese Communists confined themselves to propaganda, economic and cultural activities, and military subsidies until their forces invaded border areas of Burma and India in 1959. Although Tibet resisted invasion earlier, as it had resisted integration by Yuan Shih-k'ai and later by Chiang Kai-shek, it had for centuries been regarded as a vassal state within the Chinese empire. Undoubtedly the National Government of China would insist upon integration if it were in power. The United Nations failed to take action when, in 1951, Tibet appealed to it for aid. The issue therefore lies outside the sphere of Chinese foreign policy. It is rather an issue of human rights within a state. That the Communists have failed to respect their promises to preserve Tibetan institutions, that they have cruelly suppressed resistance designed to preserve Tibetan culture, may hardly be questioned. Their prestige in Asia has deteriorated correspondingly.

All-Chinese Irredentism

Anti-imperialism and irredentism — the redemption of territories to which the Chinese believe, or profess to believe, that they have historical claims — are major tenets of foreign policy today, as they have been since the overthrow of the Manchus. The first and second Republican governments were too weak to attempt the implementation of the Asia for Asians policy of Sun Yat-sen and Chiang Kai-shek; but it will be recalled that the National Government opposed the return of French authority to Vietnam, and also that it does not recognize the right of Chinese citizens abroad to expatriate themselves. In appraising the policy of Peking, therefore, it is important to seek evidence that it differs from that of previous governments. Does it go beyond their policies? Is it imperialistic in the sense of aiming at absorbing territory China has no valid historical claim to? What are the implications of Communist military power for international communism in Asia? What are the possibilities of nationalist resistance in Asian states toward Chinese subversionism? Are the peoples of Asia fearful of military invasion? These and other questions are pertinent to a reasoned appraisal of Communist policy.

Border-Area Disputes

Irredentism lies at the roots of Peking's unstable relations with Burma, Bhutan, Sikkim, and Nepal, all on the southern border of China. British control over them had put an end to China's vague suzerainty in the nineteenth century but boundary issues continued to plague their relations with China, issues which are highly complicated. Some progress toward settlement was made in 1954, when Communist China and Burma signed a treaty of friendship. They also have traded pieces of territory, Burma ceding to China 132 square miles in exchange for China's recognition of her title to 85 square miles previously claimed by China. Minor claims still await settlement. Peking's grant of $85,000,000 in economic aid to Burma has stimulated increased cultural, technical and commercial contacts between them. Coming as it did when Burmese sentiment was being voiced over the failure of the Chinese National government on Taiwan to withdraw troops stranded in Burma at the end of World War II, this gesture partially allayed Burmese suspicions regarding Peking's ultimate objectives.[2]

A similar improvement in Communist China's relations with Nepal appears to have resulted from the signing of a boundary treaty between them on October 5, 1961. This treaty, embodying recommendations of a joint commission, defines the boundary for five hundred miles between Nepal and Tibet. Nepal's King Mahendra described the treaty as based upon "the traditional customary boundary" and said that "all outstanding problems regarding the boundary have been solved to the satisfaction of both parties." One of the problems was the division of jurisdiction over Mount Everest, which lies on the border. Presumably China will control the mountain's northern slope, Nepal the southern. Previously both states had claimed the whole mountain.[3]

With Bhutan and Sikkim Communist China's relations have been worsened by menacing movements of Communist forces along their borders. Since regaining her independence, India, though treating these states as autonomous, claims to be the successor to the former British protectorate over them, with the right to direct their foreign policies. Thus they are pawns in play between China and India.

Peking and New Delhi

India recognized Peking as the legal government of China in 1950, and relations between China and India were cordial until 1956. In 1954 the two governments jointly proclaimed the oft-quoted and commendable "Five Principles of Competitive Coexistence": mutual

[2] When the United States government expressed disapproval of Taiwan's air-lifting American arms to its troops in Burma the troops were evacuated to Taiwan. *New York Times*, February 18, March 4, June 12, 1961.

[3] *Ibid.*, October 6, 1961.

respect for each other's territorial integrity and sovereignty, non-aggression, non-interference in each other's internal affairs, equality, and mutual benefit. Prime Minister Nehru has been a consistent critic of non-recognition of Peking and an advocate of that government's admission to the United Nations. He maintained these views even after the Communists' brutal suppression of Tibetan revolts in 1956, 1957, and 1959. He held to his belief in peaceful settlement when Chinese forces entered the Northeast Agency and Ladakh in 1958 and 1959 and clashed with Indian frontier guards. But these invasions of areas long deemed to belong to India, and the Chinese claim to thirty-five thousand square miles of the former and six thousand miles of the latter, aroused a high pitch of public feeling in India, leading Nehru to state firmly that although he was willing to negotiate rival claims India would fight to preserve her sovereignty over territory that she believed to be indisputably hers.

No legally defined boundary line exists between Tibet and Kashmir, in which Ladakh is located. The rivals rely upon differing maps based upon what each regards as valid historical arguments. Between the Northeast Agency and Tibet a boundary known as the MacMahon line was drawn by the British representative at the Simla Conference of 1913–1914, held to settle Britain's differences with China regarding Tibet. The line runs 850 miles westward from the west end of Bhutan to Kashmir through largely inaccessible mountain country. It has never been demarcated on the ground nor defined in precise geographical terms. It was drawn on the basis of available information and on the assumption that it would run about a hundred miles north of the plains of India. India holds that the line was accepted by China; the Chinese deny having accepted it. The problem is complicated by the fact that much of the disputed area is culturally Tibetan and that the Communist "liberation" of Tibet has caused a considerable flight of its people into India and other border states.

Diplomatic relations were not interrupted. Both governments assert the desire to settle their problems peaceably. Early in 1960 Premier Chou En-lai visited Nehru in New Delhi. They then agreed to study the boundary issues further. India's Communist party, though highly vocal on the validity of China's claims, is small and rent by factionalism. The prospect is for minor incidents and lengthy negotiation rather than for war.

Intervention in Korea

Communist China came to power too late to take part with the Soviets in the post-war division of Korea, designed to be temporary but still existent. Her intervention in the Korean war cost her heavily in men and money and probably saved North Korea from defeat. It cost her also condemnation by the United Nations as an aggressor. By its revelation of China's military power it both raised her standing among world powers and lowered her moral standing in Asia. Information about her current influence in North Korea is inadequate. It is believed that the Soviet Union defers to Peking but continues to share influence with that government. Both Peking and Moscow are aiding in the economic and military development of North Korea. Both have opposed UN efforts to unify Korea through free elections. The situation appears to be a stalemate, like the one in Vietnam.

Peking and Washington

The national interests, events, and group attitudes which have caused the United States to refuse recognition *de jure* to the Peking government have led that regime to direct its most vehement and most vitriolic charges of Western imperialism at the United States. American support of the Taiwan government as the government of China, inclusion of Taiwan as a bastion of American defense, opposition to China's admission to the United Nations, and other aspects of policy are the bases utilized by the Communists to pillory the United States as hostile to the people as well as to the government on the mainland. Despite this attitude Peking has dealt with Washington on a *de facto* basis in the negotiations for an armistice ending the fighting in Korea and in conversations between ambassadors of the two countries, conducted at Geneva and Warsaw sporadically over a period of five years; these talks resulted in the release of some of the Americans held in China. On the issue of Taiwan Premier Chou has taken the position that it is a domestic question which his government has the right to settle by force if necessary, but has affirmed on several occasions its readiness to discuss the settlement of the dispute between itself and the United States in the Taiwan area through peaceful negotiation. The United States has declared its willingness to negotiate but only after Peking renounces the use of force as the means of settling its territorial claims. Obviously the American view is tantamount to a denial that the Taiwan issue is solely domestic; in taking this stand the United States is on unquestionable legal ground, ground weakened, however, by its sponsorship of another Chinese regime on Taiwan. But the argument over the legal nature of the Taiwan issue was shadow-boxing. Until the United States is ready to recognize the Communist government as the legal government of China any discussion of the status and future of Taiwan is unreal.

Chinese Communist revilement of the United States found a target only secondary to the recognition and Taiwan issues in American opposition to Peking's admission to the United Nations. Each year, despite the Assembly's action of 1950 in voting the charge of aggression, the number of delegations favorable to admission has increased, but the support of the United States' opposition by Latin-American states has prevented a favorable majority vote. Communist diatribes were directed also at American aid to the rearmament of Japan, the use of Japanese territory as a military base, and the exertion of influence against Japanese recognition of and trade with mainland China. Still other shafts were aimed at SEATO (the South East Asia Treaty Organization), American military advisorship to Laos, and other aspects of American policy, determined mainly by Secretary of State John Foster Dulles. Increasingly violent Chinese outbursts were an embarrassment to Premier Khrushchev in his proclaimed desire that his announced doctrine of peaceful co-existence should be applied through summit meetings and conferences on disarmament and the control of nuclear testing. Its frustration at exclusion from the circle of great powers underlay Peking's maneuvers and will continue to do so so long as exclusion continues. The danger to world peace lies not in China's own strength but in the possibility that some military gesture of hers might draw the Soviets and the United States into Armageddon.[4]

[4] For a discussion of American policy see pp. 185–202.

Foreign Trade Policy

Communist China has sought to trade with all countries. Her foreign trade is conducted under the control of the Ministry of Foreign Trade and is actively promoted by the sending and receiving of trade missions. All but a small percentage of her trade is carried on by many thousands of state-owned corporations. These operate under the terms of contracts entered into by the ministry, which specify the total value of trade, import and export, and the commodities to be bought and sold. Prices are set on Chinese commodities by the ministry, which also determines what prices shall be paid for imports. The Bank of China administers foreign exchange according to rates set by the ministry. Thus the trade is regulated on a planned basis and is, in large degree, barter. In setting export prices the ministry may ignore profit margins, and dump commodities when it is deemed necessary to undersell competitors.

Figures on the trade, as listed, with the caution that complete assurance of their accuracy cannot be given, by Robert F. Dernberger in *International Economics of Communist China*,[5] show total trade valued at $4,625,000,000 (U.S.) in 1956. As compared with the index number 100 for 1930 the number for 1956 was 128, having risen from 14.2 in 1949. The percentage of total trade — imports and exports — with other Communist countries rose from 26 per cent in 1950 to 75 per cent in 1956. Yet the 25 per cent with non-Communist peoples amounted to $1,156,000,000, a tidy sum. While the percentage of trade with Western states declined greatly, the volume did not, because of the increase in total trade from $1,700,000,000 in 1950 to $4,625,000,000 in 1956. India, Burma, and other Asian markets accounted for much of this increase. From 1952 to 1956 the trade with the United States was but .14 per cent of the total, with the United Kingdom 1.28 per cent, with Japan 2.02 per cent. These figures contrast with those for trade with Kuomintang China from 1927 to 1930: 15.76 per cent for the United States, 7.81 per cent for the United Kingdom, and 27.17 per cent for Japan. The figures for 1952 to 1956 reflect the effects of the embargo imposed during the

[5] Edited by C. F. Remer; Ann Arbor, 1959. The total foreign trade of the United States in 1956 amounted to $30,000,000,000.

Korean war, which remains total in the United States and has been but partially eased by the United Kingdom and Japan.

During and after the economic recession of 1957, American business and labor organizations sought to influence the government to lift the embargo on non-strategic commodities.[6] The movement to reopen trade with mainland China was most vigorous in the cities of the West Coast, particularly in San Francisco. Some support came from individual members of the United States Congress, but Secretary of State Dulles stood adamant against a change of policy and was backed in this attitude by Secretary of Commerce Weeks. Apparently the American policy of economic cooperation with Japan inhibited the government from interfering with indirect trade involved in contracts between a number of American firms associated with Japanese firms trading with China. But the anomaly of a policy maintained by an administration generally favorable to business interests persisted, providing additional ammunition for Communist propaganda. It should be noted, however, that the likelihood that Peking would trade with the United States unless recognized *de jure* was slight. Some trade has been carried on with unrecognizing countries, but this cannot be regarded as a precedent that would be followed in relations with the United States, except under circumstances of dire necessity. The successive crop failures in 1960 and 1961 prompted Peking's efforts to buy surplus American grain after other foreign sources had been exhausted, efforts thwarted by the embargo.[7]

[6] H. S. Quigley, "Trade with Communist China," *Current History*, December, 1958, pp. 353–357.

[7] *San Francisco Chronicle*, November 21–22, 1961.

THE NATIONAL GOVERNMENT
ON TAIWAN

TAIWAN, known to the Western world as Formosa, lies a hundred and ten miles off the coast of China, opposite Fukien province. It was administered as part of Fukien prior to the cession to Japan in 1895. The Pescadores groups of sixty-four nearby islets and fourteen other islets are included within the area of Taiwan. Japan surrendered the area to the Allied Powers at the end of World War II. Its status remains undecided, but the Powers have acquiesced in its occupation and administration by the National Government. At the Cairo meeting in 1943 President Roosevelt, Prime Minister Churchill, and Chairman Stalin agreed that Taiwan would be returned to China. As both the National Government and the "People's" Government claim to be the legitimate government of China, each contends that the promise of the three leading trustee powers should be redeemed in its favor. The support of the Nationalist occupancy by the United States has prevented forcible seizure of the area by the Communists.

A Government in Exile

The National Government administered Taiwan as a province from 1945 to 1949. In 1949 the Nationalists were forced out of Nanking by the Communist forces, and took refuge on Taiwan. They set up there the system provided for in the constitution of 1947. Some twelve hundred members of the National Assembly followed the Leader-Generalissimo into asylum, as did the five yuan and other agencies of the administration, the Kuomintang, and the military hierarchy. This bulky structure of national agencies was superimposed upon the provincial and local organizations. With it came military forces of six hundred and fifty thousand men and more than a million private citizens, swelling the population to approximately eight million. Today it has increased to between ten and eleven million. Since the main island covers an area of only fourteen thousand square miles and has but two million acres of arable land, the added strain of the migration from the mainland upon its agriculture was severe.

An Interval of Brutality

The Kuomintang carried its monopolistic political tenets with it to Taiwan. Chiang remained a dictator, Leader of the Kuomintang, President of the Government, and Commander-in-chief of the armed forces. He did replace the Central Executive Committee of the party with a much smaller Central Reform Committee, but both Chiang and the Committee thought of reform not as liberalization of the government but as still greater disciplining of party and government officials to obey the orders of the Leader. The liberal principles of the 1947 constitution were pigeonholed.

Before the transfer of the National officials to Taiwan, a militarist, General Chen Yi — not to be confused with Premier, later Vice-President, Ch'en Ch'eng, also a general but of different character — was sent over as governor of the province. Chen Yi belonged to the era of the warlords. He treated the Taiwanese as a conquered people, collaborators with the Japanese. All but a few hundred thousand of these people were of Chinese ancestry. Under Japanese rule their living standards had risen as scientific methods were applied in agriculture. Their businessmen were prosperous and had accumulated wealth. Chen Yi and his associates expropriated their enterprises, supplanted their officers, and looted their banks and homes. This treatment provoked a revolt in 1947 which was savagely suppressed. Chen Yi was removed, but his administration left the Taiwanese in a hostile mood toward the entrance of the National Government. This administration awakened a movement for an independent state of Taiwan, a movement which grew stronger under Kuomintang methods of "tutelage."

Taiwanese Separatism

Resistance to reintegration with the mainland was organized by various leaders. The most notable resistance leader was Dr. W. I. Liao, a graduate of the University of Michigan, who set up headquarters of a provisional government, first in Hong Kong, later in Tokyo. He sent petitions to the United Nations and to the former Allied powers, asking consideration of Taiwanese claims to independence. Other leaders fled to Peking, not to voice a desire for Communist rule of Taiwan but to get help toward achieving independence. The movement relied upon the principle of self-determination proclaimed both by the Western states and by the Soviet Union. The argument ran that in the course of their development the people of Taiwan, though of Chinese descent, had become a self-conscious community; that therefore they should be permitted to decide their own destiny.

The independence movement was anathema to both Chinese governments. The National Government on Taiwan was, however, influenced by it to expand the participation of the Taiwanese people in provincial and local affairs, while keeping a stranglehold upon the central structure and continuing to apply the principle of "democratic centralism" which it had borrowed from the Soviet system in 1928. Two minor parties, the Young China party and the Social Democratic party, were permitted to function and they elected a few members to the legislative yuan. As time passed, the entrance of Taiwanese into the Kuomintang somewhat ameliorated the party's attitude. But minor-party leaders remained acidly critical of the Kuomintang's theory that one-party rule was essential to national unity. Within the Kuomintang also there were severe critics of the dominance of the military over the civil power, excessive bureaucratic restraint upon private enterprise, and arbitrary exercise of police power. The favoritism toward officials uncritical of oligarchical directives, which had weakened Kuomintang administration on the mainland, continued on Taiwan. The charges of maladministration made in 1958 against O. K. Yui, president of the executive yuan, indicated that although the constitution of 1947 was theoretically in force it was being bypassed in practice. One of those most frequently accused of arbitrary conduct was Chiang Kai-shek's son, General

Chiang Ching-kuo, head of the secret police, and entrusted with indoctrinating the troops to worship the Leader. Even the most friendly observers among foreign scholars agreed that the Kuomintang had failed to realize that its policies and program were frustrating the growth of liberalism and repelling the Taiwanese from confident cooperation.

The Will to Return

There were reasons for the failure. One of these was the fear of Communist infiltration; another the Nationalists' determination to return to the mainland, which entailed intolerable financial burdens for military purposes, and the maintenance of a civilian bureaucracy quite unnecessary for provincial purposes. Chiang and his elderly colleagues thought in terms of China, as was natural; to them Taiwan was but a temporary place of refuge. Having struggled so long and bitterly to hold China against forces which they believed to be conquerable, they were apparently incapable of appreciating the importance of reforming the party, allowing able young Taiwanese to take part freely in political life, replacing military administration with constitutional government, and retiring men who had served out their usefulness.

Economic Policy

The economic policy of the government, essentially state capitalism and restrictive of private initiative, operated, with American aid, to restore pre-war prosperity and to expand development of the area's resources, which are considerable. Agricultural products include rice, tea, sugar, various fruits, and camphor. Fishing is an important enterprise. Abundant water power enables the manufacture of fertilizers, cement, textiles, and paper. Steel works and oil refineries have been established. A diversified industrial economy exists today on Taiwan, and the general standard of living is second only to that of Japan among Asian peoples.

Though proper credit must be accorded to Chinese planning and to Chinese technicians for this remarkable progress, it could not have been made without the United States' help. Between 1951 and 1956 we contributed nearly $650,000,000 for economic development.

Subsequently the total has risen to more than a billion dollars. Agriculture has been aided by an American-Chinese joint commission on rural reconstruction. A program of land reform has reduced tenantry from forty-one per cent to sixteen per cent of the cultivated land, and to twenty per cent of its cultivators. Landlords were not subjected to confiscation but were paid for the portion of land that they were required to sell. Rents were greatly reduced and better seeds, fertilizers, and methods of farming were made available. Rural health conditions were improved by the establishment of health centers. The economic and social status of Taiwanese farmers has risen to a point where the two million civilian refugees from the mainland complain that their incomes have declined relatively, dependent as they are upon government salaries or pensions. An uneasy imbalance exists in which the refugees rule and are regarded as political carpetbaggers by the Taiwanese, who are better off economically than their rulers.

Social Progress

Social progress is reflected in Taiwan's system of public education. Many thousands of scholars and teachers were among the civilians who followed the Kuomintang to Taiwan, and their presence has made it possible to implement a program of primary, secondary, and university education. China's justly famed Academia Sinica — moved to the capital, Taipei — has taken the lead in research and publication. Related to cultural activity are the hundreds of journals and the twenty-eight newspapers of the island. Unhappily, education and journalism are so heavily staffed with refugees that Taiwanese find another cause of resentment in their exclusion from positions which they feel should be assigned to them.

Military Policy

Military policy remains in the forefront of government planning and its execution puts a disproportionate strain on the budget. Though the United States has provided training and equipment, the government's burden for the maintenance of a half million soldiers, sailors, and airmen is heavy. The refugee troops are having to be retired on pensions as over-age. They are being replaced by younger Taiwanese, who now comprise some forty per cent of the military forces. Again the Kuomintang's policy has been discriminatory, reserving the higher rankings for refugee officers, which is naturally resented.

Foreign Policy

The National Government's foreign policy has centered upon the maintenance of its international status as the legitimate or *de jure* government of China. To that end it has established embassies and legations in the forty-odd states which recognize it as such, and twenty-odd consular offices. Its representatives have been active in the Security Council, Assembly, and auxiliary bodies of the United Nations. It offered to contribute troops to the United Nations forces during the war in Korea, but the offer was declined in view of the possible complication of relations with Communist China. It has frequently reiterated its intention to return to the mainland. It has not sought recognition of Taiwan as a state.

Taiwan's existence as a government, however, has depended upon the support of the United States, with which it entered into a treaty of mutual security in 1954.[1] This treaty pledges American aid *against* attack upon Taiwan, but not *of* attack by Taiwan upon the mainland. President Eisenhower "unleashed" the Generalissimo from controls imposed by President Truman upon Taiwan's freedom to attack, but on November 23, 1958, a joint statement was issued by Secretary Dulles and President Chiang which was interpreted as renouncing the use of force by the National Government, except in defense. Only two months earlier Chiang had argued vigorously with American representatives that the time was ripe for attack. His argument made an impression; but it also increased American appreciation of the risk of being drawn into war, and of the need for Chiang's pledge to refrain from unilateral attack. The stubborn attitude of the Leader, his belief that his cause was not irretrievably lost, made difficult the relations between him and his American ally. On the American side there was some resentment that the military aid furnished at a cost of

[1] See appendix.

several billion dollars appeared not to be fully appreciated. This aid included provision of a military assistance group of between two thousand and three thousand officers, a small combat force, a large fleet, Matador and Nike missiles, and a considerable amount of up-to-date equipment in other types of arms.

Friction with the United States

The presence of American soldiers on Taiwan was desired by the Government but resented by the people, whose living conditions were far below those of the troops. In May, 1957, this feeling burst normal bounds in a riot in Taipei, during which damage was done to the American embassy and information office. The incident was provoked by a court martial's acquittal of a sergeant accused of killing a Chinese whom he had taken for a peeping Tom. It led to renewed efforts by the National government to obtain revision of the status-of-forces agreement under which United States military personnel were subject to the jurisdiction of United States military courts. The Taipei administration desired that, as in Japan and in European states where United States troops were stationed, personnel accused of criminal acts, performed when off duty, should be subject to trial in the courts of Taiwan. The issue of jurisdiction was rooted, on the Chinese side, partly in national pride, partly in the feeling that United States procedure took insufficient account of evidence presented by Chinese witnesses. On the American side the issue stemmed from differences between American and Chinese law and judicial procedure. Sentiment in the United States Congress, so far from cordiality toward limiting American jurisdiction on Taiwan, was inclined to expanding it in Europe and Japan. The desire of the National Government for jurisdiction was advanced vigorously, but with accompanying assurances that every effort would be made to calm popular antagonism and to acquaint the people with American legal principles. Consideration was given in Washington to reducing the 10,000-strong American colony, 8,500 of whom were employees of one or another United States agency. The numbers were unnecessarily large and their privileged status recalled the obsolete foreign settlements to many Chinese.

The Quemoy-Matsu Crisis

Like the Japanese, the people of Taiwan, including the refugees, were stung by Communist taunts that they were being controlled by the United States. Dependence upon another state is not welcome to any nation. And the presence of foreign troops, however well-behaved, is a constant reminder of that dependence. In Taiwan's case the situation was complicated by the known interest of the United States in utilizing the area as a bastion of its own defense. That American forces should, rather, be employed offensively to aid in reoccupation of the mainland was, to Chiang and his colleagues, the proper *raison d'être* of their presence on Taiwan. In 1958 this attitude brought Taiwan and the United States to the brink of war with Communist China over the conflicting claims of the National and the "People's" Governments to the offshore islands of Quemoy and Matsu. In 1952, with the assent, if not at the urging of Secretary Dulles and the United States military advisers to the National Government, Nationalist forces on the islands were strengthened. President Chiang considered that American encouragement of this action involved a moral commitment to aid in the defense of the islands.[2] Early in 1955 the Congress of the United States authorized President Eisenhower to employ American forces "as he deems necessary for the specific purpose of protecting Formosa and the Pescadores, including the security and protection of such related positions and territories of that area now in friendly hands, and the taking of such other measures as he judges to be required or appropriate in assuring the defense of Formosa and the Pescadores." In August, 1958, the Communists stepped up their bombardment of Quemoy and Matsu, upon which the Nationalist troops had been increased to a hundred thousand men. Chiang urged that his planes be permitted to bomb the Communist positions. For a time Secretary Dulles and the President appeared to be inclined to acquiescence, despite the risk that American planes might be drawn into the fighting. Mr. Dulles stated that the position of the United States in the whole of the Western Pacific was involved in the retention of Quemoy and Matsu by

[2] Tang Tsou, *The Embroilment Over Quemoy*, Institute of International Studies, University of Utah, 1959.

the Nationalists, and that the bombing of concentrations on the mainland might become a part of the defense of Formosa.[3] The word "might" was generally interpreted, in the United States and abroad, to mean "will." President Eisenhower, on September 11, likened the situation to the Munich crisis, and said: "I do not think that the United States can be either frightened or lured into appeasement. I believe that in taking the position of opposing aggression by force, I am taking the only position which is consistent with the vital interests of the United States and, indeed, with the peace of the world." [4] These statements appeared to express the readiness of the Secretary of State and the President to follow the lead of Chiang Kai-shek in risking world war over the possession of islands appurtenant to the mainland and, properly, under international customary law, to be regarded as part of the mainland.

That war did not result probably was owing to the counsel of American military officers and to the outspoken criticism of leading American and foreign statesmen, among them Senators Green and Fulbright, former Senator Lehman, Hugh Gaitskell, leader of the British Labour party, and U Thant, representative of Burma at the United Nations. Mr. Dulles reversed course and the Generalissimo was persuaded to accept releashment. The joint statement of November 23, 1958, above referred to, was the result of the return to wisdom. Chiang Kai-shek, however, continued to over-man Quemoy and Matsu, islands as remote from Taiwan as the mainland, with slight defensive value for Taiwan.

What Future for Taiwan?

The Taiwan issue is insoluble so long as Peking, Taipei, and Washington hold to their present attitudes. Under-Secretary of Commerce Herbert Hoover, Jr., said in March, 1956, that millions of dollars' worth of trade was being conducted between Taiwan and the mainland.[5] But the overtures addressed to the Taiwan Government by Premier Chou En-lai in June, 1956, were ignored.[6] Chou appealed

[3] *New York Times*, September 7, 1958.
[4] *Ibid.*, September 12, 1958.
[5] *Ibid.*, March 28, 1956.
[6] *Ibid.*, June 29, 1956.

for unity and promised fair treatment and jobs, without regard to past misdeeds. His argument attempted to undermine morale by references to relatives who longed for the return of the refugees. The United States, he asserted, was an undependable ally, which would ultimately desert them.

In a careful study prepared by Professor Robert A. Scalapino of the University of California in 1959, some interesting suggestions are offered toward a solution of the problem of Taiwan.[7] He does not rule out the possibility of a revolt by the eight million native inhabitants against the three million refugee Chinese. But he foresees a process of very gradual Taiwanization of the whole community, if absorption by the Chinese Communists on the mainland does not take place, through intermarriage, economic and political cooperation, and replacement of the Chinese troops by Taiwanese. A Republic of Taiwan might evolve in which the self-conscious Taiwanese people would establish and maintain a nation-state. The pretense of the refugee regime to being the government of China would be dropped, the off-shore islands would be evacuated, and the refugee officials and the civilian and military inhabitants who preferred to leave Taiwan would be protected against ill treatment and aided in establishing homes elsewhere.

It is apparent without argument that this solution, which has humanitarian appeal, envisages indefinite continuance of the present relationship of the United States to the National Government. It would require that the succeeding republic be internationally guaranteed, for obvious reasons. With the inevitable rise of China to rank with the strongest industrial and military powers such a guarantee could not be honored without war. That the United Nations would underwrite the guarantee may be doubted.

The Cairo Agreement

At the Cairo Conference of 1943, as already noted, the leaders of the United Kingdom, the United States, and the Soviet Union rec-

[7] Professor Scalapino's study is part of a Committee Print of the Committee on Foreign Relations, United States Senate, 86th Congress, 1st Session, November 1, 1959, prepared by Conlon Associates, San Francisco, California, dealing with United States relations with Asia. See pp. 139–144 of the report.

ognized that the future of Taiwan was for China to decide. This agreement undoubtedly expresses the attitude of all the Allied Powers. While all international agreements are made under the implied principle *rebus sic stantibus* (while circumstances remain unchanged), there is no reason to believe that the United States desires to treat Taiwan as a permanent military base. The most highly esteemed American expert on military strategy, Hanson Baldwin, holds that Taiwan is not essential to American defenses in the western Pacific. The United States solidly endorses present commitments but wants no part in a program of imperialism. Nor would the American people wish to stand in the way of a fair settlement between Peking and Taipei.

Such a settlement appears to be remote. It may be that the notable bargaining capacities of the Chinese people could work out a compromise, but information is lacking upon terms that might be acceptable to both governments. In the absence of a plebiscite there is no sure basis for a judgment upon the views of the Taiwanese people as a whole. Evidence that they would prefer not to be ruled by the present regime is considerable. They might prefer the status of an autonomous region under Peking to the indefinite continuance of the threat of an attempted military conquest, provided that autonomy would be genuine. Whether Peking would offer that status, and whether the Taiwanese would trust any of Peking's promises are questions unanswerable today.

The Dilemma of the United Nations

The trend of world opinion, including that in the United States, is toward admission of Communist China to the United Nations. Should that happen, the National Government would have to yield its representation of China to the "People's" Government. Whether or not Peking would consent to the representation of a Republic of Taiwan is another unknown quantity. It might do so in anticipation of an ultimate union of Taiwan with the mainland. As a member of the United Nations China may not be expected to contemplate permanent separation of Taiwan from her domain. To the Taiwanese it is less important that they live under a flag of their own than that they live well and in amity with the Chinese colossus. Their prospects for fair treatment from China within the United Nations would not be lessened and might well be improved over those attendant upon continuance of present tensions.[8]

[8] See pp. 189, 202 for United Nations action on the seating of Communist China.

DEMOCRACY'S CHANCE IN CHINA

REALISTIC, as opposed to sentimental, appraisal of Chinese politics and policies today must take account not only of current issues and invective but of the heritage of the past. To try to deal intelligently with a great people, whose rulers are exhibiting symptoms of paranoia, without weighing their past experience, is as unscientific as to attempt a medical diagnosis without reference to a patient's record of health and illness. Democracy's chance in China — one may speculate but not prophesy — may be furthered by our patient contemplation of some major historical clues to contemporary events and attitudes.

The Long-lived Empire

Chinese political thought, until the end of the nineteenth century, conceived of monarchy as divinely ordained. Restraints upon absolutism were normal and customary, not legal. They were normally effective against tyranny. If they failed, revolution might depose a ruler who had disregarded them. Stable government was ensured by an able body of civil servants. For more than two thousand years the Chinese state persisted, despite conquests and periods of rule by Mongol and Manchu invaders, who adopted Chinese principles and procedures. In all other East Asian states China was looked upon as superior in civilization and administration. Her magnificent cultural attainments were admired by Marco Polo and the scholarly European missionaries who entered the country in the sixteenth and seventeenth centuries.

Imperial government often had survived periods of economic dislocation followed by rebellion. Dynasties had fallen but had been replaced by new dynasties. Not until the nineteenth century was the throne challenged as an absolutist institution. The Manchu dynasty, shaken to its foundation by the T'aip'ing Rebellion in mid-century, was too late, a half-century after, in yielding to the advice of constitutional reformists. It succumbed to demands for a republic, and China was launched upon an uncharted sea. Since 1911 she has been seeking, so far with small success, to devise a democratic republican system which will restore her former status and stability. The ambitious plan for the first republic was devitalized within two years; the second, which was republican in name only, lasted for a decade; the third receives little more than lip service on Taiwan; the fourth is the self-styled "People's Democratic Dictatorship," the Communist totalitarianism.

The Breakdown of Authority

The Chinese republics inherited an educated aristocracy from the Empire. They inherited also a self-respecting, ethically-motivated but illiterate peasantry and proletariat. The gentry were the property-owners and public officials. They thought of government in terms of monarchy and bureaucracy. Only a few conceived of political parties as the representatives of common men. They were not without regard for the people, but they did not consider them competent to take part in politics. The people agreed. Public education was essential to their attaining competence and self-confidence. Until they were prepared to vote and hold office, good government might have been provided by the gentry — good government in the sense of the responsible paternalism required by the ethics of the Chinese family system. That was the hope of Sun Yat-sen, father of the first republic. That such good government was not provided may hardly be explained as the result of the collapse of Chinese civilization. It was the result rather of the collapse of central authority. An ethical code, however good, does not stand alone, even between individuals. It must be supported by law and law enforcement. When a code is applied to public affairs, it is incalculably dependent upon the law.

Manchu Reforms

Although the Manchu dynasty had failed to make use of Chinese resources of statesmanship, wealth, and people to comprehend and parry the impact of European and Japanese imperialism, its last reigning Emperor, Kuang Hsü, was a modernist who might, had he lived and been loyally supported by his chief minister, Yuan Shih-k'ai, have continued to encourage the progress toward constitutional monarchy begun in the closing years of his dynasty. It is true that provincial conservatives, to promote their own interests, aided the Republican Revolution, but they might have been propitiated by capable leadership backed by a loyal army. The people viewed the Manchus as aliens; but the Boxer Rebellion was directed mainly against Western controls, and it was not a country-wide movement. Though Western ideas inspired the Revolution, Western governments took no part in it. We cannot be sure how China would have changed had the Revolution failed to unseat the monarchy, but we may speculate that she might have moved as steadily as Japan toward constitutionalism.

Chinese Criticism of the West

Sun Yat-sen and Chiang Kai-shek excoriated Western governments and business interests for demeaning China and profiting at the expense of her people. Yet China profited also, from foreign administration of imperial services and from foreign educational, industrial, and medical enterprises. The Open Door doctrine advanced a principle which worked to China's advantage. Another Western doctrine — democracy — was an inspiration which Chinese liberals weigh against the injurious effects of imperialism. Sun Yat-sen died in 1925, eighteen years before the unequal treaties of the nineteenth century were completely annulled and China received recognition as a fully independent state. President Chiang acknowledged the attainment of equality in 1943 while reiterating Dr. Sun's bitter criticisms of Western imperialism.[1] To some extent these indictments were challenges to the Chinese people to exert themselves, yet they represent continued Chinese suspicion and sensitiveness toward foreign action capable of interpretation as derogatory to China. In appraising Chinese politics and policies today the West must take account of the fact that these indictments antedate the rise of communism and are significant in relation to it.

[1] Chiang Kai-shek, *China's Destiny*, New York, 1947.

The Attitude toward Russia

Eurasian Russia shares the heritage of China's past, and China's remembrance of this share need not be doubted. The U.S.S.R. aided the Chinese Communists' rise to power in only minor degree. The Soviet-Chinese alliance is a marriage of convenience. The West will fail to serve itself if it envisages Mao Tse-tung as an apostle of any prophet but himself, or as uninterested in areas formerly parts of the Chinese Empire and now restless under Soviet patronage. Japan, with the West, is the target of Chinese resentment at her imitation of the imperialistic policy which the West discarded at the Washington Conference in 1921–1922 as inconsistent with its proclaimed principle of the self-determination of nations. The future course of China's political development will not be greatly influenced by her confidence in one or another government but will be essentially determined by internal forces. This is not to say that China's relations with other peoples will not affect her future political, social, and economic order. On the contrary, it is impossible to separate any country's domestic trend from its international relations.

The Nature of the Imperial System

In attempting to foresee, through a glass darkly, the prospects for democracy in China we observe that the political genius of her people has been displayed mainly in authoritarian forms of government. Probably no one will deny that they were successful in the conduct of monarchy, nor that the advisory councils, the administrative boards, and the civil service had no legal responsibility to anyone but the reigning emperor. Such consideration as they gave to popular interests was in recognition of moral obligations, not of formal law. The route to high office was not barred to poor men, but the cost of education kept most of them from the examination cells. The small segment of the populace from which the great majority of officials came was highly influential, its influence rooted in social status, not in the process of election. Sovereignty resided in the emperor, though not always exercised by him. His "mouth was golden, his words were jade." Paternalism enlightened absolutism, but authority was absolute.

Vast China was held together by a notable civil service, a bureaucracy of scholars. Not all of them were able, and some who were able were not men of virtue. Not a few bought their way in. But as a whole they provided reliable and capable administration. That they did so in posts remote from the capital, and in provinces largely autonomous, was due to the control exercised over them by the central government through its system of appointments, censorship, inspection, and removal. Whenever that system broke down, administration broke down with it. At times the resulting misgovernment brought economic distress, accompanied by increased banditry, rioting, and peasant uprisings. Confusion might continue until a new dynasty came to power. Heaven had heard the people's complaints and had transferred its mandate. Thereupon a new cycle of the familiar pattern began.

The Gentry's Control of Policy

Why did the Chinese fail to develop a more broadly representative political organization? Why was the aristocracy content to be without a parliament of nobles and gentry? Why were its members unimpressed by European experiments with such parliaments? Does their indifference to representative government argue that it is alien to the Chinese political genius, that they are morally and spiritually so constituted as to be content with mandarinism? If an educated aristocracy prefers bosses to ballots what hope is there for democracy?

The probable answer is that the gentry in imperial China regarded themselves as adequately represented through their monopoly of executive and administrative offices. They were also the emperor's counselors on public policy. They were unchallenged by the merchant class, composed as it was of less literate proprietors of small enterprises. The merchant guilds and the bankers were not without political influence, and much of the regulation of economic activities was conducted through the guilds. But businessmen did not expect to be reckoned as entitled to have a part in the combination of monarchy, oligarchy, and bureaucracy that made up the government of imperial China. In the social scale, though many merchants were wealthy, they ranked below the farmers. As for the masses — eighty-five per cent of whom were owners of tiny farms, tenants, or farm laborers — they lived precariously, too close to the line between poverty and pauperism to be concerned with public affairs. They respected scholarship and coveted education for their children but were fortunate if they could manage to find the few coppers required for attendance at the village school. One of the most difficult questions to answer is why the Chinese, with their exalted regard for education, did not sooner provide a system of free public schools. Failure to do so seems not to have been a calculated restraint favorable to the aristocracy but part of the general assumption that social services, except in emergencies, were not the government's business. As in the West, the conception of public responsibility for social services awaited the rise of the middle classes to a status from which demands for a more liberal attitude could not be denied.

The Culture of the Masses

Chinese society was not a veneer of masters overlying a servile peasantry. Though Chinese ethics did not contemplate that men were born equal, it enjoined a superior to recognize his duties as well as his right to his superior place. The culture of the learned sifted down to the illiterate, who took pride in it. The family system did not suppress individualism or personal dignity. Men and women of humble station were self-respecting, and their sensitiveness to the respect of others was and is an outstanding characteristic. These are attributes which argue against a hasty conclusion that democracy is unadaptable to China.

The Need for Time

Half a century of experiment with republican forms is too brief a period to afford adequate evidence upon the ultimate choice the Chinese will make in their determined effort to attain modern statehood. Although liberalism has been frustrated by self-interested politicians, militarists, and dictatorial leaders both white and red, its exponents have continued to insist upon the establishment of constitutional government — constitutionalism in fact, not only in form. The roll-call of democratically-minded statesmen and scholars, businessmen and

journalists, who have worked to implement republicanism, is creditable. Many have lost their lives in the cause of freedom. They and
others have left their marks on the constitutions of 1912, 1923, and
1947.[2] Worthy of remark also is the enthusiasm shown by the masses
toward opportunities offered them at intervals to share in political
activities. They despise regimentation.

Tutelage Neglected

Republican government is a difficult system to operate. New re-
publics in Asia have in many instances reverted to military bureaucracy. In essence this has been the recourse of the Kuomintang — the
Nationalist party of China — since the suffocation of the first republic
by Yuan Shih-k'ai. Students differ about the justification for this policy. It would seem that the Chinese people, despite their illiteracy,
were ready for introduction into political life on a more generous
scale than was accorded them by the dominant party and its Leader.
As before noted, culture in its broader sense is not limited to the literate upper crust. The people are seasoned in the art of getting along
with one another, which is the art of politics. "Tutelage" might better
have been attended with participation in the pattern of progress laid
down by Sun Yat-sen, since one learns by doing while being instructed in how things are done. Dr. Sun hoped that his plans would
be followed, but after his death they were pigeonholed by the tradi-
tionalist right wing of the Kuomintang, buttressed by the army. The
National Government also repudiated promises of social and economic reforms on the premise that they were Communist-inspired,
forgetful of the fact that they had been formulated by Sun Yat-sen.
These departures from the liberal principles of the party's founders
lost it much of the confidence of the most respected elements — the
intellectuals and the peasantry. The Kuomintang has not recovered
from the effects of its shift away from its early liberalism.

Communism Aided by Japan

Communism entered China in the midst of the chaotic era of the
warlords, the *tuchün*. Affiliating with the Kuomintang, its agents gave

[2] See appendix for the constitution of 1947.

some aid to the Nationalist revival and return to power. As the Communist aims to seize control became clear, the break with the Kuomintang was inevitable. In taking advantage of the internal strife to make war on China, Japan provided the Communists with the opportunity to develop military strength and to win the peasants' confidence by fighting the Japanese and introducing reform measures which the Kuomintang had repudiated. The subsequent downfall of the National Government probably was owing in considerable degree to its loss of the peasants' confidence. The Communists capped the explosive powder of agrarian discontent with a warhead more powerful than the superior armament of the Government. The warhead was the promise of a better life.

In power at Peking the Communists not only used as justification the landlords' resistance to expropriation to massacre hundreds of thousands of the gentry, but followed the example of repudiation by collectivizing land they had parceled out among the peasantry. The "democratic dictatorship" is indeed a dictatorship such as China has never before known; as for the "democratic" part, though there are various forms of democracy none can exist as a partner of dictatorship. Mao and his comrades, however, have shown awareness of the masses' preference for economic and social as contrasted with political reforms by expanding educational opportunities for young and old, increasing food production, improving public health facilities, and raising the position of women.

Deference to Democracy

The two party dictatorships of the right and left bear striking resemblances to each other. Both are dominated by men who have headed them for a generation and who won and now hold power as military leaders. Both permit the unpropertied and illiterate to vote and to discuss political issues but not to decide policy. Both treat complaisant intellectuals well. Both use secret police and soldiers to silence criticism. Both are raising the standards of the welfare of the masses. Both nourish resentment toward the Western influence in Asia. There are liberals in both camps but they are at present unable to exert effective influence.

Both systems are in name democratic republics, in fact bureaucracies in which democratic types of representation may be regarded as agencies of tutelage. Both governments aspire to implement the impressive guarantees of civil rights written into their constitutions. Both rest legally upon universal suffrage. Control of elections by the ruling parties prevents our regarding either junta's popular assemblies as broadly representative advisory bodies; but we may assume that experience in them will contribute to the growth of democracy. We lack comparative scientific studies that would permit comparison of the two embryonic approaches to truly popular parliaments. But it should be reassuring to the West that both systems reject in principle any hypothesis that the Chinese people are incapable of or disinclined toward democracy.

Keys to Freedom

Western history teaches that possessors of power do not relinquish it willingly. Relatively well-educated classes in Western states have had to struggle for political rights against the tradition that only those with a "stake in the country," attested by ownership of property, were entitled to vote and hold office. American women were not enfranchised until 1920. In China the *principle* of democracy has arrived. But a long, rough road lies ahead to popular understanding of its meaning, realization of its value, and insistence upon its transfer from paper to practice. Historical and contemporary forces retarding progress along this road can be overcome by new elements — social and physical science — leavening the lump of illiteracy and poverty. These forces obviously are brought to bear through the processes of education. The education of China's masses must be envisioned as a longtime process, but the whole lump need not be leavened before the advent of constitutional government. The Chinese people are culturally conditioned to enlightened leadership motivated by consideration for their welfare. Every country, democratic or not, relies upon informed leadership. In every country such leadership is impeded by elements hostile or indifferent to it. Already China has a reservoir of middle-aged and younger men and women scientifically and culturally prepared for leadership. Evidence is considerable that they are straining at the leash of dictatorship. Mass education cannot but strengthen their influence in a civilization so respectful of moderation in social relations.

Not the least of the potential influences toward the progress of education in China is the association which her intellectuals may enjoy with Western scholars. The majority of Chinese scholars have no choice but to remain on the mainland whether or not they are converts to Maoism. To hold themselves aloof from this enlightened and respected element, as American scholars have been required to do by the Department of State, is to throw sand on the embers of liberalism and to deny encouragement to those from whose ranks liberal leadership is most likely to come.

The Chinese Will Decide

We noted earlier that the Chinese people are sensitive in the matter of personal dignity but have not associated it with political equality. Sun Yat-sen called upon them to put the attainment of national equality before individual liberty. Chiang Kai-shek and Mao Tse-tung have followed Sun in his incitement to nationalism. In the West the new nations which emerged in the nineteenth century accepted the well-tried doctrine that political liberty and freedom in economic enterprise must march together. But with the rise of communism to power in the Soviet Union this doctrine was forced to defend itself. Rival economic theories and interests became dominant divisive forces between the East and the West. The Communist challenge to the free-enterprise system raised doubts in Asia and Africa about the relation of individual liberty to economic betterment. Democracy as a way of political life is challenged along with its economic ally, free enterprise, and is faced with the great task of proving its right to be recognized as the best hope of mankind. To do so it must take more thoughtful account of Asian and African traditions and conditions. It cannot expect that Western political development will be duplicated in China or elsewhere in Asia. It would be presumptuous to predict what the future form of Chinese society will be but we have found evidence to indicate that it will not be totalitarian communism. To the property-conscious, family-centered Chinese free enterprise is preferable to state capitalism, which is the actual system in communist countries today. But they do not equate free enterprise with large-scale private capitalism as it has evolved in the West and in Japan. As for political liberty, they want it but are, as a people, unaware of its full meaning. They will be influenced toward awareness, and toward adaptation of democracy to Chinese conditions by humane application of principles conducive to mutual confidence. Granted that principles of policy are more easily formulated than implemented, we lose sight of them amidst the complexities of day-to-day developments unless we keep them in the forefront of our thinking.

Desirable Principles of Policy

The principles of good policy are not new. They are:

1. Mutual recognition of and by all states in accordance with general practice under international law.

2. Mutual practice of the right of self-determination of a state's political and economic systems.

3. Co-existence, involving normal relations between states and non-interference in each other's affairs.

4. International jurisdiction over all disputes deemed by the Assembly of the United Nations to be international in character.

5. Membership of all states in the United Nations, subject to acceptance of obligations under the Charter.

All nations are responsible for the application of these principles. For that there is need of patience, knowledge, understanding, and sympathy. These essentials must contend with ignorance, suspicion, ultra-nationalism, and fear. They contend also with the contemporary obsession with the necessity of haste, which demands quick decisions and determined, even forceful, action. On the other hand they are supported by the world-wide premonition of the consequences of nuclear war. While the balance of power persists there may be time for reason to prevail over passion.

WHAT POLICY FOR THE UNITED STATES?

WHETHER to recognize the People's Government at Peking as the legal government of China remains undecided by the government of the United States after more than a decade of Communist control of the mainland. In earlier chapters the positions of Peking and Taipei relative to the United States have been noted. Although our subject is Chinese, not American, politics it seems desirable to conclude with a viewing of the Chinese scene from this side of the Pacific. Why has our government, under both Democratic and Republican leadership, and with consistent accord between the Administration and the Congress, held firmly to the course of non-recognition? Are the reasons given for this policy well-considered? Has the policy redounded to the national interest of the United States, and to world interest in disarmament and peace? Has it helped or hindered the prospects for democracy in China?

American Policy Explained

The Department of State, on August 11, 1958, issued a "Memorandum on United States Policy Regarding Non-Recognition of Communist China." Until the Kennedy Administration indicates otherwise, this document stands as our most comprehensive and authoritative statement of policy toward China. It begins by saying that:

Policy toward Communist China has been an important issue since the Communists came to power there. In the United States the issue is a very real one to the vast majority of the people. As a result of Chinese and Korean Communist aggression in Korea the United States suffered 142,000 casualties, bringing tragedy to communities all over the country. Nevertheless, despite the emotions thus engen-

NOTE: Portions of this chapter were published in "Toward Reappraisal of Our China Policy," *Virginia Quarterly Review*, Summer, 1959.

dered, and the abhorrence of the American people for the brutality and utter lack of morality of Communist systems, the policy of the United States toward China has necessarily been based on objective considerations of American interest. It also reflects a continuing appraisal of all available facts.

Though this memorandum gives assurance that American policy is not inflexible the condition it lays down for a change of policy is that "the situation in the Far East shall so change in its basic elements as to call for a radically different evaluation of the threat Chinese Communist policies pose to the United States and free world security interests."

The Nature of the Threat

Two basic considerations underlie the conviction that recognition of the Communist regime would produce no tangible benefits and would materially assist "Chinese Communist attempts to extend Communist dominion throughout Asia." These are (1) that the Soviet bloc "is engaged in a long-range struggle to destroy the way of life of the free countries of the world and bring about the global dominion of communism," and (2) that the free countries of East Asia are "peculiarly vulnerable" to the threat of communism. The United States must "neutralize" this threat, not only to save East Asian peoples for the free world but to secure other free nations from the consequences of Communist control of East Asian resources and points of vantage. "The extension of diplomatic recognition by a great power normally carries with it not only increased access to international councils but also enhanced international standing and prestige." Denial of recognition handicaps the affected regime and thus limits its ability to pursue its policies. American recognition of the regime would "confuse and demoralize" East Asian nations, which might either resort to "desperate measures" or "seek the best terms possible from Peiping." It might also lead Chinese abroad to cease supporting Taiwan or to act subversively against the countries they live in.

Other Reasons for Non-recognition

Recognition is being withheld on these additional grounds: (1) that the Communists have not completed the conquest of the country. The "generally recognized" government of the Republic of China controls Taiwan with a "sizeable military force." Although this force "presents a significant deterrent to renewed Chinese Communist aggression," recognition of Peiping "would seriously cripple, if not destroy altogether," the Taiwan government. That government now is "enabled to challenge the claim of the Chinese Communists to represent the Chinese people and keeps alive the hopes of those Chinese who are determined eventually to free their country of Communist rule"; (2) that American recognition "would inevitably lead to the seating of Peiping in the United Nations," which would "vitiate if not destroy the U.N. as an instrument for the maintenance of international peace."

Ten Questions

Informed and thoughtful Americans have questioned the policy of non-recognition from its inception. The advent of a new Administration warrants a review of the most debated questions. They are:

1. Would recognition aid the Communist states' struggle for world dominion?

2. Would it be demoralizing to the new states of Asia?

3. What consequences would be likely to follow the admission of Communist China to the United Nations?

4. What is the obligation of the United States toward the free world?

5. Is non-recognition consistent with international law?

6. What is the legal status and political significance of Taiwan?

7. What are the strategic and political implications of our relationship to Taiwan?

8. Would recognition be injurious to American prestige?

9. Would recognition produce no tangible results for the United States?

10. Has *de facto* recognition served and will it continue to serve our purposes?

The following discussion is indebted to many persons who have written or spoken their views, but it embodies primarily my own reflections.

1. Would recognition aid the Communist states' struggle for world dominion?

Global dominion may be read to mean military conquest. But American policy increasingly emphasizes the prospect of using other methods of influencing undeveloped or pre-industrial economies: economic, cultural, and psychological, for example. These methods are equally available to the democracies. True, Communist China's attraction for peoples of related culture works for her, but not as an ally of force. Their reaction to the brutal treatment of Tibet should be proof that the smaller nations of Asia are as alert to the danger of Communist imperialism as they are suspicious of the motives or possible consequences of aid from former colonial powers of the West. True also, they are impressed by China's economic progress under communism. But the West is on firm ground in its potential for demonstrating that economic progress can be accompanied by personal liberty if it avoids alliances with rightist dictatorship. Too little weight has been ascribed to the nationalist spirit of the newly independent countries, which is neither pro-Communist nor anti-Communist. It is a compensating force against their military vulnerability.

2. Would recognition of Peking be demoralizing to East Asian states?

There are two available indices pertinent to an answer to this question. Both of them appear to run counter to an affirmative reply. One is the extent of the recognition accorded to Taipei on the one hand and to Peking on the other. The other is the attitude of United Nations members toward the admission of Peking to that organization. During the past decade forty-one governments have recognized Peking as the *de jure* government of China. Among them are Britain, Norway, Sweden, Denmark, Finland, The Netherlands, and Switzerland. In Asia and Africa twenty-four governments, only three of which are Communist — North Korea, Mongolia, and North Vietnam (Vietminh) — now recognize Peking, while but twenty-six recognize Taipei. Of the fifty-five states maintaining diplomatic relations with Taipei, twenty-one are in the Americas. Only eight European states continue to recognize Taipei. Fourteen governments recognize neither Chinese regime. These figures include eight non-members of the

United Nations. They also include the Vatican, thus totaling a hundred and ten.

In the 1958 vote of the United Nations Assembly upon whether or not to consider seating Peking twenty-eight delegations voted for consideration, forty-four opposed and nine abstained from voting. After the Soviet Union, the most urgent proponent of consideration was India. In the 1959 test vote twenty-nine delegations voted for consideration, forty-four opposed and nine abstained. In 1960, thirty-four delegations were for consideration, forty-two opposed and twenty-two abstained. Of the seventeen new members admitted to the United Nations between the 1959 and the 1960 votes on this issue, 3 voted for consideration, 13 abstained and one did not vote. Not one of the new member states voted against consideration.[1]

Evidence upon the factors which influenced one or another government to recognize Peking or to favor Communist China's admission to the United Nations is inadequate to a confident conclusion. There are Communist parties of varying strength in most countries, but they control the government in but three states of Asia other than mainland China — North Korea, Mongolia, and Vietminh. It is reasonable to assume that the principal basis for recognition has been the *de facto* situation. Coupled therewith may be the felt need of diplomatic relations for commercial purposes. Whatever the influencing factor, it seems clear that the burden of proof rests upon one who

[1] In 1960 the following states voted for consideration: Afghanistan, Albania, Bulgaria, Burma, Cambodia, Ceylon, Cuba, Czechoslovakia, Denmark, Ethiopia, Finland, Ghana, Guinea, Hungary, India, Indonesia, Iraq, Ireland, Mali, Morocco, Nepal, Nigeria, Norway, Poland, Romania, Senegal, Soviet Union, Sudan, Sweden, Ukraine, United Arab Republic, White Russia, Yemen, and Yugoslavia. Total 34.

Voting against consideration: Argentina, Australia, Belgium, Bolivia, Brazil, Britain, Canada, Chile, China, Colombia, Costa Rica, Dominican Republic, Ecuador, El Salvador, France, Greece, Guatemala, Haiti, Honduras, Iran, Italy, Japan, Jordan, Lebanon, Liberia, Luxemburg, Mexico, The Netherlands, New Zealand, Nicaragua, Pakistan, Panama, Paraguay, Peru, The Philippines, South Africa, Spain, Thailand, Turkey, United States, Uruguay, and Venezuela. Total 42.

Abstaining: Austria, Cameroon, Central African Republic, Chad, French Congo, Cyprus, Dahomey, Gabon, Iceland, Israel, Ivory Coast, Laos, Libya, Malagasy, Malaya, Niger, Portugal, Saudi Arabia, Somalia, Togo, Tunisia, Voltaic Republic. Total 22.

Not voting: The Congo (formerly Belgian). Total 1.

holds that a change in American policy would be demoralizing to Asian governments.

3. What consequences would be likely to follow the admission of Communist China to the United Nations?

The figures cited above indicate an increasing doubt among United Nations members that admission would be other than beneficial. The importance of a nation of seven hundred million people renders absurd its exclusion from the world organization. This realistic view underlay the statement of Britain's Foreign Secretary, Lord Home, when he told the House of Commons on February 8, 1961, that "the facts of international life" required the seating of Peking in the United Nations. This view had been expressed as early as 1950 by Secretary-General Hammarskjöld. Apprehension of added discord within the United Nations is countered by the hope that with recognition of equality Communist China would be held to a corresponding sense of international responsibility. Peking would not be free to pursue its own objectives without regard for world opinion. It is clear today, also, that while Peking still "inclines toward" Moscow the degree of its inclination has diminished since 1949. Again, Communist China faces tremendous problems of internal construction. Good conduct in the United Nations would contribute to relationships helpful to solving these problems. For the indefinite future she has far less to gain by war than by peace. Apparently the sentiment that despite her intervention in the Korean war she is entitled to the opportunity to measure up to Charter requirements as a "peace-loving" nation is growing among United Nations members.

4. What is the obligation of the United States toward the free world?

The concept that the United States, because of its great wealth, power, experience in democracy, and unselfish motives, has a unique responsibility for the preservation and expansion of the free world, is a high and valid one. This concept underlies the Monroe and Open Door doctrines and our attempt to save democracy from Kaiserism and Hitlerism. But it may lead to failure to take full account of the sensitiveness of other peoples — even of our friends — or of their natural belief that several heads may reach wiser judgments than one.

Unfriendly or skeptical governments may question the purity of our motives. Skepticism among nations is inevitable so long as each, in practice, seeks first the national interest. It is utopian to think that they will cease to do so. The most that can be hoped for is that they will deal with one another in international councils and in a spirit of cooperation.

No government has supported the use of international procedures more consistently than that of the United States since the founding of the United Nations. While it may hardly be argued that we have diverged from this principle in a legal sense, in exerting our great influence to sway the United Nations voting on the admission of Peking, can it be denied that we have diverged in a political sense? Or that success so far attained has been offset by a decline in many states of confidence in American statesmanship?

5. Is non-recognition consistent with international law?

The Department of State has hitherto, in relation to Communist China, taken the position that recognition *de jure*, i.e., of the Peking government as a legal entity, may be decided upon as a matter of national policy, independently of any obligation under international law. This view is not in accord with the normal practice of states, including the United States. We have, in a majority of cases, applied the criteria laid down by Thomas Jefferson: control of the national territory, general acceptance by the inhabitants, an actually functioning administration, and acceptance of international obligations. Throughout the world and in the United States, it is recognized that the Peking government is solidly established, is functioning effectively, and is not seriously threatened by opposing elements nor by the Taiwan government. Without negotiation the attitude of Peking toward its international obligations cannot be determined.

This is not to deny that recognition is an act of policy. Obviously it is. However, a member of the international community is bound by international law in the exercise of its policy-making power. Otherwise there could be no international community. The absence from international law of the firm sanctions of municipal law does not justify disregard of international law. Rather it imposes upon governments a heavier moral responsibility to respect that law. Americans put great emphasis upon moral principles in international affairs. We open the way to the charge of insincerity if we fail to apply such principles in so perilous a situation, one that involves the risk of nuclear war. Certainly the international community seeks constantly to raise moral standards. But up to the present the act of recognition has not been held to signify approval of the moral standards of the recognized state. Our prompt acceptance of the new government of Iraq should be sufficient evidence of this fact. There are numerous cases in point. For one government to presume to judge the moral standards of another can hardly lead to anything but the old battle between the pot and the kettle. No one member or bloc may assume the duty that rests upon the whole community.

6. What is the legal status and political significance of Taiwan?

Japan acquired Taiwan in 1896 after her defeat of China, and governed the island and appurtenant islets until 1945. Defeated in the Pacific war, Japan was dispossessed by the Allied Powers, who permitted the National Government of China to assume the administration of Taiwan. However, no peace treaty was signed until 1951. At that time Japan surrendered the area to the Allied Powers, not to China nor to either the Taipei or the Peking government. Since 1951 there has been no international determination of its status. Both the "National Government of the Republic of China" and the "People's Government of the People's Republic of China" claim it as part of China. Award to China means award to a recognized government of China. Both Taipei and Peking claim to be the true government of China. Thus the issue of recognition is interwoven with that of Taiwan's future status. Both Mao Tse-tung and his premier Chou En-lai have declared that "it is inconceivable that there can be diplomatic relations between China and the United States without a settlement of the dispute between the two countries in the Taiwan region." [2] They insist that American military forces must be withdrawn, leaving the future of Taiwan to be settled between Peking and Taipei.

In 1943 at Cairo President Roosevelt, Prime Minister Churchill, and Generalissimo Chiang Kai-shek agreed that Taiwan should be restored to the "Republic" of China; that the words "National Gov-

[2] Edgar Snow, "A Report from Red China," *Look*, January 31, 1961.

ernment" were omitted is not significant, since at that date there existed but one central regime. Stalin adhered to the agreement at Potsdam in 1945. Subsequently it has been assumed generally that the governments signatory to the 1951 Treaty of San Francisco would support the Cairo agreement. As observed in an earlier chapter, the rise of an autonomist movement among the native-born Taiwanese has become a third complicating factor.

7. What are the strategic and political implications of the United States' position relative to Taiwan?

That Taiwan is today included within the American perimeter of defense has been fully demonstrated. The area is viewed by this country as part of the free world, to the defense of which our military position (see above, pp. 167–168) is officially regarded as crucially important. Until the outbreak of hostilities in Korea the Truman Administration had not adopted this view but had indicated that Taiwan was an internal Chinese issue.[3] The North Korean attack on South Korea induced the shift to resumption of military aid to Formosa and the neutralization of the Taiwan Strait. In 1951 Dean Rusk, then Assistant Secretary of State for Far Eastern Affairs, said that "We recognize the National Government of the Republic of China, even though the territory under its control is severely restricted. We believe it more authentically represents the views of the great body of the people of China, particularly their historic demand for independence from foreign control." [4] In 1954 Communist China's reemphasized indication of intention to extend her area of control to include Taiwan led the United States to enter into a defense pact with Taipei. Under the pact this country is committed to defend the area but not to support Taipei should that government attack the mainland, nor to act with it in defense of Quemoy and Matsu. The United States is granted and accepts the right to dispose its forces in and

[3] White House press release, January 5, 1950. President Truman stated that: "The United States has no desire to obtain special rights or privileges or to establish military bases on Formosa at this time. Nor does it have any intention of utilizing its armed forces to interfere in the present situation. The United States will not pursue a course which will lead to involvement in the civil conflict in China. Similarly, the United States Government will not provide military aid or advice to Chinese forces on Formosa."

[4] Bulletin of the Department of State, May 28, 1951.

about Taiwan and the Pescadores in accordance with mutual agreement upon the need of such action. Chiang's effort to expand the coverage of the treaty in 1958 failed but the original provisions are to hold indefinitely unless denounced by either party upon a year's notice.

Obviously, American official concepts of Taiwan's importance to the defense of the United States hinge upon our view of strategic necessities, which changed with the demonstration of Communist Chinese military power in Korea and the focusing of Peking's hate campaign upon this country.[5] Clearly, the United States has no thought of appropriating Taiwan but regards itself as morally bound to save its people and a former ally from engulfment by communism. Taiwan is also a significant bastion for the defense of our allies, Japan and the Philippines. Though it should not be overlooked that Japan's people are apprehensive of possible involvement should our military position in Japan be utilized in the defense of Taiwan, the ruling forces there, which appear to be destined for indefinite control of the government, have asked only that it be consulted before our facilities are used for operations outside Japan.

It is unlikely that Peking will accept the United States' demand that it renounce the use of force as a precondition to negotiation about the future status of Taiwan. Were it to do so on condition of admission to the United Nations recourse might be had to the agencies and procedures of that organization, including the International Court of Justice, for settlement of this complicated issue. The Communist government's present lack of interest in United Nations membership so long as the National Government remains on Taiwan may or may not import objection to an autonomous regime there during consideration of a settlement. Taking part as a United Nations member in the consideration would put Peking in a position from which refusal to accept its result would be difficult to justify.

[5] Doak Barnett points to former Secretary of State Acheson's assertion in 1958 that "on four occasions between 1948 and 1950 the highest American military authorities concluded that it was not essential to the United States' vital interests that Taiwan be retained in friendly hands" (*Communist China and Asia*, p. 419).

8. Would recognition of Peking injure American prestige?

A great country has a natural reluctance to depart from a set line of policy. Prestige marches with firmness in the exercise of power and refusal to be influenced by threats or malicious propaganda. If well-grounded in the respect and confidence of other governments it rivals military strength as an ally of diplomacy. Respect and confidence develop from appreciation of intelligent and considerate use of power.

The United States has not relied solely upon power to maintain prestige. It has sought consistently the good will of other peoples through concern that agreement with its policies shall not rest upon fear, and it has eschewed the supercilious self-assurance of nineteenth-century imperialism. Faced today with a challenge to its most cherished ideals and to its dominant economic interests, and conscious of responsibilities which over-tax its experience, it may over-estimate the importance of prestige based upon power. It may under-estimate considerations which undermine prestige. The United States need not fear loss of prestige through a change of policy. No state would regard American recognition of Peking as a confession of fear or weakness, approval of communism, or an intent to desert our friends. The governments which now recognize Peking will hardly contemn this country for agreeing with them; a majority of other states are awaiting our lead. The opportunity for cooperative planning and action would increase rather than diminish.

9. Would recognition produce no tangible results for the United States?

Taking trade as the principal "tangible" result that may be foreseen, American business and labor leaders and organizations have been urging since 1953 that the embargo imposed in 1950 upon all United States trade with mainland China be modified in favor of non-military goods.[6] In 1957 that country's foreign trade amounted to between four and five billion U.S. dollars, and was shared by most non-Communist countries. Peking reported an over-all increase of fourteen per cent in 1958. Though our economists foresee no con-

---

[6] This author's survey of anti-embargoism appeared in *Current History*, December, 1958.

siderable market if trade channels are reopened, American industries and shipping companies argue that they should be able to compete before the field is pre-empted by others. A number of Congressmen have endorsed this effort, and important newspapers have supported it with vigorous editorials. It is remarkable that our businessmen, particularly those on the West coast, have been able to make so little impression upon this aspect of policy. Observable here is an illustration of Jacob Viner's well-known thesis that economic diplomacy is not controlled by bankers and businessmen but by governments.

10. Has de facto *recognition served, and will it continue to serve American purposes?*

American policy, acknowledging as it has that the Communist regime is in fact in control of mainland China, has held that it is not necessary to have formal diplomatic relations with a government in order to deal with it. This is true. Some gain has accrued from our *de facto* recognition of Peking. The hostilities in Korea were terminated, a similar result was reached regarding Vietnam, and release of most of the Americans imprisoned in China was effected. It is possible, but not probable, that trade might be carried on — as it now is with several non-recognizing states — if the embargo were lifted. Peking, however, has desired and presumably still desires *de jure* recognition not only for its practical advantages but as a badge of equality. Its resentment at not receiving it is a psychological bar to rational handling of major problems. The usefulness of *de facto* dealings declines as resentment grows. It is entirely unlikely, for example, that such dealings would serve for the establishment of inspection stations for implementing an international program to control bomb-testing.

There are other important purposes to be served. At present non-recognition is a bar to reciprocity in cultural, scientific, and informational relations. When countries deny entrance to each other's scholars and journalists they obstruct channels to objective judgment of conditions that underlie policy. American contacts with Chinese liberals who may value them as leverage for criticism of totalitarianism are prevented. Agencies of mutual understanding widely believed to be more efficacious than official procedures are unable to function.

How this situation can be construed as contributory to the advancement of democracy or the prospects for world peace is difficult to comprehend.

Barriers to Flexibility

As previously noted, the condition laid down in 1958 for a change in the United States policy was that "the situation in the Far East shall so change in its basic elements as to call for a radically different evaluation of the threat Communist policies pose to the United States and free world security interests." Under the Truman Administration Secretary of State Acheson had hoped that the threat would diminish, the dust would settle, and normal relations would become possible. Even after the Korean conflict the Eisenhower Administration continued in that hope. Obviously the opposite happened. Peking's attitude toward the United States was more hostile in 1960 than at any time since 1949. Meanwhile the number of states recognizing Peking and favorable to seating its representatives in the United Nations had increased, suggesting that the governments of the free world doubted that non-recognition protected their security. Evidences of strain in the Moscow-Peking axis could be viewed as another change of "basic elements" in the Far Eastern situation. However, American attachment to a former ally, and military assessment of the strategic value of Taiwan continued to bar the way to a change of policy.

Signs of Change

When the Kennedy Administration took office there were indications that American policy toward China might be modified. During the "Great Debate" that preceded the 1960 elections, Senator Kennedy's view that the Chinese coastal islands of Quemoy and Matsu were not of major concern to the United States seemed to portend a change in the wind should he become President. It semed unlikely that Lord Home, Britain's Foreign Secretary, would have said in Parliament that Communist China ought to be seated in the United Nations unless his government believed or knew that President Kennedy was of the same opinion.[7] In June, 1961, reports were published

[7] *Eastern World*, London, March, 1961, p. 11.

that Washington was considering what attitude to take if another government were to propose that Peking be admitted to the United Nations.[8] Previously steps were taken to establish diplomatic relations with the Republic of Mongolia, for the purposes of determining whether or not it is independent of Moscow and of having a listening post near to Peking. Recognition was to be accompanied by support of Mongolia's admission to the United Nations, which Nationalist China had vetoed in 1955 on the ground that it was a Soviet satellite.[9] And in March, 1961, Washington and Peking resumed conversations on minor issues through their ambassadors at Warsaw.

Resistance to Change

When Chairman Mao and Premier Chou En-lai, who had hoped that the New Frontier might not embrace Taiwan, found that it did so their stepped-up torrent of anti-Americanism played into the hands of American opponents of change. In February, 1961, the Committee of One Million, which has on its steering committee the odd combination of Senator Paul Douglas and Representative Francis Walter, announced that 54 Senators and 285 Representatives had endorsed its statement that Communist China ought not to be admitted to the United Nations.[10] In July, 1961, the Senate voted 76 to 0 to oppose recognition of Peking and its admission to the United Nations. Senator Fulbright, chairman of the Foreign Relations Committee, explained the vote as a "Republican ritual, a hangover from the Joseph McCarthy era." [11] Said Fulbright: "We are prisoners of our past mistakes." In August, 1961, the House voted 395–0 for the same resolution. The Daughters of the American Revolution reaffirmed their plea for stronger support of the Taiwan regime.[12]

Support for Change

There were, however, proponents of a more realistic policy. The General Synod of the newly formed United Church of Christ, repre-

---

[8] *New York Times,* June 24, July 7, 1961.
[9] *Ibid.,* April 21, 1961.
[10] *Ibid.,* February 21, 1961.
[11] *San Francisco Chronicle,* August 1, 1961.
[12] *New York Times,* April 22, 1961.

senting two million members of the former Congregational and Evan-
gelical and Reformed Churches voted for recognition and admission.[13] Clarence Morse, chairman of the Federal Maritime Board in
the Eisenhower Administration, called for recognition as a move toward influencing the Chinese Communist experiment, saying: "In my
personal opinion, this inability [to exert influence], voluntarily assumed on our part, is one of the greatest tragedies in our international
relations of the postwar decade." [14] An editorial in the *San Francisco
Chronicle*, which supported Richard Nixon in 1960 for the presidency of the United States, chastised the Democratic party for being
"so flabby that it refuses to cast a single vote against a Republican
ritual." The editor called for change, saying: "The longer this farce
goes on, the farce of pretending that a nation of 700 million people
does not exist, the more ridiculous it becomes. Historians will one
day marvel at the fact that in the mid-Twentieth Century the United
States Government chose to make ignorance and self-deception national policies." [15]

No Change of Policy

Those who hoped for a more realistic policy were disappointed.
The State Department declared that Lord Home's statement "was
not the result of any consultation between our two governments,"
adding that so long as Communist China demanded the expulsion of
what her Foreign Minister called the Chiang Kai-shek clique as the
condition of her entrance into the United Nations it "was doubtful
whether there are many in this country or abroad who feel that the
Communist Chinese should gain admittance on these terms." [16] Secretary of State Rusk evaded the issue of the comparatively small percentage of the Chinese people under the jurisdiction of the National
Government, introducing instead the concept of cultural representa-

[13] *Ibid.*, July 7, 1961.
[14] *San Francisco Chronicle*, February 2, 1961.
[15] *Ibid.*, August 1, 1961. It may be noted here that as early as October, 1949,
in a round-table discussion at the State Department, a majority of member specialists on the Far East from our universities favored consideration of recognition. The minutes of the three-day meeting were not published but were
mimeographed under the title *Transcript of Round Table Discussion on American Policy toward China*, Department of State, undated.
[16] *New York Times*, February 10, 1961.

tion. He said that we recognize that "the leadership from the main-land, not just government officials but their professors, their scholars, their scientists, their artists, that came over there [to Formosa] were to us and are a much more genuine representation of the China that we have known and the great traditions of China than what appeared on the mainland at that time [1951]." But when asked whether he would still say that Chiang's government is "an authentic representa-tive" of the people of China Mr. Rusk replied: "I'm talking in this context about the great cultural heritage of China. I think you would find a more direct expression of that in Formosa than you would find in another regime." [17] In another interview he recognized that "if we go into a nuclear weapons test-ban situation, this would make no sense unless all those who might be in a position to develop nuclear weapons were members of the party, or, if we were in a general dis-armament arrangement involving conventional forces, such an ar-rangement would not be realistic unless it included all of those who had powerful armed forces at their disposal." [18]

In response to an invitation from President Kennedy Vice Presi-dent and Premier Ch'en Ch'eng of the National Government on Tai-wan visited the United States. In a joint communiqué issued by the President and Mr. Ch'en on August 2, 1961, the President reaffirmed American support of China's National Government and our deter-mination to continue to oppose the admission of the Chinese Com-munist regime to the United Nations. He and Mr. Ch'en expressed agreement that developments in the economic and social field "pro-vide vivid proof that the Communist regime cannot meet the genuine needs and desires of the Chinese people." The President said also that "in contrast with the disregard of human rights manifested by the Chinese Communist regime" the unprecedented economic and social progress on Taiwan "was accomplished without violence to the great traditions and human values which have been cherished throughout history by the Chinese people." [19]

Mr. Ch'en tried to persuade the President against recognition of

[17] Press release, Department of State, No. 111, March 6, 1961.
[18] *Ibid.*, No. 63, February 10, 1961.
[19] *New York Times*, August 3, 1961.

Mongolia and support for Mongolia's admission to the United Nations. Whether the United States discontinued its plan to recognize Mongolia in response to his plea or for other reasons was not explained. At any rate it did so, but it continued its support of admitting Mongolia to the United Nations in the hope that this attitude would aid toward winning the votes of new African states against the admission of Peking.[20] Eventually the Taiwan government refrained from voting on the admission of Mongolia after twelve African states threatened to vote for the admission of Peking. Thus Mongolia was admitted on October 25, 1961, in a package deal that linked her admission with that of Mauritania, protégé of the African states. Neither the United States nor Nationalist China took part in the voting on Mongolia in the Security Council, recorded as nine to none.[21]

A Change in Tactics

Doubt that the 1961 United Nations Assembly would vote for another year's moratorium on consideration of the seating of Peking led the United States government to change its tactics but not to change its policy. It supported a New Zealand proposal for debate on the question of China's representation, which was approved by the Assembly's steering committee on September 21, 1961. A Soviet proposal for discussion of "the restoration of the lawful rights of the People's Republic of China in the United Nations" also was approved by the steering committee. Our delegation stated its willingness to debate on both proposals but made it clear that we would continue to oppose Peking's admission.[22]

The change of tactics was embodied in a double-barreled plan. The first barrel contained a charge that the question of admission was a substantive matter which required for decision a two-thirds majority in the Assembly. Hitherto the Assembly has decided such questions by simple majority vote. The second barrel, to be fired if the first missed its mark, reportedly was suggested by the British gov-

[20] *Ibid.*, August 12, 1961.
[21] *Ibid.*, October 26, 1961. It may be noted here that among the non-aligned states which met in conference at Belgrade in September, 1961, only those having diplomatic relations with Peking joined in recommending its admission to the United Nations during the 1961 session (*ibid.*, September 7, 1961).
[22] *San Francisco Chronicle*, September 22, 1961.

ernment. It would aim at setting up a special Assembly committee to consider the matter of representation and to report to the 1962 session.[23]

The United Nations Votes "No"

Assembly debate on the issue of Chinese representation began on December 1 and was concluded on December 15, 1961. The election of five states — Syria, Sierra Leone, Mongolia, Mauritania, and Tanganyika — to membership during the 1961 session had increased it to 104. Although some fifty delegations took part, the discussion was perfunctory. Observers reported a pervading sense, most objectively voiced by Canada, of the futility of further postponement of Peking's admission, but many members were more deeply concerned with other problems: the replacement of Secretary General Hammarskjöld, the pacifying of the Congo, and the increasing tension in Berlin. The Soviet Union's demand that the Chinese Nationalist delegation be ousted antagonized members, who offered, however, no feasible plan for seating two Chinese delegations. The recent chill in Peking's relations with India, and the above-noted "package deal" of the "Brazzaville" states of Africa with Taipei tended to discourage serious consideration of a pre-ordained decision. However, the United States made doubly sure of a vote favorable to Taipei by moving to treat the issue as important, or substantive, requiring a two-thirds vote for the passage of the Soviet resolution to seat Peking and to unseat the Nationalist delegation. The motion was passed but proved unnecessary. No resolution was introduced for an interim study committee to report to the 1962 session, though Canada, Sweden, and four other states were known to favor such action. The Assembly voted 48 to 37, with 19 abstaining, against Communist China's admission.[24] Thus the trend of opinion during the past two years, re-

[23] *New York Times*, September 16, 1961.

[24] States voting for admission: Afghanistan, Albania, Britain, Bulgaria, Burma, Byelorussia, Cambodia, Ceylon, Cuba, Czechoslovakia, Denmark, Ethiopia, Finland, Ghana, Guinea, Hungary, India, Indonesia, Iraq, Mali, Mongolia, Morocco, Nepal, Norway, Pakistan, Poland, Rumania, Sierra Leone, Somalia, Soviet Union, Sudan, Sweden, Syria, Ukraine, United Arab Republic, Yemen, Yugoslavia.
States voting against admission: Argentina, Australia, Belgium, Bolivia,

flected in Britain's shift to support for admission, failed to sway the decision.

The Outlook

It must be assumed that for an unpredictable period the governments of the United States and the People's Republic of China will be without regular diplomatic relations with one another. In view of the long history of confident relations between the American and Chinese people it may fairly be asked whether Washington and Peking are reflecting the general will of their citizens. Do these policies reflect the will of the political leaders themselves? Are the policies in fact policies? Or are they procedures to postpone having policies, induced by mutual fear and frustration? Have these procedures succeeded in advancing prospects for democracy and world peace?

Mao Tse-tung, Chou En-lai, and their comrades in the Politburo show little understanding of the obstacles to the attainment by the American people of a realistic perspective toward China's situation. They can point to American mistakes in policy and procedure. But they cannot divide the American people from their government. And they know that the United States has the best record of any major power in relations with China, that it has no imperialist ambitions toward Asia, and that our people want peace and co-existence with honor. By turning off the flow of vitriol Peking can contribute to a less confused state of the American public mind.

On our part Americans can contribute by rethinking the Chinese problem in the light of history, some of it very recent. It is to be hoped that the time has not passed when both Washington and Peking will substitute reason for emotion, knowledge for propaganda. The alternative was well-expressed in a recent address by Dean John C. Bennett of the Union Theological Seminary of New York, reported

Brazil, Cameroon, Canada, Chile, China, Colombia, Costa Rica, Dominican Republic, Ecuador, El Salvador, France, Gabon, Greece, Guatemala, Haiti, Honduras, Iran, Ireland, Italy, Japan, Jordan, Laos, Liberia, Libya, Luxembourg, Malagasy, Malaya, Mauritania, Mexico, New Zealand, Nicaragua, Panama, Paraguay, Peru, Philippines, Senegal, South Africa, Spain, Tanganyika, Thailand, Turkey, United States, Uruguay, Venezuela.

States abstaining: Austria, Central African Republic, Chad, Congo, Congo Republic, Cyprus, Dahomey, Iceland, Israel, Ivory Coast, Lebanon, Netherlands, Niger, Nigeria, Portugal, Saudi Arabia, Togo, Tunisia, Upper Volta.

in the *New York Times* of October 28, 1961: "The temptation to turn the cold war into a holy crusade is ever with us and in so far as we yield to it we make impossible the tolerance and humanism which must yet come into international relations if there is to be a future for mankind."

Appendixes, Recommended Readings, Index

THE CONSTITUTION OF THE NATIONAL REPUBLIC OF CHINA (Effective December 25, 1947)

PREAMBLE

The National Assembly of the Republic of China, by virtue of the mandate received from the whole body of citizens, in accordance with the teachings of Dr. Sun Yat-sen, founder of the Republic of China, and in order to consolidate the power of the state, safeguard the rights of the people, ensure social security, and promote the welfare of the people, hereby adopt this Constitution to be promulgated and enforced throughout the land for faithful and perpetual observance by all.

CHAPTER 1 — GENERAL PROVISIONS

ARTICLE 1 — The Republic of China founded on the *San Min Chu I* (Three People's Principles*), is a democratic republic of the people, governed for the people and by the people.

ARTICLE 2 — The sovereignty of the Republic of China resides in the whole body of citizens.

ARTICLE 3 — Persons possessing the nationality of the Republic of China are citizens of the Republic of China.

ARTICLE 4 — The territory of the Republic of China comprises its original areas. It shall not be altered except by resolution of the National Assembly.

ARTICLE 5 — All racial groups of the Republic of China shall enjoy equality.

ARTICLE 6 — The National flag of the Republic of China shall have a red background with a blue sky and a white sun in the upper left corner.

CHAPTER 2 — RIGHTS AND DUTIES OF THE PEOPLE

ARTICLE 7 — All citizens of the Republic of China, irrespective of sex, religion, race, class, or party affiliation shall be equal before the law.

ARTICLE 8 — Freedom of person shall be guaranteed to the people. No person may, except in case of *flagrante delicto* as otherwise provided for by law, be arrested or detained except through a judicial or a police organ in compliance with legal procedure. No person may be tried or punished except by a law court in accordance with legal procedure. Any arrest, detention, trial, or punishment, if not in accordance with legal procedure, may be resisted.

---

* The Three People's Principles are the Principle of Nationalism, the Principle of Democracy, and the Principle of People's Livelihood.

When a person is arrested or detained on suspicion of having committed a crime, the organ responsible therefor shall in writing inform the said person and his designated relatives or friends of the reason for the arrest or detention, and shall, within twenty-four hours, turn him over to a competent court for trial. The said person, or any other person, may petition the competent court to demand from the organ concerned the surrender, within twenty-four hours, of the said person to the court for trial.

The court may not reject the petition mentioned in the preceding section, nor may it order the organ concerned to make an investigation and report first. The organ concerned may not refuse to execute or delay in executing the writ of the court for surrender of the said person for trial.

When a person is arrested or detained illegally, he or any other person may petition the court for investigation. The court may not reject such a petition, and shall, within twenty-four hours, make the investigation with the organ concerned, and proceed with the case in accordance with law.

ARTICLE 9 — No person may, except those in active military service, be subject to trial by a military court.

ARTICLE 10 — The people shall have the freedom of domicile and of change of domicile.

ARTICLE 11 — The people shall have the freedom of speech, academic instruction, writing, and publication.

ARTICLE 12 — The people shall have the freedom of secrecy of correspondence.

ARTICLE 13 — The people shall have the freedom of religious belief.

ARTICLE 14 — The people shall have freedom of assembly and of association.

ARTICLE 15 — The right to exist, the right to work, and the right of property shall be guaranteed to the people.

ARTICLE 16 — The people shall have the right to present petitions, file complaints, or institute legal proceedings.

ARTICLE 17 — The people shall have the right of election, recall, initiative, and referendum.

ARTICLE 18 — The people shall have the right to take public examinations and to hold public offices.

ARTICLE 19 — The people shall have the duty of paying taxes in accordance with law.

ARTICLE 20 — The people shall have the duty of performing military service in accordance with law.

ARTICLE 21 — The people shall have the right and duty of receiving citizen's education.

ARTICLE 22 — All other liberties and rights of the people that are not inimical to social order or public interest shall be guaranteed under the Constitution.

ARTICLE 23 — None of the liberties and rights enumerated in the preceding articles may, except as warranted by reasons of preventing infringement on the liberties of other persons, averting an imminent crisis, maintaining social order, or advancing public interest, be restricted by law.

ARTICLE 24 — Any public functionary who, in violation of law, infringes upon the liberties or rights of any person shall, besides being subject to disciplinary measures in accordance with the law, be responsible under criminal and civil laws. The injured person may, in accordance with law, claim indemnity from the state for damage sustained.

CHAPTER 3 — THE NATIONAL ASSEMBLY

ARTICLE 25 — The National Assembly shall, in accordance with provisions of this Constitution, exercise political power on behalf of the whole body of citizens.

ARTICLE 26 — The National Assembly shall be composed of the following representatives:

(1) — One representative to be elected by every *hsien* (county), municipality, or area of an equivalent status. In case the population exceeds five hundred thousand, one additional representative shall be elected for every additional five hundred thousand. What constitutes an area equivalent to a *hsien* or to a municipality shall be determined by law.

(2) — Representatives to be elected by Mongolia, four from every league and one from every special banner.*

(3) — The number of representatives to be elected from Tibet shall be determined by law.

(4) — The number of representatives to be elected by various racial groups in the border regions shall be determined by law.

(5) — The number of representatives to be elected by Chinese nationals residing abroad shall be determined by law.

(6) — The number of representatives to be elected by occupational groups shall be determined by law.

(7) — The number of representatives to be elected by women's organizations shall be determined by law.

ARTICLE 27 — The functions and powers of the National Assembly shall be as follows:

(1) — Election of the President and the Vice-President.

(2) — Recall of the President or the Vice-President.

(3) — Amendment of the Constitution.

(4) — Ratification of amendments to the Constitution proposed by the Legislative Yuan.

With respect to the exercise of the powers of initiative and referendum, besides what is stipulated in the preceding third and fourth sections, the National Assembly shall institute measures pertaining thereto and enforce them, after the said two powers shall have been exercised in one-half of the *hsien* and municipalities of the whole country.

ARTICLE 28 — Representatives to the National Assembly shall be elected every six years.

The terms of office of the representatives to each National Assembly shall terminate on the day of convocation of the next National Assembly. Incumbent government officials may not be elected representatives to the National Assembly in constituencies where they hold office.

ARTICLE 29 — The National Assembly shall be summoned by the President to meet ninety days prior to the date of expiration of the term of each presidency.

ARTICLE 30 — The National Assembly may, in any of the following circumstances, convene in extraordinary session:

(1) — When, in accordance with the provisions of Article 49 of this Constitution, it is necessary to hold a supplementary election of the President and the Vice-President;

---

* League and banner are administrative units in Mongolia.

(2) — When, in accordance with a resolution of the Control Yuan, an impeachment of the President or the Vice-President is instituted;

(3) — When, in accordance with a resolution of the Legislative Yuan, an amendment to the Constitution is proposed;

(4) — When it is convened upon a petition of over two-fifths of the representatives of the National Assembly.

When an extraordinary session is called in accordance with the preceding first or second section, the President of the Legislative Yuan shall issue the notice of convocation; when called in accordance with the preceding third or fourth section, such session shall be summoned by the President of the Republic.

ARTICLE 31 — The National Assembly shall meet at the seat of the Central Government.

ARTICLE 32 — No representative to the National Assembly shall be held responsible outside the Assembly for opinions he may have expressed or for votes he may have cast in sessions of the Assembly.

ARTICLE 33 — While the Assembly is in session, no representative to the National Assembly shall, except in case of *flagrante delicto*, be arrested or detained without the permission of the National Assembly.

ARTICLE 34 — The organization of the National Assembly, the election and recall of representatives to the National Assembly, and the procedure of the exercise of the functions and powers of the National Assembly shall be prescribed by law.

CHAPTER 4 — THE PRESIDENT

ARTICLE 35 — The President is the head of the state and represents the Republic of China in official foreign relations.

ARTICLE 36 — The President shall command the land, sea, and air forces of the whole country.

ARTICLE 37 — The President shall, in accordance with law, promulgate laws and issue mandates with the counter-signature of the President of the Executive Yuan, or of both the President of the Executive Yuan and the Heads of Ministries or Commissions concerned.

ARTICLE 38 — The President shall, in accordance with the provisions of this Constitution, exercise the powers of concluding treaties, declaring war, and making peace.

ARTICLE 39 — The President may, in accordance with law, declare martial law with the approval or confirmation of the Legislative Yuan. When the Legislative Yuan deems it necessary it may, by resolution, request the President to rescind such law.

ARTICLE 40 — The President shall, in accordance with law, exercise the power of granting general amnesties, pardons, remission of sentences, and restitution of civil rights.

ARTICLE 41 — The President shall, in accordance with law, appoint and remove civil and military officers.

ARTICLE 42 — The President may, in accordance with law, confer honors and award decorations.

ARTICLE 43 — In case of a natural calamity, an epidemic, or a serious national financial or economic crisis which necessitates that emergency measures be taken, the President, during the recess of the Legislative Yuan, may, by resolution of the Executive Yuan Council and in accordance with the Emergency Decrees Law, issue an emergency decree expedient and necessary to cope with the situation. Such a decree shall, within one month after issuance, be presented to the Legislative Yuan for confirmation; in case the Legislative Yuan dissents, the said decree shall immediately become null and void.

ARTICLE 44 — In case of any difference of opinion arising among the different Yuan that is not covered by the Constitution, the President may summon a meeting of the presidents of the Yuan concerned for consultation to settle the difference.

ARTICLE 45 — Any citizen of the Republic of China having attained to the age of forty years is eligible to the office of the President or the Vice-President.

ARTICLE 46 — The election of the President and the Vice-President shall be prescribed by law.

ARTICLE 47 — The term of office of the President and the Vice-President shall be six years. They may be elected for a second term.

ARTICLE 48 — The President shall, at the time of his inauguration, take an oath as follows: "I do solemnly and sincerely swear before the people of the whole country that I will observe the Constitution, faithfully perform my duties, promote the welfare of the people, safeguard the security of the state, and will not betray the trust of the people. Should I betray my oath, I shall be willing to submit myself to severe punishment from the state."

ARTICLE 49 — In the event of the President's office becoming vacant, the Vice-President shall succeed to the Presidency until the expiration of the presidential term. In case both the President's and the Vice-President's office should become vacant, the President of the Executive Yuan shall discharge the duties of the President's office. In accordance with the provisions of Article 30 of the Constitution, an extraordinary session of the National Assembly shall be convened for the purpose of holding a supplementary election of the President and the Vice-President, who shall hold office until the completion of the unfinished term of the former President.

In case the President should become unable to attend to office due to any cause, the Vice-President shall discharge the duties of his office. In case both the President and the Vice-President should become unable to attend to office, the President of the Executive Yuan shall discharge the duties of the President's office.

ARTICLE 50 — The President shall retire from office on the day his term expires. If by that time the succeeding President shall not have yet been elected, or, if already elected, both the President and the Vice-President shall not have yet been inaugurated, the President of the Executive Yuan shall discharge the duties of the President's office.

ARTICLE 51 — The period for the President of the Executive Yuan to discharge the duties of the President's office shall not exceed three months.

ARTICLE 52 — The President, except in the case of rebellion or treason, shall not, without having been recalled or released from office, be liable to criminal prosecution.

CHAPTER 5 — ADMINISTRATION

ARTICLE 53 — The Executive Yuan is the highest administrative organ of the state.

ARTICLE 54 — The Executive Yuan shall have a President, a Vice-

President, a number of Heads of various Ministries and Commissions, and a number of Executive Members without portfolio.

ARTICLE 55 — The President of the Executive Yuan shall be appointed by the President of the Republic with the consent of the Legislative Yuan. During the recess of the Legislative Yuan, if the President of the Executive Yuan resigns or if his office becomes vacant, the Vice-President of the Yuan shall discharge the duties of the office of the President of the Executive Yuan. The President of the Republic shall, within forty days, request the Legislative Yuan to summon a meeting for consent to his nominee to the presidency of the Executive Yuan.

Pending consent of the Legislative Yuan to the said nominee, the Vice-President of the Executive Yuan shall discharge the duties of the office of the President of the Yuan.

ARTICLE 56 — The Vice-President, the Heads of the various Ministries and Commissions, and the Executive Members without portfolio of the Executive Yuan shall be appointed by the President of the Republic upon the recommendation of the President of the Executive Yuan.

ARTICLE 57 — The Executive Yuan shall be responsible to the Legislative Yuan in accordance with the following provisions:

(1) — The Executive Yuan has the responsibility to present to the Legislative Yuan its administrative policies and its administrative reports. Members of the Legislative Yuan have, in the sessions of the Legislative Yuan, the right to interpellate the President and the Heads of the various Ministries and Commissions of the Executive Yuan.

(2) — If the Legislative Yuan dissents to any important policy of the Executive Yuan, it may, by resolution, ask the Executive Yuan to alter such policy. With respect to such resolution, the Executive Yuan may, with the approval of the President of the Republic, request the Legislative Yuan for reconsideration. If, in reconsideration, two-thirds of the attending members of the Legislative Yuan uphold the original resolution, the President of the Executive Yuan shall either abide by the same or resign from office.

(3) — If the Executive Yuan deems a resolution passed by the Legislative Yuan on a statutory, budgetary, or treaty bill difficult and inexpedient for execution, it may, with the approval of the President of the Republic, request, within ten days after the delivery of the said resolution to the Executive Yuan, the Legislative Yuan for reconsideration. If, in reconsideration, two-thirds of the attending members of the Legislative Yuan uphold the original resolution, the President of the Executive Yuan shall either abide by the same or resign from office.

ARTICLE 58 — The Executive Yuan shall have an Executive Yuan Council to be composed of its President, Vice-President, and the Heads of the various Ministries and Commissions and the Executive Members without portfolio of the Executive Yuan, with the Yuan President as chairman.

Prior to the submission to the Legislative Yuan of any statutory or budgetary bill or any bill concerning declaration of martial law, granting of general amnesty, declaration of war, conclusion of peace, treaties, or other important affairs, or concerning matters of common concern to the various ministries and commissions, the President and the Heads of the various Ministries and Commissions of the Executive Yuan shall present the same to the Executive Yuan Council for discussion and decision.

ARTICLE 59 — The Executive Yuan shall, three months before the beginning of every fiscal year, present to the Legislative Yuan the budget for the following fiscal year.

ARTICLE 60 — The Executive Yuan shall, within four months after the end of every fiscal year, present the budget statement to the Control Yuan.

ARTICLE 61 — The organization of the Executive Yuan shall be prescribed by law.

CHAPTER 6 — LEGISLATION

ARTICLE 62 — The Legislative Yuan is the highest legislative organ of the state to be composed of Members elected by the people. It shall exercise the legislative power on behalf of the people.

ARTICLE 63 — The Legislative Yuan shall have the power to decide upon any statutory or budgetary bill or any bill concerning martial law, general amnesty, declaration of war, conclusion of peace, treaties, and other important affairs of the state.

ARTICLE 64 — Members of the Legislative Yuan shall be elected in accordance with the following provisions:

(1) — Those elected by provinces and by municipalities under the direct jurisdiction of the National Government, five from each province or municipality with a population of less than three million; and, in case of a population exceeding three million, one additional member for every additional one million persons.

(2) — Those elected by Mongolian leagues.

(3) — Those elected by Tibet.

(4) — Those elected by various racial groups in border regions.

(5) — Those elected by Chinese nationals residing abroad.

(6) — Those elected by occupational groups.

The election of the Members of the Legislative Yuan and the allotment of their number in the preceding second and sixth sections shall be determined by law.

The number of women members in Section 1 of this article shall be determined by law.

ARTICLE 65 — Members of the Legislative Yuan shall serve a term of three years, and are re-eligible. The general election shall be completed within three months prior to the expiration of each term of office.

ARTICLE 66 — The Legislative Yuan shall have a President and a Vice-President to be elected by and from among the Members of the Legislative Yuan.

ARTICLE 67 — The Legislative Yuan may organize various committees. Such committees may invite government officials and private persons concerned to be present at their meetings for consultation.

ARTICLE 68 — The Legislative Yuan shall hold two regular sessions every year, to be convened by itself. The first session shall last from February to the end of May, and the second session from September to the end of December. When necessary, a session may be extended.

ARTICLE 69 — In any of the following circumstances, the Legislative Yuan may hold an extraordinary session:

(1) — At the request of the President of the Republic.

(2) — Upon the petition of more than one-fourth of the Members of the Legislative Yuan.

ARTICLE 70 — The Legislative Yuan shall not make proposals for an increase in the expenditures listed in the budget presented by the Executive Yuan.

ARTICLE 71 — At meetings of the Legislative Yuan, the Presidents of the various Yuan concerned and the Heads of the various Ministries and Commissions concerned may be present to present their views.

ARTICLE 72 — Statutory bills passed by the Legislative Yuan shall be sent to the President of the Republic and to the Executive Yuan. The President shall, within ten days after their receipt, promulgate them. The President may proceed with them in accordance with the provisions of Article 57 of the Constitution.

ARTICLE 73 — No Member of the Legislative Yuan shall be held responsible outside of the Yuan for opinions he may have expressed and votes he may have cast in sessions of the Yuan.

ARTICLE 74 — No Members of the Legislative Yuan may, except in case of *flagrante delicto*, be arrested or detained without the permission of the Legislative Yuan.

ARTICLE 75 — No Member of the Legislative Yuan may concurrently hold a public office.

ARTICLE 76 — The organization of the Legislative Yuan shall be prescribed by law.

CHAPTER 7 — JUDICIARY

ARTICLE 77 — The Judicial Yuan is the highest judicial organ of the state and shall have jursidiction over civil, criminal, and administrative suits involving public functionaries.

ARTICLE 78 — The Judicial Yuan shall have the power to interpret the Constitution and also the power to unify the interpretations of laws and decrees.

ARTICLE 79 — The Judicial Yuan shall have a President and a Vice-President, who shall be appointed by the President of the Republic with the consent of the Control Yuan.

The Judicial Yuan shall have a number of Grand Judges to attend to matters stipulated in Article 78 of the Constitution, who shall be appointed by the President with the consent of the Control Yuan.

ARTICLE 80 — Judges shall be independent of party affiliations and shall, in accordance with law, have independence in the exercise of their functions, subject to no interference of any kind.

ARTICLE 81 — The Judges shall hold office for life. No Judge may be removed from office unless he shall have been subject to criminal or disciplinary punishment or shall have been declared to be under interdiction. No Judge may, except in accordance with law, be suspended, transferred, or have his salary reduced.

ARTICLE 82 — The organization of the Judicial Yuan and the law courts of various grades shall be prescribed by law.

CHAPTER 8 — EXAMINATION

ARTICLE 83 — The Examination Yuan is the highest examination organ of the state and shall attend to matters relating to examination, appointment, personnel registration, ranks, work records, salaries, promotion and transfers, security of tenures, commendation, compensation, retirement, pensions, et cetera.

ARTICLE 84 — The Examination Yuan shall have a President and a Vice-President and a number of Examination Members who shall be appointed by the President of the Republic, with the consent of the Control Yuan.

ARTICLE 85 — In the selection of public functionaries, the system of examinations by open competition shall be enforced, quotas of candidates shall be prescribed severally according to provinces and areas, and examinations shall be held in designated districts. No person may be appointed to a public office without having passed an examination.

ARTICLE 86 — The following qualifications shall be determined and registered through examination by the Examination Yuan in accordance with law:

(1) — Qualifications for appointment as public functionaries.

(2) — Qualifications for practice in specialized professions and as technicians.

ARTICLE 87 — The Examination Yuan may, with respect to matters under its charge, present statutory bills to the Legislative Yuan.

ARTICLE 88 — Examination Members shall be independent of party affiliations and shall, in accordance with law, have independence in the exercise of their functions.

ARTICLE 89 — The organization of the Examination Yuan shall be prescribed by law.

CHAPTER 9 — CONTROL

ARTICLE 90 — The Control Yuan is the highest organ of control of the state and shall exercise the powers of consent, impeachment, rectification, and auditing.

ARTICLE 91 — The Control Yuan shall be composed of Control Members, to be elected by provincial and municipal councils, the local district councils of Mongolia and Tibet, and overseas Chinese communities. The allotment of their respective numbers shall be made in accordance with the following provisions:

(1) — Five members from every province.

(2) — Two members from every municipality under the direct jurisdiction of the National Government.

(3) — Eight members from Mongolian leagues and banners.

(4) — Eight members from Tibet.

(5) — Eight members from Chinese nationals residing abroad.

ARTICLE 92 — The Control Yuan shall have a President and a Vice-President, to be elected by and from among the Control Members.

ARTICLE 93 — Control Members shall serve a term of six years and are eligible for re-election.

ARTICLE 94 — When the Control Yuan exercises the power of consent in accordance with the Constitution, it shall do so by resolutions of a majority of its attending members.

ARTICLE 95 — The Control Yuan, in the exercise of its censorial powers, may request the Executive Yuan and its Ministries and Commissions to present to it for perusal orders issued by them and related documents.

ARTICLE 96 — The Control Yuan, according to the nature of the work of the Executive Yuan and its Ministries and Commissions, may appoint severally a number of committees to investigate their administration with a view to finding out whether or not there is any violation of law or any neglect of duty on the part of the Executive Yuan and of its Ministries and Commissions.

ARTICLE 97 — The Control Yuan may, on the basis of the investigations and resolutions of its committees, propose measures of rectification to be sent to the Executive Yuan and its Ministries and Commissions concerned, with request to effect improvement.

When the Control Yuan deems a public functionary in the central or a local government guilty of neglect of duty or violation of law, it may propose measures of rectification or institute an impeachment. If the criminal law is involved, the case shall be turned over to a law court.

ARTICLE 98 — Any impeachment by the Control Yuan of a public functionary in a central or a local government shall be instituted upon the proposal of more than one Control Member and the endorsement, after due consideration, of more than nine Control Members.

ARTICLE 99 — In the institution of impeachment of personnel of the Judicial Yuan or of the Examination Yuan for neglect of duty or violation of law, the provisions of Articles 95, 97, and 98 shall be applicable.

ARTICLE 100 — Any impeachment of the President or the Vice-President of the Republic by the Control Yuan shall be instituted upon the proposal of more than one-fourth and the endorsement, after due consideration, of the majority, of the entire membership of the Yuan, and the same shall be brought before the National Assembly.

ARTICLE 101 — No Control Member shall be held responsible outside the Yuan for opinions he may have expressed or for votes he may have cast in sessions of the Yuan.

ARTICLE 102 — No Control Member may, except in case of *flagrante delicto*, be arrested or detained without the permission of the Control Yuan.

ARTICLE 103 — No Control Member may concurrently hold a public office or engage in a professional practice.

ARTICLE 104 — In the Control Yuan, there shall be an Auditor-General, who shall be appointed by the President of the Republic with the consent of the Legislative Yuan.

ARTICLE 105 — The Auditor-General shall, within three months after the presentation of the budget statement by the Executive Yuan, complete the auditing thereof in accordance with law, and submit an auditing report to the Legislative Yuan.

ARTICLE 106 — The organization of the Control Yuan shall be prescribed by law.

CHAPTER 10 — POWERS OF THE CENTRAL AND LOCAL GOVERNMENTS

ARTICLE 107 — The following matters shall be subjects of legislation and execution by the Central Government:

(1) — Foreign affairs.

(2) — National defense and military affairs concerning national defense.

(3) — Nationality law, and criminal, civil, and commercial laws.

(4) — Judicial system.

(5) — Aviation, national highways, state-owned railways, navigation, postal, and telegraph services.

(6) — Central Government finance and national revenues.

(7) — Demarcation between national and provincial or *hsien* revenues.

(8) — State-operated economic enterprises.

(9) — Currency system and state banks.

(10) — Weights and measures.

(11) — Policies of international trade.

(12) — Financial and economic matters of an international nature.

(13) — Other matters of the Central Government as stipulated in the Constitution.

ARTICLE 108 — The following matters shall be subjects of legislation and execution by the Central Government. Their execution may be delegated to the provincial and *hsien* governments:

(1) — General rules governing provincial and *hsien* self-government.

(2) — Division of administrative areas.

(3) — Forestry, mining, and commerce.

(4) — Educational system.

(5) — Banking and exchange systems.

(6) — Shipping and coastal fishery.

(7) — Public utilities.

(8) — Cooperative enterprises.

(9) — Water and land communication, and transportation covering more than two provinces.

(10) — Water conservancy, waterways, and agricultural and pastoral enterprises covering more than two provinces.

(11) — Personnel registration, ranks, appointment, supervision, and protection of officials in the Central and local governments.

(12) — Land legislation.

(13) — Labor legislation and other social legislation.

(14) — Eminent domain.

(15) — National census and statistics.

(16) — Immigration and land reclamation.

(17) — Police system.

(18) — Public health.

(19) — General relief, compensation and unemployment relief.

(20) — Preservation of ancient books, articles, and landmarks of cultural value.

With respect to the preceding sections, the province may enact separate laws and rules, provided these do not contravene national laws.

ARTICLE 109 — The following matters shall be subjects of legislation and execution by the province. Their execution may be delegated to the *hsien*:

(1) — Provincial education, provincial public health, provincial industries, and provincial communications.

(2) — Management and disposal of provincial property.

(3) — Provincial and municipal administration.

(4) — Province-operated enterprises.

(5) — Provincial cooperative enterprises.

(6) — Provincial agriculture and forestry, provincial water conservancy, provincial fishery and animal-husbandry, and provincial public works.

(7) — Provincial finance and provincial revenue.

(8) — Provincial debts.

(9) — Provincial banks.

(10) — Enforcement of provincial police administration.

(11) — Provincial charitable and public welfare enterprises.

(12) — Other matters delegated in accordance with national legislation.

Any of the items in the preceding section covering more than two provinces may, except as otherwise provided for by law, be undertaken jointly by the provinces concerned.

When any province, in undertaking the items in the first section, finds its funds insufficient, it may, by resolution of the Legislative Yuan, receive a subsidy from the National Treasury.

ARTICLE 110 — The following matters shall be subjects of legislation and execution by the *hsien*:

(1) — *Hsien* education, *hsien* public health, *hsien* industries, and *hsien* communications.

(2) — Management and disposal of *hsien* property.

(3) — *Hsien*-operated enterprises.

(4) — *Hsien* cooperative enterprises.

(5) — *Hsien* agriculture and forestry, *hsien* water conservancy, *hsien* fishery and animal husbandry, and *hsien* public works.

(6) — *Hsien* finance and *hsien* revenue.

(7) — *Hsien* debts.

(8) — *Hsien* banks.

(9) — Administration of *hsien* policing and defense.

(10) — *Hsien* charitable and public welfare enterprises.

(11) — Other matters delegated in accordance with national legislation and the provincial self-government law.

Any of the items in the preceding sections covering more than two *hsien* may, except as otherwise provided for by law, be undertaken jointly by the *hsien* concerned.

ARTICLE 111 — Should there occur any matter not enumerated in Articles 107, 108, 109, and 110, the same shall fall within the jurisdiction of the Central government if it is of national nature, of the province if it is of provincial nature, and of the *hsien* if it is of *hsien* nature. Any dispute over jurisdiction shall be settled by the Legislative Yuan.

CHAPTER 11 — LOCAL GOVERNMENT SYSTEM

PART I — THE PROVINCE

ARTICLE 112 — A Province may convene a Provincial Assembly to enact, in accordance with the General Rules of Provincial and *Hsien* Self-Government, a provincial self-government law, provided the same does not contravene the Constitution.

The organization of the Provincial Assembly and the election of the representatives shall be prescribed by law.

ARTICLE 113 — The provincial self-government law should contain the following provisions:

(1) — In the province, there shall be a Provincial Council. Members of the Provincial Council shall be elected by the people of the province.

(2) — In the Province, there shall be a Provincial Government with a Provincial Governor, to be elected by the people of the province.

(3) — Relationship between the province and the *hsien*.

The legislative power of the province shall be exercised by the Provincial Council.

ARTICLE 114 — The provincial self-government law, after enactment, shall be immediately submitted to the Judicial Yuan. The Judicial Yuan, if it deems any part thereof unconstitutional, shall declare null and void the article or articles contradictory to the Constitution.

ARTICLE 115 — If, in its enforcement, the provincial self-government law encounters serious obstacles on account of any of the articles therein, the Judicial Yuan shall first summon the parties concerned to present their views. Then the Presidents of the Executive Yuan, Legislative Yuan, Judicial Yuan, Examination Yuan, and Control Yuan shall form a committee, with the President of the Judicial Yuan as chairman, to propose formulas for settlement.

ARTICLE 116 — The provincial laws and regulations that are in contravention of National Laws shall be null and void.

ARTICLE 117 — In case doubt arises as to whether or not a provincial law or regulation contravenes a National Law, interpretation thereon shall be made by the Judicial Yuan.

ARTICLE 118 — The self-government of municipalities under the direct jurisdiction of the National Government shall be stipulated by law.

ARTICLE 119 — The local self-government system of the Mongolian leagues and banners shall be stipulated by law.

ARTICLE 120 — The self-government system of Tibet shall be guaranteed.

PART 2 — THE HSIEN

ARTICLE 121 — The *hsien* shall enforce self-government.

ARTICLE 122 — The *hsien* may convene a *Hsien* Assembly and enact, in accordance with the General Rules of the Provincial and *Hsien* Self-Government, a *hsien* self-government law, provided the same does not contravene the Constitution or the provincial self-government law.

ARTICLE 123 — People of the *hsien*, with respect to matters concerning *hsien* self-government, shall exercise the rights of initiative and referendum in accordance with law, and, in regard to the Magistrate and other *hsien* self-government officers, shall exercise the rights of election and recall in accordance with law.

ARTICLE 124 — In the *hsien,* there shall be a *Hsien* Council. Members of the *Hsien* Council shall be elected by the people of the *hsien*.

The legislative power of the *hsien* shall be exercised by the *Hsien* Council.

ARTICLE 125 — *Hsien* laws and regulations that are in contravention of National Laws or provincial laws and regulations shall be null and void.

ARTICLE 126 — In the *hsien*, there shall be a *Hsien* Government with a *Hsien* Magistrate, to be elected by the people of the *hsien*.

ARTICLE 127 — The *Hsien* Magistrate shall attend to the enforcement of *hsien* self-government and to the execution of matters delegated by central and provincial governments.

ARTICLE 128 — The provisions governing the *hsien* shall apply *mutatis mutandis* to the municipality.

CHAPTER 12 — ELECTION, RECALL, INITIATIVE, AND REFERENDUM

ARTICLE 129 — The elections stipulated in the Constitution, except when otherwise provided for by the Constitution, shall be by universal, equal, and direct suffrage, and by secret ballot.

ARTICLE 130 — Any citizen of the Republic of China having attained to the age of twenty years shall have the right of suffrage in accordance with law. Unless otherwise provided for by the Constitution and laws, any citizen having attained to the age of twenty-three years shall have the right to be elected in accordance with law.

ARTICLE 131 — All candidates in the election stipulated in the Constitution shall openly campaign for election.

ARTICLE 132 — Coercion or inducement shall be strictly forbidden in elections. Suits arising in connection with elections shall be tried by the courts.

ARTICLE 133 — A person elected may, in accordance with law, be recalled by his constituency.

ARTICLE 134 — In the elections, the minimum number of women to be elected shall be fixed, and measures pertaining thereto shall be prescribed, by law.

ARTICLE 135 — Measures with respect to the number and election of representatives of citizens in interior areas whose conditions of living and habits are peculiar to their section shall be prescribed by law.

ARTICLE 136 — The people's exercise of their two rights of initiative and referendum shall be stipulated by law.

CHAPTER 13 — FUNDAMENTAL NATIONAL POLICIES

PART 1 — NATIONAL DEFENSE

ARTICLE 137 — The national defense of the Republic of China shall have as its aim the safeguarding of the national security and the preservation of world peace. The organization of national defense shall be prescribed by law.

ARTICLE 138 — The land, sea, and air forces of the whole land shall, independent of individual, regional, or party affiliation, be loyal to the state and shall protect the people.

ARTICLE 139 — No political party or faction or individual may make use of armed force as an instrument in a struggle for political power.

ARTICLE 140 — No military man in active service may concurrently hold a civil office.

PART 2 — FOREIGN POLICY

ARTICLE 141 — The foreign policy of the Republic of China shall, in a spirit of independence and initiative and on the basis of the principles of equality and reciprocity, cultivate good neighborliness with other nations and respect treaties and the United Nations Charter in order to protect the rights and interests of overseas Chinese nationals, promote international cooperation, advance international justice, and ensure world peace.

PART 3 — NATIONAL ECONOMY

ARTICLE 142 — National economy shall be based on the Principle of the People's Livelihood for equitable distribution of land ownership and control of capital in order to obtain a well-balanced development of public economy and private livelihood.

ARTICLE 143 — All land within the territory of the Republic of China shall in principle belong to the whole body of citizens. Private ownership of land, acquired by the people in accordance with law, shall be protected and restricted by law. Privately owned land shall be liable to taxation according to its value and the government may buy such land according to its value.

Mines embedded in the land and natural power which may be economically utilized for public benefit shall belong to the state and shall in no way be affected by the people's acquisition of the right of ownership over such land.

If any land has an increase in its value not through exertion of labor and the employment of capital, the state shall levy thereon an increment tax, the proceeds of which shall be enjoyed by the people in common.

In the distribution and adjustment of land, the state shall, as a principle, assist self-farming landowners and persons who make use of the land by themselves, and shall also regulate their appropriate areas of operation.

ARTICLE 144 — Public utilities and other enterprises of monopolistic nature shall, as a principle, be under public operation. The same may, if permitted by law, be operated by citizens.

ARTICLE 145 — With respect to private wealth and privately operated enterprises, the state shall restrict them by law if they are deemed obstructive to the balanced development of public economy and private livelihood. Co-operative enterprises shall receive encouragement and assistance by the state.

Citizens' productive enterprises and foreign trade shall receive encouragement, guidance, and protection by the state.

ARTICLE 146 — The state shall, through the employment of scientific techniques, develop water conservancy, increase the productivity of the land, improve agricultural conditions, plan for the utilization of land, and exploit agricultural resources in order to bring about the industrialization of agriculture.

ARTICLE 147 — The Central Government, in order to attain a balanced economic development among the provinces, shall extend appropriate aid to undeveloped provinces.

The province, in order to attain a balanced economic development among the *hsien*, shall extend appropriate aid to undeveloped *hsien*.

ARTICLE 148 — Within the territorial bounds of the Republic of China, all goods shall be permitted to flow freely.

ARTICLE 149 — Private financial institutions shall, in accordance with law, be subject to state control.

ARTICLE 150 — The state shall extensively establish financial institutions for the people to relieve unemployment.

ARTICLE 151 — With respect to Chinese nationals residing abroad, the state shall foster and ensure the development of their economic enterprises.

PART 4 — SOCIAL SECURITY

ARTICLE 152 — The state shall provide opportunity of employment to people who are capable of work.

ARTICLE 153 — The state, in order to improve the livelihood of laborers and farmers and to increase their productive technical skill, shall enact laws and carry out the policies for their protection.

Women and children engaged in labor shall, according to their age and physical condition, be accorded special protection.

ARTICLE 154 — Capital and labor shall, on the principle of harmony and cooperation, promote productive enterprises. Mediation and arbitration of disputes between capital and labor shall be stipulated by law.

ARTICLE 155 — The state, in order to promote social welfare, shall enforce a social insurance system. To the aged, the infirm, and the crippled among the people who are unable to earn a living, and to victims of unusual calamities, the state shall extend appropriate assistance and relief.

ARTICLE 156 — The state, in order to secure the foundation of national existence and development, shall protect motherhood and carry out the policy of promoting the welfare of women and children.

ARTICLE 157 — The state, in order to improve national health, shall extensively establish sanitation and infant health protection enterprises and a system of socialized medical service.

PART 5 — EDUCATION AND CULTURE

ARTICLE 158 — Education and culture shall have as their aim the development among citizens of a national spirit, a democratic spirit, national morality, sound and healthy physique, sciences, and the knowledge and ability to earn a living.

ARTICLE 159 — Citizens shall have equal opportunity to receive education.

ARTICLE 160 — All children of the school age from six to twelve years shall receive primary education free, and those who are poor shall be supplied with textbooks by the government.

All citizens beyond school age who have not received primary education shall receive supplementary education free, and shall also be supplied with textbooks by the government.

ARTICLE 161 — Governments of various grades shall extensively establish scholarships to aid students who, possessing a good record in scholarship and conduct, are financially unable to pursue advanced studies.

ARTICLE 162 — All public and private educational institutions in the country shall, in accordance with law, be subject to state supervision.

ARTICLE 163 — The state shall pay due attention to the balanced development of education in various areas and shall promote social education in order to raise the cultural standard of the citizens in general. Educational and cultural expenses of border regions and undeveloped regions shall be subsidized by the National Treasury. The more important local educational and cultural enterprises may be undertaken or subsidized by the Central Government.

ARTICLE 164 — Expenditure for educational, scientific, and cultural purposes shall be, in case of the Central Government, not less than fifteen per cent of the total National Budget, in case of the province, not less than twenty-five per cent of the total provincial budget, and in case of the *hsien*, not less than thirty-five per cent of the total *hsien* budget. Educational and cultural foundations established in accordance with law shall, together with their property, be protected.

ARTICLE 165 — The state shall safeguard the livelihood of those who work in the fields of education, sciences, and arts, and shall, in accord with the development of national economy, raise their scale of treatment from time to time.

ARTICLE 166 — The state shall encourage scientific discoveries and inventions and shall protect ancient landmarks and articles of historical, cultural, or artistic value.

ARTICLE 167 — The state shall extend encouragement or subsidies to the following enterprises of individuals:

(1) — Educational enterprises in the country which have been operated with good records by private individuals.

(2) — Educational enterprises of Chinese nationals residing abroad which have been operated with good records.

(3) — Persons who have made discoveries in learning or in techniques.

(4) — Persons who have long been engaged in education and with good records.

PART 6 — BORDER REGIONS

ARTICLE 168 — The state shall accord legal protection to the status of the racial groups in the border regions, and shall render special assistance to their undertakings of local self-government.

ARTICLE 169 — The state shall positively undertake and foster the development of education, culture, communications, water conservancy, public health, and other economic and social enterprises of the racial groups in the border regions. With respect to the utilization of land, the state shall, according to the climate and the nature of the soil and in the light of what is deemed suitable to the life and habits of the people, protect the land and assist its development.

CHAPTER 14 — ENFORCEMENT AND AMENDMENT OF THE CONSTITUTION

ARTICLE 170 — The term "law," as used in the Constitution, denotes a law that shall have been passed by the Legislative Yuan and promulgated by the President of the Republic.

ARTICLE 171 — Laws that are in contravention of the Constitution shall be null and void. When doubt arises as to whether or not a law is in contravention of the Constitution, interpretation thereon shall be made by the Judicial Yuan.

ARTICLE 172 — Ordinances that are in contravention of the Constitution or laws shall be null and void.

ARTICLE 173 — The power to interpret the Constitution resides in the Judicial Yuan.

ARTICLE 174 — Amendments to the Constitution shall be made in accordance with one of the following procedures:

(1) — Upon the proposal of one-fifth of the total number of the representatives of the National Assembly and by a resolution of three-fourths of the representatives present at a meeting having a quorum of two-thirds of the entire Assembly, an amendment may be made.

(2) — Upon the proposal of one-fourth of the members of the Legislative Yuan and by a resolution of three-fourths of the members present at a meeting having a quorum of three-fourths of the members of the Yuan, an amendment may be drawn up and submitted to the National Assembly for ratification. Such a proposed amendment to the Constitution shall, six months before the coming into session of the National Assembly, be published publicly.

ARTICLE 175 — Matters provided by the Constitution which require procedures of enforcement shall be prescribed by law.

The preparatory procedure for the enforcement of the Constitution shall be decided upon by the National Assembly which shall have adopted the Constitution.

THE CONSTITUTION OF THE PEOPLE'S REPUBLIC OF CHINA (Effective September 20, 1954)

PREAMBLE

In the year 1949, after more than a century of heroic struggle, the Chinese people, led by the Communist Party of China, finally achieved their great victory in the people's revolution against imperialism, feudalism, and bureaucrat-capitalism; and so brought to an end a long history of oppression and enslavement and founded the People's Republic of China, a people's democratic dictatorship. The system of people's democracy — new democracy — of the People's Republic of China guarantees that China can in a peaceful way banish exploitation and poverty and build a prosperous and happy socialist society.

From the founding of the People's Republic of China to the attainment of a socialist society is a period of transition. During the transition the fundamental task of the state is, step by step, to bring about the socialist industrialization of the country and, step by step, to accomplish the socialist transformation of agriculture, handicrafts, and capitalist industry and commerce. In the last few years our people have successfully carried out a series of large-scale struggles: the reform of the agrarian system, resistance to American aggression and aid to Korea, the suppression of counter-revolutionaries, and the rehabilitation of the national economy. As a result, the necessary conditions have been created for planned economic construction and gradual transition to socialism.

The First National People's Congress of the People's Republic of China, at its first session held in Peking, the capital, solemnly adopted the constitution of the People's Republic of China on September 20, 1954. This Constitution is based on the Common Program of the Chinese People's Political Consultative Conference of 1949, and is an advance on it. It consolidates the gains of the Chinese people's revolution and the political and economic victories won since the founding of the People's Republic of China; and, moreover, it reflects the basic needs of the state in the period of transition, as well as the general desire of the people as a whole to build a socialist society.

In the course of the great struggle to establish the People's Republic of China, the people of our country forged a broad people's democratic united front, composed of all democratic classes, democratic parties and groups, and popular organizations, and led by the Communist Party of China. This people's democratic united front will continue to play its part in mobilizing and rallying the whole people in common struggle to fulfill the fundamental task of the state during the transition and to oppose enemies within and without.

All nationalities of our country are united in one great family of free and equal nations. This unity of China's nationalities will continue to gain in strength, founded as it is on ever-growing friendship and mutual aid among themselves, and on the struggle against imperialism, against public enemies of the people within the nationalities, and against both dominant-nation chauvinism and local nationalism. In the course of economic and cultural development, the state will concern itself with the needs of the different nationalities, and, in the matter of socialist transformation, pay full attention to the special characteristics in the development of each.

China has already built an indestructible friendship with the great Union of Soviet Socialist Republics and the People's Democracies; and the friendship between our people and peace-loving people in all other countries is growing day by day. Such friendship will be constantly strengthened and broadened. China's policy of establishing and extending diplomatic relations with all countries on the principle of equality, mutual benefit, and mutual respect for each other's sovereignty and territorial integrity, which has already yielded success, will continue to be carried out. In international affairs our firm and consistent policy is to strive for the noble cause of world peace and the progress of humanity.

CHAPTER 1 — GENERAL PRINCIPLES

ARTICLE 1 — The People's Republic of China is a people's democratic state led by the working class and based on the alliance of workers and peasants.

ARTICLE 2 — All power in the People's Republic of China belongs to the people. The organs through which the people exercise power are the National People's Congress and the local people's congresses.

The National People's Congress, the local people's congresses and other organs of state practice democratic centralism.

ARTICLE 3 — The People's Republic of China is a single multi-national state.

All the nationalities are equal. Discrimination against, or oppression of, any nationality, and acts which undermine the unity of the nationalities are prohibited.

All the nationalities have freedom to use and foster the growth of their spoken and written languages, and to preserve or reform their own customs or ways.

Regional autonomy applies in areas where people of national minorities live in compact communities. National autonomous areas are inalienable parts of the People's Republic of China.

ARTICLE 4 — The People's Republic of China, by relying on the organs of state and the social forces, and by means of socialist industrialization and socialist transformation, ensures the gradual abolition of systems of exploitation and the building of a socialist society.

ARTICLE 5 — At present, the following basic forms of ownership of means of production exist in the People's Republic of China: state ownership, that is, ownership by the whole people; cooperative ownership, that is, collective ownership by the working masses; ownership by individual working people; and capitalist ownership.

ARTICLE 6 — The state sector of the economy is a socialist sector, owned by the whole people. It is the leading force in the national economy and the material basis on which the state carries out socialist transformation. The state ensures priority for the development of the state sector of the economy.

All mineral resources and waters, as well as forests, undeveloped land, and other resources which the state owns by law, are the property of the whole people.

ARTICLE 7 — The cooperative sector of the economy is either socialist, when collectively owned by the working masses, or semi-socialist, when in part collectively owned by the working masses. Partial collective ownership by the working masses is a transitional form by means of which individual peasants, individual handicraftsmen and other individual working people organize themselves in their advance towards collective ownership by the working masses.

The state protects the property of the cooperatives, encourages, guides, and helps the development of the cooperative sector of the economy. It regards the promotion of producers' cooperatives as the chief means for the transformation of individual farming and individual handicrafts.

ARTICLE 8 — The state protects the right of peasants to own land and other means of production according to law.

The state guides and helps individual peasants to increase production and encourages them to organize producers', supply and marketing, and credit cooperatives voluntarily.

The policy of the state towards rich-peasant economy is to restrict and gradually eliminate it.

ARTICLE 9 — The state protects the right of handicraftsmen and other non-agricultural individual working people to own means of production according to law.

The state guides and helps individual handicraftsmen and other non-agricultural individual working people to improve their enterprise and encourages them to organize producers', and supply and marketing cooperatives voluntarily.

ARTICLE 10 — The state protects the right of capitalists to own means of production and other capital according to law.

The policy of the state towards capitalist industry and commerce is to use, restrict, and transform them. The state makes use of the positive sides of capitalist industry and commerce which are beneficial to national welfare and the people's livelihood, restricts their negative sides which are not beneficial to national welfare and the people's livelihood, encourages and guides their transformation into various forms of state-capitalist economy, gradually replacing capitalist ownership with ownership by the whole people; and this it does by means of control exercised by administrative organs of state, the leadership given by the state sector of the economy, and supervision by the workers.

The state forbids capitalists to engage in unlawful activities which injure the public interest, disrupt the social-economic order, or undermine the economic plan of the state.

ARTICLE 11 — The state protects the right of citizens to own lawfully-earned incomes, savings, houses, and other means of life.

ARTICLE 12 — The state protects the right of citizens to inherit private property according to law.

ARTICLE 13 — The state may, in the public interest, buy, requisition, or nationalize land and other means of production both in cities and countryside according to provisions of law.

ARTICLE 14 — The state forbids any person to use his private property to the detriment of the public interest.

ARTICLE 15 — By economic planning, the state directs the growth and transformation of the national economy to bring about the constant increase of productive forces, in this way enriching the material and cultural life of the people and consolidating the independence and security of the country.

ARTICLE 16 — Work is a matter of honor for every citizen of the People's Republic of China who is able to work. The state encourages citizens to take an active and creative part in their work.

ARTICLE 17 — All organs of state must rely on the masses of the people, constantly maintain close contact with them, heed their opinions, and accept their supervision.

ARTICLE 18 — All servants of the state must be loyal to the people's democratic system, observe the Constitution and the law, and strive to serve the people.

ARTICLE 19 — The People's Republic of China safeguards the people's democratic system, suppresses all treasonable and counter-revolutionary activities, and punishes all traitors and counter-revolutionaries.

The state deprives feudal landlords and bureaucrat-capitalists of political rights for a specific period of time according to law; at the same time it provides them with a way to earn a living, in order to enable them to reform through work and become citizens who earn their livelihood by their own labor.

ARTICLE 20 — The armed forces of the People's Republic of China belong to the people; their duty is to safeguard the gains of the people's revolution and the achievements of national construction, and to defend the sovereignty, territorial integrity, and security of the country.

CHAPTER 2 — THE STATE STRUCTURE

SECTION I. THE NATIONAL PEOPLE'S CONGRESS

ARTICLE 21 — The National People's Congress is the highest organ of state authority in the People's Republic of China.

ARTICLE 22 — The National People's Congress is the only legislative authority in the country.

ARTICLE 23 — The National People's Congress is composed of deputies elected by provinces, autonomous regions, municipalities directly under the central authority, the armed forces, and Chinese resident abroad.

The number of deputies to the National People's Congress, including those representing national minorities, and the manner of their election, are prescribed by electoral law.

ARTICLE 24 — The National People's Congress is elected for a term of four years.

Two months before the term of office of the National People's Congress expires, its Standing Committee must complete the election of deputies to the succeeding National People's Congress. Should exceptional circumstances arise preventing such an election, the term of office of the sitting National People's Congress may be prolonged until the first session of the succeeding National People's Congress.

ARTICLE 25 — The National People's Congress meets once a year, convened by its Standing Committee. It may also be convened whenever its Standing Committee deems this necessary or one-fifth of the deputies so propose.

ARTICLE 26 — When the National People's Congress meets, it elects a praesidium to conduct its sittings.

ARTICLE 27 — The National People's Congress exercises the following functions and powers:

(1) to amend the Constitution;
(2) to enact laws;

(3) to supervise the enforcement of the Constitution;

(4) to elect the Chairman and the Vice-Chairman of the People's Republic of China;

(5) to decide on the choice of the Premier of the State Council upon recommendation by the Chairman of the People's Republic of China, and of the component members of the State Council upon recommendation by the Premier;

(6) to decide on the choice of the Vice-Chairman and other members of the Council of National Defense upon recommendation by the Chairman of the People's Republic of China;

(7) to elect the President of the Supreme People's Court;

(8) to elect the Chief Procurator of the Supreme People's Procuratorate;

(9) to decide on the national economic plans;

(10) to examine and approve the state budget and the financial report;

(11) to ratify the status and boundaries of provinces, autonomous regions, and municipalities directly under the central authority;

(12) to decide on general amnesties;

(13) to decide on questions of war and peace; and

(14) to exercise such other functions and powers as the National People's Congress considers necessary.

ARTICLE 28 — The National People's Congress has power to remove from office:

(1) the Chairman and the Vice-Chairman of the People's Republic of China;

(2) the Premier and Vice-Premiers, Ministers, Heads of Commissions, and the Secretary-General of the State Council;

(3) the Vice-Chairman and other members of the Council of National Defense;

(4) the President of the Supreme People's Court; and

(5) the Chief Procurator of the Supreme People's Procuratorate.

ARTICLE 29 — Amendments to the Constitution require a two-thirds majority vote of all the deputies to the National People's Congress.

Laws and other bills require a simple majority vote of all the deputies to the National People's Congress.

ARTICLE 30 — The Standing Committee of the National People's Congress is a permanently acting body of the National People's Congress.

The Standing Committee is composed of the following members, elected by the National People's Congress: the Chairman; the Vice-Chairmen; the Secretary-General; and other members.

ARTICLE 31 — The Standing Committee of the National People's Congress exercises the following functions and powers:

(1) to conduct the election of deputies to the National People's Congress;

(2) to convene the National People's Congress;

(3) to interpret the laws;

(4) to adopt decrees;

(5) to supervise the work of the State Council, the Supreme People's Court, and the Supreme People's Procuratorate;

(6) to annul decisions and orders of the State Council which contravene the Constitution, laws, or decrees;

(7) to revise or annul inappropriate decisions issued by the government authorities of provinces, autonomous regions, and municipalities directly under the central authority;

(8) to decide on the appointment or removal of any Vice-Premier, Minister,

Head of Commission, or the Secretary-General of the State Council when the National People's Congress is not in session;

(9) to appoint or remove the Vice-Presidents, judges, and other members of the Judicial Committee of the Supreme People's Court;

(10) to appoint or remove the Deputy Chief Procurators, procurators, and other members of the Procuratorial Committee of the Supreme People's Procuratorate;

(11) to decide on the appointment or recall of plenipotentiary representatives to foreign states;

(12) to decide on the ratification or abrogation of treaties concluded with foreign states;

(13) to institute military, diplomatic, and other special titles and ranks;

(14) to institute and decide on the award of state orders, medals, and titles of honor;

(15) to decide on the granting of pardons;

(16) to decide, when the National People's Congress is not in session, on the proclamation of a state of war in the event of armed attack on the country or in fulfillment of international treaty obligations concerning common defense against aggression;

(17) to decide on general or partial mobilization;

(18) to decide on the enforcement of martial law throughout the country or in certain areas; and

(19) to exercise such other functions and powers as are vested in it by the National People's Congress.

ARTICLE 32 — The Standing Committee of the National People's Congress exercises its functions and powers until a new Standing Committee is elected by the succeeding National People's Congress.

ARTICLE 33 — The Standing Committee of the National People's Congress is responsible to the National People's Congress and reports to it.

The National People's Congress has power to recall members of its Standing Committee.

ARTICLE 34 — The National People's Congress establishes a Nationalities Committee, a Bills Committee, a Budget Committee, a Credentials Committee, and other necessary committees.

The Nationalities Committee and the Bills Committee are under the direction of the Standing Committee of the National People's Congress when the National People's Congress is not in session.

ARTICLE 35 — The National People's Congress, or its Standing Committee if the National People's Congress is not in session, may, if necessary, appoint commissions of inquiry for the investigation of specific questions.

All organs of state, people's organizations, and citizens concerned are obliged to supply necessary information to these commissions when they conduct investigations.

ARTICLE 36 — Deputies to the National People's Congress have the right to address questions to the State Council, or to the Ministries and Commissions of the State Council, which are under obligation to answer.

ARTICLE 37 — No deputy to the National People's Congress may be arrested or placed on trial without the consent of the National People's Congress or, when the National People's Congress is not in session, of its Standing Committee.

ARTICLE 38 — Deputies to the National People's Congress are subject to the supervision of the units which elect them. These electoral units have power to replace at any time the deputies they elect, according to the procedure prescribed by law.

SECTION 2. THE CHAIRMAN OF THE PEOPLE'S REPUBLIC OF CHINA

ARTICLE 39 — The Chairman of the People's Republic of China is elected by the National People's Congress. Any citizen of the People's Republic of China who has the right to vote and stand for election and has reached the age of thirty-five is eligible for election as Chairman of the People's Republic of China.

The term of office of the Chairman of the People's Republic of China is four years.

ARTICLE 40 — The Chairman of the People's Republic of China, in pursuance of decisions of the National People's Congress or the Standing Committee of the National People's Congress, promulgates laws and decrees; appoints or removes the Premier, Vice-Premiers, Ministers, Heads of Commissions and the Secretary-General of the State Council; appoints or removes the Vice-Chairman and other members of the Council of National Defense; confers state orders, medals, and titles of honor; proclaims general amnesties and grants pardons; proclaims martial law; proclaims a state of war; and orders mobilization.

ARTICLE 41 — The Chairman of the People's Republic of China represents the People's Republic of China in its relations with foreign states, receives foreign diplomatic representatives, and, in pursuance of decisions of the Standing Committee of the National People's Congress, appoints or recalls plenipotentiary representatives to foreign states and ratifies treaties concluded with foreign states.

ARTICLE 42 — The Chairman of the People's Republic of China commands the armed forces of the country, and is Chairman of the Council of National Defense.

ARTICLE 43 — The Chairman of the People's Republic of China, whenever necessary, convenes a Supreme State Conference and acts as its chairman.

The Vice-Chairman of the People's Republic of China, the Chairman of the Standing Committee of the National People's Congress, the Premier of the State Council, and other persons concerned take part in the Supreme State Conference.

The Chairman of the People's Republic of China submits the views of the Supreme State Conference on important affairs of state of the National People's Congress, its Standing Committee, the State Council, or other bodies concerned for their consideration and decision.

ARTICLE 44 — The Vice-Chairman of the People's Republic of China assists the Chairman in his work. The Vice-Chairman may exercise such part of the functions and powers of the Chairman as the Chairman may entrust to him.

The provisions of Article 39 of the Constitution governing the election and term of office of the Chairman of the People's Republic of China apply also to the election and term of office of the Vice-Chairman of the People's Republic of China.

ARTICLE 45 — The Chairman and the Vice-Chairman of the People's Republic of China exercise their functions and powers until the new Chairman and Vice-Chairman elected by the succeeding National People's Congress take office.

ARTICLE 46 — Should the Chairman of the People's Republic of China be incapacitated for a prolonged period by reason of health, the functions of Chairman shall be exercised by the Vice-Chairman.

Should the office of Chairman of the People's Republic of China fall vacant, the Vice-Chairman succeeds to the office of Chairman.

SECTION 3. THE STATE COUNCIL

ARTICLE 47 — The State Council of the People's Republic of China, that is, the Central People's Government, is the executive organ of the highest state authority; it is the highest administrative organ of state.

ARTICLE 48 — The State Council is composed of the following members: the Premier; the Vice-Premiers; the Ministers; the Heads of Commissions; and the Secretary-General.

The organization of the State Council is determined by law.

ARTICLE 49 — The State Council exercises the following functions and powers:

(1) to formulate administrative measures, issue decisions and orders, and verify their execution, in accordance with the Constitution, laws and decrees;

(2) to submit bills to the National People's Congress or its Standing Committee;

(3) to coordinate and lead the work of Ministries and Commissions;

(4) to coordinate and lead the work of local administrative organs of state throughout the country;

(5) to revise or annul inappropriate orders and directives issued by Ministers or by Heads of Commissions;

(6) to revise or annul inappropriate decisions and orders issued by local administrative organs of state;

(7) to put into effect the national economic plans and provisions of the state budget;

(8) to control foreign and domestic trade;

(9) to direct cultural, educational, and public health work;

(10) to administer affairs concerning the nationalities;

(11) to administer affairs concerning Chinese resident abroad;

(12) to protect the interests of the state, to maintain public order, and to safeguard the rights of citizens;

(13) to direct the conduct of external affairs;

(14) to guide the building up of the defense forces;

(15) to ratify the status and boundaries of autonomous *chou*, counties, autonomous counties, and municipalities;

(16) to appoint or remove administrative personnel according to provisions of law; and

(17) to exercise such other functions and powers as are vested in it by the National People's Congress or its Standing Committee.

ARTICLE 50 — The Premier directs the work of the State Council and presides over its meetings.

The Vice-Premiers assist the Premier in his work.

ARTICLE 51 — The Ministers and Heads of Commissions direct the work of their respective departments. They may issue orders and directives within the jurisdiction of their respective departments and in accordance with laws and decrees, and decisions and orders of the State Council.

ARTICLE 52 — The State Council is responsible to the National People's

Congress and reports to it, or, when the National People's Congress is not in session, to its Standing Committee.

SECTION 4. THE LOCAL PEOPLE'S CONGRESSES AND LOCAL PEOPLE'S COUNCILS

ARTICLE 53 — The administrative division of the People's Republic of China is as follows:

(1) The country is divided into provinces, autonomous regions, and municipalities directly under the central authority;

(2) Provinces and autonomous regions are divided into autonomous *chou*, counties, autonomous counties, and municipalities; and

(3) Counties and autonomous counties are divided into *hsiang*, nationality *hsiang*, and towns.

Municipalities directly under the central authority and other large municipalities are divided into districts. Autonomous *chou* are divided into counties, autonomous counties, and municipalities.

Autonomous regions, autonomous *chou*, and autonomous counties are all national autonomous areas.

ARTICLE 54 — People's congresses and people's councils are established in provinces, municipalities directly under the central authority, counties, municipalities, municipal districts, *hsiang*, nationality *hsiang*, and towns.

Organs of self-government are established in autonomous regions, autonomous *chou*, and autonomous counties. The organization and work of organs of self-government are specified in Section 5 of Chapter 2 of the Constitution.

ARTICLE 55 — Local people's congresses at all levels are the organs of government authority in their respective localities.

ARTICLE 56 — Deputies to the people's congresses of provinces, municipalities directly under the central authority, counties, and municipalities divided into districts are elected by the people's congresses of the next lower level; deputies to the people's congresses of municipalities not divided into districts, municipal districts, *hsiang*, nationality *hsiang*, and towns are directly elected by the voters.

The number of deputies to local people's congresses and the manner of their election are prescribed by electoral law.

ARTICLE 57 — The term of office of the provincial people's congresses is four years. The term of office of the people's congresses of municipalities directly under the central authority, counties, municipalities, municipal districts, *hsiang*, nationality *hsiang*, and towns is two years.

ARTICLE 58 — The local people's congresses at every level ensure the observance and execution of laws and decrees in their respective administrative areas; draw up plans for local economic and cultural development and for public works; examine and approve local budgets and financial reports; protect public property; maintain public order; safeguard the rights of citizens and the equal rights of national minorities.

ARTICLE 59 — The local people's congresses elect, and have power to recall, members of the people's councils at corresponding levels.

The people's congresses at county level and above elect, and have power to recall, the presidents of people's courts at corresponding levels.

ARTICLE 60 — The local people's congresses adopt and issue decisions within the limits of the authority prescribed by law.

The people's congresses of nationality *hsiang* may, within the limits of the authority prescribed by law, take specific measures appropriate to the characteristics of the nationalities concerned.

The local people's congresses have power to revise or annul inappropriate decisions and orders issued by people's councils at corresponding levels.

The people's congresses at county level and above have power to revise or annul inappropriate decisions issued by people's congresses at the next lower level as well as inappropriate decisions and orders issued by people's councils at the next lower level.

ARTICLE 61 — Deputies to the people's congresses of provinces, municipalities directly under the central authority, counties, and municipalities divided into districts are subject to supervision by the units which elect them; deputies to the people's congresses of municipalities not divided into districts, municipal districts, *hsiang*, nationality *hsiang*, and towns are subject to supervision by their electorates. The electoral units and electorates which elect the deputies to the local people's congresses have power at any time to recall their deputies according to the procedure prescribed by law.

ARTICLE 62 — Local people's councils, that is, local people's governments, are the executive organs of local people's congresses at corresponding levels, and are the administrative organs of state in their respective localities.

ARTICLE 63 — A local people's council is composed, according to its level, of the provincial governor and deputy provincial governors; or the mayor and deputy mayors; or the county head and deputy county heads; or the district head and deputy district heads; or the *hsiang* head and the deputy *hsiang* heads; or the town head and deputy town heads, as the case may be; together with council members.

The term of office of a local people's council is the same as that of the people's congress at corresponding levels.

The organization of local people's councils is determined by law.

ARTICLE 64 — The local people's councils administer their respective areas within the limits of the authority prescribed by law.

The local people's councils carry out the decisions issued by people's congresses at corresponding levels and decisions and orders issued by administrative organs of state at higher levels.

The local people's councils issue decisions and orders within the limits of the authority prescribed by law.

ARTICLE 65 — The people's councils at county level and above direct the work of all their subordinate departments and of people's councils at lower levels, and also appoint or remove personnel of organs of state according to provisions of law.

The people's councils at county level and above have power to suspend the carrying out of inappropriate decisions by people's congresses at the next lower level; and to revise or annul inappropriate orders and directives issued by their subordinate departments, and inappropriate decisions and orders issued by people's councils at lower levels.

ARTICLE 66 — The local people's councils are responsible to the people's congresses at corresponding levels and to the administrative organs of state at the next higher level, and report to them.

The local people's councils throughout the country are administrative organs of state, and are subordinate to and under the coordinating direction of the State Council.

SECTION 5. THE ORGANS OF SELF-GOVERNMENT OF
NATIONAL AUTONOMOUS AREAS

ARTICLE 67 — The organs of self-government of all autonomous regions, autonomous *chou*, and autonomous counties are formed in accordance with the basic principles governing the organization of local organs of state as specified in Section 4 of Chapter 2 of the Constitution. The form of each organ of self-government may be determined in accordance with the wishes of the majority of the people of the nationality or nationalities enjoying regional autonomy in a given area.

ARTICLE 68 — In all autonomous regions, autonomous *chou*, and autonomous counties where a number of nationalities live together, each nationality is entitled to appropriate representation on the organs of self-government.

ARTICLE 69 — The organs of self-government of all autonomous regions, autonomous *chou*, and autonomous counties exercise the functions and powers of local organs of state as specified in Section 4 of Chapter 2 of the Constitution.

ARTICLE 70 — The organs of self-government of all autonomous regions, autonomous *chou*, and autonomous counties exercise autonomy within the limits of the authority prescribed by the Constitution and the law.

The organs of self-government of all autonomous regions, autonomous *chou*, and autonomous counties administer their own local finances within the limits of the authority prescribed by law.

The organs of self-government of all autonomous regions, autonomous *chou*, and autonomous counties organize their local public security forces in accordance with the military system of the state.

The organs of self-government of all autonomous regions, autonomous *chou*, and autonomous counties may draw up statutes governing the exercise of autonomy or separate regulations suited to the political, economic, and cultural characteristics of the nationality or nationalities in a given area, which statutes and regulations are subject to endorsement by the Standing Committee of the National People's Congress.

ARTICLE 71 — In performing their duties, organs of self-government of all autonomous regions, autonomous *chou*, and autonomous counties employ the spoken and written language or languages commonly used in the locality.

ARTICLE 72 — The higher organs of state should fully safeguard the right of organs of self-government of all autonomous regions, autonomous *chou*, and autonomous counties to exercise autonomy, and should assist the various national minorities in their political, economic, and cultural development.

SECTION 6. THE PEOPLE'S COURTS AND THE PEOPLE'S PROCURATORATE

ARTICLE 73 — In the People's Republic of China judicial authority is exercised by the Supreme People's Court, local people's courts, and special people's courts.

ARTICLE 74 — The term of office of the President of the Supreme People's Court and presidents of local people's courts is four years.

The organization of people's courts is determined by law.

ARTICLE 75 — The system of people's assessors applies, in accordance with law, to judicial proceedings in the people's courts.

ARTICLE 76 — Cases in the people's courts are heard in public unless otherwise provided for by law. The accused has the right to defense.

ARTICLE 77 — Citizens of all nationalities have the right to use their own spoken and written languages in court proceedings. The people's courts are to provide interpretation for any party unacquainted with the spoken or written language commonly used in the locality.

In an area where people of national minorities live in compact communities or where a number of nationalities live together, hearings in people's courts are conducted in the language commonly used in the locality, and judgments, notices, and all other documents of the people's courts are made public in such language.

ARTICLE 78 — In administering justice the people's courts are independent, subject only to the law.

ARTICLE 79 — The Supreme People's Court is the highest judicial organ.

The Supreme People's Court supervises the judicial work of local people's courts and special people's courts; people's courts at higher levels supervise the judicial work of people's courts at lower levels.

ARTICLE 80 — The Supreme People's Court is responsible to the National People's Congress and reports to it; or, when the National People's Congress is not in session, to its Standing Committee. Local people's courts are responsible to the local people's congresses at corresponding levels and report to them.

ARTICLE 81 — The Supreme People's Procuratorate of the People's Republic of China exercises procuratorial authority over all departments of the State Council, all local organs of state, persons working in organs of state, and citizens, to ensure observance of the law. Local organs of the people's procuratorate and special people's procuratorates exercise procuratorial authority within the limits prescribed by law.

Local organs of the people's procuratorate and the special people's procuratorates work under the leadership of the people's procuratorates at higher levels, and all work under the coordinating direction of the Supreme People's Procuratorate.

ARTICLE 82 — The term of office of the Chief Procurator of the Supreme People's Procuratorate is four years.

The organization of people's procuratorates is determined by law.

ARTICLE 83 — In the exercise of their authority local organs of the people's procuratorate are independent and are not subject to interference by local organs of state.

ARTICLE 84 — The Supreme People's Procuratorate is responsible to the National People's Congress and reports to it; or, when the National People's Congress is not in session, to its Standing Committee.

CHAPTER 3 — FUNDAMENTAL RIGHTS AND DUTIES OF CITIZENS

ARTICLE 85 — Citizens of the People's Republic of China are equal before the law.

ARTICLE 86 — Citizens of the People's Republic of China who have reached the age of eighteen have the right to vote and stand for election whatever their nationality, race, sex, occupation, social origin, religious belief, education, property status, or length of residence, except insane persons and persons deprived by law of the right to vote and stand for election.

Women have equal rights with men to vote and stand for election.

ARTICLE 87 — Citizens of the People's Republic of China enjoy freedom of speech, freedom of the press, freedom of assembly, freedom of association, freedom of procession, and freedom of demonstration. The state guarantees to citizens enjoyment of these freedoms by providing the necessary material facilities.

ARTICLE 88 — Citizens of the People's Republic of China enjoy freedom of religious belief.

ARTICLE 89 — Freedom of the person of citizens of the People's Republic of China is inviolable. No citizen may be arrested except by decision of a people's court or with the sanction of a people's procuratorate.

ARTICLE 90 — The homes of citizens of the People's Republic of China are inviolable, and privacy of correspondence is protected by law.

Citizens of the People's Republic of China enjoy freedom of residence and freedom to change their residence.

ARTICLE 91 — Citizens of the People's Republic of China have the right to work. To guarantee enjoyment of this right, the state, by planned development of the national economy, gradually creates more employment, and better working conditions and wages.

ARTICLE 92 — Working people in the People's Republic of China have the right to rest and leisure. To guarantee enjoyment of this right, the state prescribes working hours and holidays for workers and office employees; at the same time it gradually expands material facilities to enable working people to rest and build up their health.

ARTICLE 93 — Working people in the People's Republic of China have the right to material assistance in old age, and in case of illness or disability. To guarantee enjoyment of this right, the state provides social insurance, social assistance, and public health services and gradually expands these facilities.

ARTICLE 94 — Citizens of the People's Republic of China have the right to education. To guarantee enjoyment of this right, the state establishes and gradually extends the various types of schools and other cultural and educational institutions.

The state pays special attention to the physical and mental development of young people.

ARTICLE 95 — The People's Republic of China safeguards the freedom of citizens to engage in scientific research, literary and artistic creation, and other cultural pursuits. The state encourages and assists creative work in science, education, literature, art, and other cultural pursuits.

ARTICLE 96 — Women in the People's Republic of China enjoy equal rights with men in all spheres of political, economic, cultural, social, and domestic life.

The state protects marriage, the family, and the mother and child.

ARTICLE 97 — Citizens of the People's Republic of China have the right to bring complaints against any person working in organs of state for transgression of law or neglect of duty by making a written or verbal statement to any organ of state at any level. People suffering loss by reason of infringement by persons working in organs of state of their rights as citizens have the right to compensation.

ARTICLE 98 — The People's Republic of China protects the proper rights and interests of Chinese resident abroad.

ARTICLE 99 — The People's Republic of China grants the right of asylum to any foreign national persecuted for supporting a just cause, for taking part in the peace movement, or for engaging in scientific activity.

ARTICLE 100 — Citizens of the People's Republic of China must abide by the Constitution and the law, uphold discipline at work, keep public order, and respect social ethics.

ARTICLE 101 — The public property of the People's Republic of China is sacred and inviolable. It is the duty of every citizen to respect and protect public property.

ARTICLE 102 — It is the duty of citizens of the People's Republic of China to pay taxes according to law.

ARTICLE 103 — It is the sacred duty of every citizen of the People's Republic of China to defend the homeland.

It is an honorable duty of citizens of the People's Republic of China to perform military service according to law.

CHAPTER 4 — NATIONAL FLAG, NATIONAL EMBLEM, CAPITAL

ARTICLE 104 — The national flag of the People's Republic of China is a red flag with five stars.

ARTICLE 105 — The national emblem of the People's Republic of China is: in the center, Tien An Men (Gate in Peking) under the light of five stars, framed with ears of grain, and with a cogwheel at the base.

ARTICLE 106 — The capital of the People's Republic of China is Peking.

THE CONSTITUTION OF THE COMMUNIST PARTY OF CHINA (Effective September 26, 1956)

GENERAL PROGRAM

The Communist Party of China is the vanguard of the Chinese working class, the highest form of its class organization. The aim of the Party is the achievement of socialism and communism in China.

The Communist Party of China takes Marxism-Leninism as its guide to action. Only Marxism-Leninism correctly sets forth the laws of development of society and correctly charts the path leading to the achievement of socialism and communism. The Party adheres to the Marxist-Leninist world outlook of dialectical and historical materialism, and opposes the world outlook of idealism and metaphysics. Marxism-Leninism is not a dogma, but a guide to action. It demands that in striving to build socialism and communism we should proceed from reality, apply the principles of Marxism-Leninism in a flexible and creative way for the solution of various problems arising out of the actual struggle, and thus continuously develop the theory of Marxism-Leninism. Consequently, the Party in its activities upholds the principle of integrating the universal truth of Marxism-Leninism with the actual practice of China's revolutionary struggle, and combats all doctrinaire or empiricist deviations.

In the year 1949, after long years of revolutionary struggle and revolutionary wars, the Communist Party of China and the people of the whole country overthrew the rule of imperialism, feudalism, and bureaucratic capitalism and founded the People's Republic of China — a people's democratic dictatorship led by the working class and based on the alliance of workers and peasants. Following this, the Party led the masses of the people in accomplishing the democratic revolution in most parts of the country and achieving great successes in the struggle for the establishment of a socialist society. During the period of transition from the founding of the People's Republic of China to the attainment of a socialist society, the fundamental task of the Party is to complete, step by step, the socialist transformation of agriculure, handicrafts, and capitalist industry and commerce and to bring about, step by step, the industrialization of the country.

A decisive victory has already been attained in every field in the socialist transformation of our country. It is the task of the Communist Party of China to transform, by continuing to adopt correct methods, what now remains of capitalist ownership into ownership by the whole people, to transform what remains of individual ownership by working people into collective ownership by the working masses, to uproot the system of exploitation, and to remove all the causes that give rise to such a system. In the process of building up a socialist society, the principle "from each according to his ability, to each according to his work" should be brought into effect step by step; and all former exploiters should be reformed in a peaceful manner to become working people living by their own labor. The Party must continue to pay attention to the elimination of capitalist factors and influences in the economic, political, and ideological fields, and make determined efforts to mobilize and unite all the positive forces throughout the country that can be mobilized and united for the purpose of winning a complete victory for the great cause of socialism.

The victory of the socialist revolution has opened up illimitable possibilities for the development of the productive forces of society. It is the task of the Communist Party of China to develop the national economy in a planned way so as to bring about the industrialization of the country as rapidly as possible, and to effect the technological transformation of the national economy in a planned, systematic way so that China may possess a powerful modernized industry, a modernized agriculture, modernized communications and transport, and a modernized national defense. In order to achieve industrialization and bring about a continuous growth of the national economy, priority must be given to the development of heavy industry, and at the same time a due proportion must be maintained between heavy industry and light industry, and between industry as a whole and agriculture. The Party must do everything possible to stimulate progress in China's science, culture, and technology so as to catch up with the world's advanced levels in these fields. The basic object of all Party work is to satisfy the material and cultural needs of the people to the maximum possible extent. Therefore, it is necessary that the living conditions of the people should improve steadily on the basis of increased production. This is also a requisite for stimulating the people's enthusiasm for production.

Our country is a multi-national state. Because of historical reasons, the development of many of the national minorities has been hindered. The Communist Party of China must make special efforts to raise the status of the national minorities, help them to attain self-government, endeavor to train cadres from among them, accelerate their economic and cultural advance, bring about complete equality between all the nationalities, and strengthen the unity and fraternal relations among them. Social reforms among the nationalities must be carried out by the respective nationalities themselves in accordance with their own wishes, and by taking steps in conformity with their special characteristics. The Party opposes all tendencies to great-nation chauvinism and local nationalism, both of which hamper the unity of nationalities. Special attention must be paid to the prevention and correction of tendencies of great-Hanism on the part of Party members and government workers of Han nationality.

The Communist Party of China must work untiringly to consolidate the people's democratic dictatorship in our country, which is the guarantee for the success of the socialist cause in China. The Party must fight for a fuller development of the democratic life of the nation and strive for the constant improvement of its democratic institutions. The Party must work in every way to fortify the fraternal alliance of workers and peasants, to consolidate the united front of all patriotic forces, and to strengthen its lasting cooperation with the other democratic parties as well as democrats without party affiliations. Since the imperialists and counter-revolutionary remnants are bent on undermining the cause of the Chinese people, it is imperative for the Party to heighten its revolutionary vigilance and wage determined struggles against those forces which endanger our country's independence and security and those elements who try to wreck socialist construction in our country. The Party must work together with the people of the whole country to bring about the liberation of Taiwan.

The Communist Party of China advocates a foreign policy directed to the safeguarding of world peace and the achievement of peaceful coexistence between countries with different systems. The Party stands for the establishment and development of diplomatic, economic, and cultural relations between China and other countries and for the broadening and strengthening of friendly relations between the Chinese people and the peoples of all other countries of the world. The Party is resolutely opposed to any act of aggression against China by imperialist countries and to any imperialist plans for a new war; it supports all efforts made by the peoples and governments of other countries to uphold peace and promote friendly relations between nations, and expresses its sympathy for all struggles in the world against imperialism and colonialism. The Party endeavors to develop and strengthen China's friendship with all other countries in the camp of peace, democracy, and socialism headed by the Soviet Union, to strengthen proletarian internationalism and to learn from the experiences of the world communist movement. It supports the struggle of the Communists, progressives, and laboring people of the whole world for the progress of mankind, and educates its members and the Chinese people in the spirit of internationalism, as expressed in the slogan "Proletarians of all lands, unite!"

The Communist Party of China puts into practice all that it advocates through the activity of the Party organizations and membership among the masses and through the conscious efforts made by the people under its guidance. For this reason it is necessary to constantly develop the tradition of following the mass line in Party work. The Party's ability to continue to give correct leadership depends on whether or not it can, through analysis and synthesis, systematically summarize the experience and opinions of the masses, turn the resulting ideas into the policy of the Party and then, as a result of the Party's propaganda and organizational work among the masses, transform this policy into the views and action of the masses themselves, testing the correctness of Party policy, and supplementing and revising it in the course of mass activity. It is the duty of the Party leadership to ensure that in the endless repetition of this process of "coming from the masses and going back to the masses" the level of the Party members' understanding and that of the masses are continually raised and the cause of the Party and the people is constantly advanced. The Party and its members must, therefore, maintain close and extensive ties with the workers, peasants, intellectuals, and other patriots and strive constantly to make such ties ever stronger and more widespread. Every Party member must understand that the interests of the Party and those of the people are one, and responsibility to the Party and responsibility to the people are identical. Every Party member must whole-heartedly serve the people, constantly consult them, pay heed to their opinions, concern himself with their well-being, and strive to help realize their wishes. Now that the Communist Party of China is a party in power, it must especially conduct itself with modesty and prudence, guard against self-conceit and impatience, and make the maximum effort in every Party organization, state organ, and economic unit to combat any bureaucratic practice which estranges the masses or leads to isolation from the realities of life.

The organizational principle of the Communist Party of China is democratic centralism, which means centralism on the basis of democracy and democracy under centralized guidance. The Party must take effective measures to promote inner-Party democracy, encourage the initiative and creative ability of all Party members and of all local and primary Party organizations, and strengthen the lively contact between the higher and lower Party organizations. Only in this way can the Party effectively extend and strengthen its ties with the masses of the people, give correct and timely leadership, and adapt itself flexibly to various concrete conditions and local characteristics. And only in this way can Party life be invigorated and the cause of the Party advance on an ever wider scale and at an ever greater pace. Only on this basis, furthermore, can centralism and the unity of the Party be consolidated and its discipline be voluntarily, not mechanically, observed. Democratic centralism demands that every Party organization should strictly abide by the principle of collective leadership coupled with individual responsibility and that every Party member and Party organization should be subject to Party supervision from above and from below.

Democracy within the Party must not be divorced from centralism. The Party is a united militant organization, welded together by a discipline which is obligatory on all its members. Without discipline it would be impossible for the Party to lead the state and the people to overcome their powerful enemies and achieve socialism and communism. As the highest form of class organization, the Party must strive to play a correct role as the leader and core in every aspect of the country's life and must combat any tendency to departmentalism, which reduces the Party's role and weakens its unity. Solidarity and unity are the very life of the Party, the source of its strength. It is the sacred duty of every Party member to pay constant attention to the safeguarding of the solidarity of the Party and the consolidation of its unity. Within the Party, no action which violates the Party's political line or organizational principles is permissible, nor is it permissible to carry on factional activities or activities aimed at splitting the Party, to act independently of the Party, or to place the individual above the collective body of the Party.

No political party or person can be free from shortcomings and mistakes in work. The Communist Party of China and its members must constantly practice criticism and self-criticism to expose and eliminate their shortcomings and mistakes so as to educate themselves and the people. In view of the fact that the Party plays the leading role in the life of the state and society, it is all the more necessary that it should make stringent demands on every Party organization and member and promote criticism and self-criticism; and in particular, it should encourage and support criticism from below within the Party as well as criticism of the Party by the people, and should prohibit any suppression of criticism. The Party must prevent and resist corrosion by bourgeois and petty-bourgeois ways of thinking and styles of work and guard against and defeat any Rightist or "Leftist" opportunist deviation inside the Party. In the case of Party members who have committed mistakes, the Party should, in the spirit of "curing the illness to save the patient," allow them to remain in its ranks and receive education, and help them to correct their mistakes, provided such mistakes can be corrected within the Party and the erring Party member himself is prepared to correct his mistakes. As for those who persist in their mistakes and carry on activities detrimental to the Party, it is essential to wage a determined struggle against them even to the point of expelling them from the Party.

The Communist Party of China requires all its members to place the Party's interests above their personal interests, to be diligent and unpretentious, to study and work hard, to unite the broad masses of the people, and to overcome all difficulties in order to build China into a great, mighty, prosperous, and advanced socialist state, and on this basis to advance towards the achievement of the loftiest ideal of mankind — communism.

CHAPTER 1 — MEMBERSHIP

ARTICLE 1 — Membership of the Party is open to any Chinese citizen who works and does not exploit the labor of others, accepts the program and Constitution of the Party, joins and works in one of the Party organizations, carries out the Party's decisions, and pays membership dues as required.

ARTICLE 2 — Party members have the following duties:

(1) To strive to study Marxism-Leninism and unceasingly raise the level of their understanding;

(2) To safeguard the Party's solidarity and consolidate its unity;

(3) To faithfully carry out Party policy and decisions and energetically fulfill the tasks assigned them by the Party;

(4) To strictly observe the Party Constitution and the laws of the state and behave in accordance with communist ethics, no exception being made for any Party member, whatever his services and position;

(5) To place the interests of the Party and the state, that is, the interests of the masses of the people, above their personal interests, and in the event of any conflict between the two, to submit unswervingly to the interests of the Party and the state, that is, the interests of the masses;

(6) To serve the masses heart and soul, to strengthen their ties with the masses, to learn from them, to listen with an open mind to their wishes and opinions and report these without delay to the Party, to explain Party policy and decisions to the people;

(7) To set a good example in their work and constantly raise their productive skill and professional ability;

(8) To practice criticism and self-criticism, expose shortcomings and mistakes in work and strive to overcome and correct them; to report such shortcomings and mistakes to the leading Party bodies, up to and including the Central Committee; and to fight both inside and outside the Party against everything which is detrimental to the interests of the Party and the people;

(9) To be truthful and honest with the Party and not to conceal or distort the truth;

(10) To be constantly on the alert against the intrigues of the enemy, and to guard the secrets of the Party and the state.

Party members who fail to fulfill any of the above-mentioned duties shall be criticized and educated. Any serious infraction of these duties, splitting of Party unity, breaking of the laws of the state, violation of Party decisions damaging Party interests, or deception towards the Party constitutes a violation of Party discipline, and disciplinary action shall be taken against it.

ARTICLE 3 — Party members enjoy the following rights:

(1) To participate in free and practical discussion at Party meetings or in the Party press on theoretical and practical questions relating to Party policy;

(2) To make proposals regarding the Party's work and give full play to their creative ability in their work;

(3) To elect and be elected within the Party;

(4) To criticize any party organization or any functionary at Party meetings;

(5) To ask to attend in person when a Party organization decides to take

disciplinary action against them or make an appraisal of their character and work;

(6) To reserve their opinions or submit them to a leading body of the Party in case they disagree with any Party decision, which, in the meanwhile, they must carry out unconditionally;

(7) To address any statement, appeal, or complaint to any Party organization, up to and including the Central Committee.

Party members and responsible members of Party organizations who fail to respect these rights of a Party member shall be criticized and educated. Infringement of these rights constitutes a violation of Party discipline, and disciplinary action shall be taken against it.

ARTICLE 4 — Only persons of 18 years old and upwards are eligible for Party membership.

Applicants for Party membership must undergo the procedure of admission individually.

New members are admitted to the Party through a Party branch. An applicant must be recommended by two full Party members, and is admitted as a probationary member after being accepted by the general membership meeting of a Party branch and approved by the next higher Party committee; he may become a full Party member only after the completion of a probationary period of a year.

Under special conditions, Party committees at county or municipal level and above have the power to admit new members to the Party directly.

ARTICLE 5 — Party members who recommend an applicant for admission to the Party must furnish the Party, in all sincerity and with a full sense of responsibility, with truthful information about the applicant's ideology, character, and personal history and must explain the Party program and Constitution to the applicant.

ARTICLE 6 — Before approving the admission of an applicant for Party membership, the Party committee concerned must assign a Party functionary to have a detailed conversation with the applicant and carefully examine his application form, the opinions of his recommenders, and the decision made by the Party branch on his application.

ARTICLE 7 — During the probationary period, the Party organization concerned shall give the probationary member an elementary Party education and observe his political qualities.

Probationary members have the same duties as full members. They enjoy the same rights as full members except that they have no right to elect or be elected or to vote on any motion.

ARTICLE 8 — When the probationary period of a probationary member has expired, the Party branch to which he belongs must discuss without delay whether he is qualified to be transferred to full membership. The application for such a transfer must be accepted by a general membership meeting of the said Party branch and approved by the next higher Party committee.

When the probationary period of a probationary member has expired, the Party organization concerned may prolong it for a period not exceeding a year if it finds it necessary to continue to observe him. If a probationary member is found to be unfit for transfer to full membership, his status as probationary member shall be annulled.

Any decision by a Party branch to prolong the probationary period of a probationary member or to deprive him of his status as probationary member must be approved by the next higher Party committee.

ARTICLE 9 — The probationary period of a probationary member begins from the day when the general membership meeting of a Party branch accepts him as probationary member. The Party standing of a Party member dates from the day when the general membership meeting of a Party branch accepts his transfer to full membership.

ARTICLE 10 — Party members transferring from one Party organization to another become members of the latter organization.

ARTICLE 11 — Party members are free to withdraw from the Party. When a Party member asks to withdraw, the Party branch to which he belongs shall, by decision of its general membership meeting, strike his name off the Party rolls and report the matter to the next higher Party committee for registration.

ARTICLE 12 — A Party member who, over a period of six months and without proper reasons, fails to take part in Party life or to pay membership dues is regarded as having quitted the Party himself. The Party branch to which this member belongs shall, by decision of its general membership meeting, strike his name off the Party rolls and report the matter to the next higher Party committee for registration.

ARTICLE 13 — Party organizations at all levels may, according to each individual case, take disciplinary measures against any Party member who violates Party discipline, such as warning, serious warning, removal from posts held in the Party, placing on probation within the Party, or expulsion from the Party.

The period in which a Party member is placed on probation shall not exceed two years. During this period, the rights and duties of the Party member concerned are the same as those of a probationary member. If after a Party member has been placed on probation the facts show that he has corrected his mistakes, his rights as a full Party member shall be restored and the period in which he is placed on probation will be reckoned in his Party standing. If he is found to be unfit for Party membership, he shall be expelled from the Party.

ARTICLE 14 — Any disciplinary measure taken against a Party member must be decided on by a general membership meeting of the Party branch to which he belongs and must be approved by a higher Party control commission or higher Party committee.

Under special conditions, a Party branch committee or a higher Party committee has the power to take disciplinary measures against a Party member, but they must be subject to approval by a higher Party control commission or higher Party committee.

ARTICLE 15 — Any decision to remove a member or alternate member of the Party committee of a county, an autonomous county, a municipality, a province, an autonomous region, or a municipality directly under the central authority, or an autonomous *chou* from the said committee, to place him on probation or to expel him from the Party must be taken by the Party congress that has elected the said member. In conditions of urgency, such decision may be taken by a two-thirds majority vote at a plenary session of the Party committee to which the member belongs, but it must be subject to approval by the next higher Party committee. A primary Party organization has no power to take decisions on removing a member or alternate member of a higher Party committee from the said committee, or placing him on probation or expelling him from the Party.

ARTICLE 16 — Any decision to remove a member or alternate member of the Central Committee of the Party from the Central Committee, to place him on probation or to expel him from the Party must be taken by the National

Party Congress. In conditions of urgency, such decision may be taken by a two-thirds majority vote of the Central Committee at its plenary session, but it must be subject to subsequent confirmation by the next session of the National Party Congress.

ARTICLE 17 — Expulsion from the Party is the most severe of all inner-Party disciplinary measures. In taking or approving such a decision, all Party organizations must exercise the utmost caution, thoroughly investigate and study the facts and material evidence of the case, and listen carefully to the statement made in his own defense by the Party member concerned.

ARTICLE 18 — When a Party organization discusses or decides on a disciplinary measure against a Party member, it must, barring special circumstances, notify the member concerned to attend the meeting to defend himself. When disciplinary action is decided upon, the person against whom such action is taken must be told the reasons for it. If he disagrees, he may ask for a reconsideration of his case and address an appeal to higher Party committees, to Party control commissions, up to and including the Central Committee. Party organizations at all levels must deal with such appeals seriously or forward them promptly; no suppression is permitted.

CHAPTER 2 — ORGANIZATIONAL STRUCTURE AND ORGANIZATIONAL PRINCIPLES OF THE PARTY

ARTICLE 19 — The Party is formed on the principle of democratic centralism.

Democratic centralism means centralism on the basis of democracy and democracy under centralized guidance. Its basic conditions are as follows:

(1) The leading bodies of the Party at all levels are elected.

(2) The highest leading body of the Party is the National Party Congress, and the highest leading body in each local Party organization is the local Party congress. The National Party Congress elects the Central Committee and the local Party congresses elect their respective local Party committees. The Central Committee and local Party committees are responsible to their respective Party congresses to which they should report on their work.

(3) All leading bodies of the Party must pay constant heed to the views of their lower organizations and the rank-and-file Party members, study their experiences, and give prompt help in solving their problems.

(4) Lower Party organizations must present periodical reports on their work to the Party organizations above them and ask in good time for instructions on questions which need decision by higher Party organizations.

(5) All Party organizations operate on the principle of combining collective leadership with individual responsibility. All important issues are to be decided on collectively, and at the same time, each individual is enabled to play his part to the fullest possible extent.

(6) Party decisions must be carried out unconditionally. Individual Party members shall obey the Party organization, the minority shall obey the majority, the lower Party organizations shall obey the higher Party organizations and all constituent Party organizations throughout the country shall obey the National Party Congress and the Central Committee.

ARTICLE 20 — Party organizations are formed on a geographical or industrial basis.

The Party organization in charge of Party work in a defined area is regarded as the highest of all the constituent Party organizations in that area.

The Party organization in charge of Party work in a particular production or work unit is regarded as the highest of all the constituent Party organizations in that unit.

ARTICLE 21 — The highest leading bodies of the Party organizations at various levels are as follows:

(1) For the whole country, it is the National Party Congress. When the National Party Congress is not in session, it is the Central Committee elected by the National Party Congress;

(2) For a province, autonomous region, or municipality directly under the central authority, it is the provincial, autonomous regional or municipal Party congress. When the congress is not in session, it is the provincial, autonomous regional or municipal Party committee elected by the congress.

For an autonomous *chou*, it is the autonomous *chou* Party congress. When the congress is not in session, it is the autonomous *chou* committee elected by the congress;

(3) For a county, autonomous county or municipality, it is the county, autonomous county, or municipal Party congress. When the congress is not in session, it is the county, autonomous county, or municipal committee elected by the congress;

(4) For primary units (factories, mines, and other enterprises, *hsiang*, nationality *hsiang*, towns and agricultural producers' cooperatives, offices, schools, streets, companies of the People's Liberation Army and other primary units), it is the delegate meeting or the general membership meeting of the particular primary unit. When the delegate meeting or general membership meeting of the primary unit is not in session, it is the primary Party committee, the committee of a general Party branch, or the committee of a Party branch elected by the delegate meeting or the general membership meeting.

ARTICLE 22 — Party elections must fully reflect the will of the electors. The list of candidates for election put forward by the Party organization or by electors must be discussed by the electors.

Election is by secret ballot. Electors shall be ensured the right to criticize or reject any candidate, or nominate a person who is not on the list.

In an election in a primary Party organization, voting may be by a show of hands if voting by ballot is impossible. In such cases, each candidate shall be voted upon separately, and voting on a whole list of candidates is forbidden.

ARTICLE 23 — Party electing units have the power to replace any member they have elected to a Party congress or Party committee during his term of office.

When a local Party congress is not in session, a higher Party committee, if it deems it necessary, may transfer or appoint responsible members of a lower Party organization.

ARTICLE 24 — In places where, because of special circumstances, it is impossible for the time being to call Party congresses or general membership meetings to elect Party committees, such Party committees may be elected at Party conferences or appointed by higher Party organizations.

ARTICLE 25 — The functions and powers of the central Party organizations and those of the local Party organizations shall be appropriately divided. All questions of a national character or questions that require a uniform decision for the whole country shall be handled by the central Party organizations so as to contribute to the centralism and unity of the Party. All questions of a local character or questions that need to be decided locally shall be handled by the local Party organizations so as to find solutions appropriate to the local conditions. The functions and powers of higher local Party organizations and those of lower local Party organizations shall be appropriately divided according to the same principle.

Decisions taken by lower Party organizations must not run counter to those made by higher Party organizations.

ARTICLE 26 — Before decisions on Party policy are made by leading bodies of the Party, lower Party organizations and members of the Party committees may hold free and practical discussions inside the Party organizations and at Party meetings and submit their proposals to the leading bodies of the Party. However, once a decision is taken by the leading bodies of the Party, it must be accepted. Should a lower Party organization find that a decision made by a higher Party organization does not suit the actual conditions in its locality or in its particular department, it should request the higher Party organization concerned to modify the decision. If the higher Party organization still upholds its decision, then the lower Party organization must carry it out unconditionally.

On policy of a national character, before the central leading bodies of the Party have made any statement or decision, departmental and local Party organizations and their responsible members are not permitted to make any public statement or make their own decisions on it, although they may discuss it among themselves and make suggestions to the central leading bodies.

ARTICLE 27 — The newspapers issued by Party organizations at all levels must publicize the decisions and policy of the central Party organizations, of higher Party organizations, and of their own Party organizations.

ARTICLE 28 — The formation of a new Party organization or the dissolution of an existing Party organization must be decided on by the next higher Party organization.

ARTICLE 29 — To facilitate direction of the work in various localities, the Central Committee may, if it deems it necessary, establish a bureau of the Central Committee as its representative body for an area embracing several provinces, autonomous regions, and municipalities directly under the central authority. A provincial or autonomous regional committee may, if it deems it necessary, establish a regional committee or an organization of equal status as its representative body for an area embracing a number of counties, autonomous counties, and municipalities. The Party committee of a municipality directly under the central authority, or of a municipality, county, or autonomous county may, if it deems it necessary, establish a number of district committees as its representative bodies within its area.

ARTICLE 30 — Party committees at all levels may, as the situation requires, set up a number of departments, commissions, or other bodies to carry on work under their own direction.

CHAPTER 3 — CENTRAL ORGANIZATIONS OF THE PARTY

ARTICLE 31 — The National Party Congress is elected for a term of five years.

The number of delegates to the National Party Congress and the procedure governing their election and replacement and the filling of vacancies shall be determined by the Central Committee.

A session of the National Party Congress shall be convened once a year by the Central Committee. Under extraordinary conditions, it may be postponed or convened before its due date as the Central Committee may decide. The

Central Committee must convene a session of the National Party Congress if one-third of the delegates to the National Party Congress or one-third of the Party organizations at provincial level so request.

ARTICLE 32 — The functions and powers of the National Party Congress are as follows:

(1) To hear and examine the reports of the Central Committee and other central organs;

(2) To determine the Party's line and policy;

(3) To revise the Constitution of the Party;

(4) To elect the Central Committee.

ARTICLE 33 — The Central Committee of the Party is elected for a term of five years. The number of members and alternate members of the Central Committee shall be determined by the National Party Congress. Vacancies on the Central Committee shall be filled by alternate members in order of established precedence.

ARTICLE 34 — When the National Party Congress is not in session, the Central Committee directs the entire work of the Party, carries out the decisions of the National Party Congress, represents the Party in its relations with other parties and organizations, sets up various Party organs and directs their activities, takes charge of and allocates Party cadres.

The Central Committee guides the work of the central state organs and people's organizations of a national character through leading Party members' groups within them.

ARTICLE 35 — The Party organizations in the Chinese People's Liberation Army carry on their work in accordance with the instructions of the Central Committee. The General Political Department in the People's Liberation Army, under the direction of the Central Committee, takes charge of the ideological and organizational work of the Party in the army.

ARTICLE 36 — The Central Committee meets in plenary session at least twice a year to be convened by the Political Bureau of the Central Committee.

ARTICLE 37 — The Central Committee elects at its plenary session the Political Bureau, the Standing Committee of the Political Bureau, and the Secretariat, as well as the chairman, vice-chairman, and general secretary of the Central Committee.

When the Central Committee is not in plenary session, the Political Bureau and its Standing Committee exercise the powers and functions of the Central Committee.

The Secretariat attends to the daily work of the Central Committee under the direction of the Political Bureau and its Standing Committee.

The chairman and vice-chairmen of the Central Committee are concurrently chairman and vice-chairmen of the Political Bureau.

The Central Committee may, when it deems it necessary, have an honorary chairman.

CHAPTER 4 — PARTY ORGANIZATIONS IN PROVINCES, AUTONOMOUS REGIONS, MUNICIPALITIES DIRECTLY UNDER THE CENTRAL AUTHORITY, AND AUTONOMOUS *CHOU*

ARTICLE 38 — The Party congress for a province, autonomous region, or municipality directly under the central authority is elected for a term of three years.

The number of delegates to such a Party congress and the procedure governing their election and replacement and the filling of vacancies shall be determined by the Party committee in the given area.

The Party congress for a province, autonomous region, or municipality directly under the central authority shall be convened once a year by the Party committee in the area.

ARTICLE 39 — The Party congress for a province, autonomous region, or municipality directly under the central authority hears and examines the reports of the Party committee and other organs in the area, discusses and decides on questions relating to policy and work of a local character in its area, elects the Party committee for the area, and elects delegates to the National Party Congress.

ARTICLE 40 — The Party committee of a province, autonomous region, or municipality directly under the central authority is elected for a term of three years. The number of members and alternate members of the committee shall be determined by the Central Committee. Vacancies on the committee shall be filled by alternate members of the committee in order of established precedence.

The Party committee of a province, autonomous region, or municipality directly under the central authority shall, when the Party congress for the given area is not in session, carry out the decisions and directives of the Party in that area, direct all work of a local character, set up various Party organs and direct their activities, take charge of and allocate Party cadres in accordance with the regulations laid down by the Central Committee, direct the work of leading Party members' groups in local state organs and people's organizations and systematically report on its work to the Central Committee.

ARTICLE 41 — The Party committee of a province, autonomous region, or municipality directly under the central authority shall meet in full session at least three times a year.

The Party committee of a province, autonomous region, or municipality directly under the central authority elects at its plenary session its standing committee and secretariat. The standing committee exercises the powers and functions of the Party committee when the latter is not in plenary session. The secretariat attends to the daily work under the direction of the standing committee.

The members of the secretariat and those of the standing committee of the Party committee of a province, autonomous region, or municipality directly under the central authority, must be approved by the Central Committee. Members of the secretariat must be Party members of at least five years' standing.

ARTICLE 42 — Party organizations in an autonomous *chou* carry on their work under the direction of a provincial or autonomous regional Party committee.

The Party congress and Party committee for an autonomous *chou* are constituted in the same manner as those for a province, autonomous region, or municipality directly under the central authority.

The Party congress and Party committee for an autonomous *chou* are elected for a term of two years.

An autonomous *chou* Party congress elects delegates to the provincial or autonomous regional Party congress.

The members of the secretariat and those of the standing committee of an autonomous *chou* Party committee must be approved by the Central Committee. The secretaries must be Party members of at least three years' standing.

CHAPTER 5 — COUNTY, AUTONOMOUS COUNTY, AND MUNICIPAL PARTY ORGANIZATIONS

ARTICLE 43 — The Party congress for a county, autonomous county, or municipality is elected for a term of two years.

The number of delegates to the congress and the procedure governing their election and replacement and the filling of vacancies shall be determined by the Party committee in the area.

The Party congress for a county, autonomous county or municipality shall be convened once a year by the Party committee in the area.

ARTICLE 44 — The Party congress for a county, autonomous county, or municipality hears and examines the reports of the Party committee and other organs in the area, discusses and decides on questions relating to the policy and work of a local character in its area, elects the Party committee for the area and elects delegates to the provincial or autonomous regional Party congress.

The Party congress for a county, autonomous county, or municipality under the jurisdiction of an autonomous *chou* elects delegates only to the Party congress of the said autonomous *chou*.

ARTICLE 45 — The Party committee of a county, autonomous county, or municipality is elected for a term of two years. The number of members and alternate members of the committee shall be determined by the provincial or autonomous regional Party committee concerned. Vacancies on the committee shall be filled by alternate members of the committee in order of established precedence.

When the Party congress for a county, autonomous county, or municipality is not in session, the Party committee in the area carries out Party decisions and directives in that area, directs all work of a local character, sets up various Party organs and directs their activities, takes charge of and allocates Party cadres in accordance with the regulations laid down by the Central Committee, directs the work of leading Party members' groups in local government organs and people's organizations, and systematically reports on its work to higher Party committees.

ARTICLE 46 — The Party committee of a county, autonomous county, or municipality shall meet in plenary session at least four times a year.

The county, autonomous county, or municipal party committee elects at its plenary session its standing committee and secretary, and, if necessary, a secretariat. The standing committee exercises the powers and functions of the Party committee when the latter is not in plenary session. The secretary or the secretariat attends to the daily work under the direction of the standing committee.

The members of the secretariat and those of the standing committee must be approved by the provincial or autonomous regional Party committee. In the case of a city with a population of 500,000 or more, or in the case of a key industrial city, such members must be approved by the Central Committee. The secretaries of the Party committee of a county, autonomous county, or municipality must be Party members of at least two years' standing. In the case of a city with a population of 500,000 or more, or in the case of a key industrial city, the secretaries of the Party committee must be Party members of at least five years' standing.

CHAPTER 6 — PRIMARY ORGANIZATIONS OF THE PARTY

ARTICLE 47 — Primary Party organizations are formed in factories, mines, and other enterprises, in *hsiang* and nationality *hsiang*, in towns, in agricultural producers' cooperatives, in offices, schools, and streets, in companies of the People's Liberation Army and in other primary units where there are three or more full Party members. When a primary unit contains less than three full Party members, no primary Party organization should be established, but these members together with the probationary members in their unit may either form a group or join the primary Party organization of a nearby unit.

ARTICLE 48 — Primary Party organizations take the following organizational forms:

(1) A primary Party organization with one hundred or more Party members may, by decision of the next higher Party committee, hold a delegate meeting or a general membership meeting to elect a primary Party committee. Under the primary Party committee a number of general branches or branches may be formed in accordance with divisions based on production, work, or residence. Under a general Party branch a number of Party branches may be formed. The committee of a general Party branch is elected by a general membership meeting or a delegate meeting of the said general branch. The committee of a Party branch is elected by the general membership meeting of the said branch. The committee of the primary Party organization or of the general Party branch has the power to approve decisions made by a branch on the admission of new members and on disciplinary measures against Party members.

Under special conditions, an individual primary Party organization with less than one hundred members may, by decision of the next higher Party committee, establish a primary Party committee.

(2) A primary Party organization with fifty or more Party members may, by decision of the next higher Party committee, set up a general branch committee to be elected by a general membership meeting or a delegate meeting. Under a general branch committee a number of branches may be formed in accordance with divisions based on production, work, or residence. The general branch committee has the power to approve decisions made by a branch on the admission of new members and on disciplinary measures against Party members.

Under special conditions, a general branch committee may, by decision of the next higher Party committee, be set up in a primary Party organization whose membership is less than fifty but whose work requires a general branch committee, or in a primary Party organization whose membership numbers one hundred or more but whose work does not require a primary Party committee.

(3) A primary Party organization with less than fifty members may, by decision of the next higher Party committee, set up a branch committee to be elected by a general membership meeting, and has the power to make decisions on the admission of new members and on disciplinary measures against Party members.

(4) Groups may be formed under a general Party branch or a Party branch.

ARTICLE 49 — A primary Party organization which has set up its own primary committee shall convene a delegate meeting at least once a year. A general Party branch shall hold a general membership meeting or a delegate meeting at least twice a year. A Party branch shall hold a general membership meeting at least once in three months.

The delegate meeting or general membership meeting of a primary Party organization hears and examines the reports of the primary Party committee, the general branch committees, or the branch committees, discusses and decides on questions relating to work in its own unit, elects the primary Party committee, the general Party branch committees, or the branch committees, and elects delegates to the higher Party congress.

The primary Party committee, the general Party branch committee, and the branch committee are elected for a term of one year. The number of members of these committees shall be determined by their respective next higher Party committees.

A primary Party committee shall elect a secretary and from one to four deputy secretaries. If necessary, it may elect a standing committee. The general branch committee and the branch committee shall each elect a secretary, and, if necessary, one to three deputy secretaries.

A Party branch with less than ten members only elects a secretary or in addition a deputy secretary, but no branch committee needs to be formed.

A Party group shall elect a leader and, if necessary, a deputy leader.

ARTICLE 50 — Primary Party organizations must cement the ties of the workers, peasants, intellectuals, and other patriotic people with the Party and its leading bodies. The general tasks of primary Party organizations are as follows:

(1) To carry on propaganda and organizational work among the masses and put into practice what the Party advocates, and the decisions of higher Party organizations;

(2) To pay constant heed to the sentiments and demands of the masses and report them to higher Party organizations, to pay constant attention to the material and cultural life of the masses and strive to improve it;

(3) To recruit new Party members, to collect membership dues, to appraise the character and work of Party members, and to maintain Party discipline among the membership;

(4) To organize Party members to study Marxism-Leninism and the Party's policy and experience and raise the level of their ideology and political understanding;

(5) To lead the masses to take an active part in the political life of the country;

(6) To lead the masses to give full play to their activity and creative ability, to strengthen labor discipline and to ensure the fulfillment of production and work plans;

(7) To promote criticism and self-criticism, to expose and eliminate shortcomings and mistakes in work, and to wage struggles against the violation of laws and discipline, against corruption and waste, and against bureaucracy;

(8) To educate the Party members and the masses to sharpen their revolutionary vigilance and to be constantly on the alert to combat the disruptive activities of the class enemy.

ARTICLE 51 — Primary Party organizations in enterprises, villages, schools, and army units should guide and supervise the administrative bodies and mass organizations in their respective units in the energetic fulfillment of the decisions of higher Party organizations and higher state organs and in ceaselessly improving their work.

Since special conditions obtain in public institutions and organizations, the primary Party organizations therein are in no position to guide and supervise their work, but they should give ideological and political supervision to all Party members in the said institutions and organizations, including those who hold leading administrative posts. The primary Party organizations should also take a constant interest in improving the work in their respective units, strengthen labor discipline, combat bureaucracy, and report without delay any shortcomings in the work to the administrative chiefs of the given units and to higher Party organizations.

CHAPTER 7 — CONTROL ORGANS OF THE PARTY

ARTICLE 52 — The Party's Central Committee, the Party committees of the provinces, autonomous regions, municipalities directly under the central authority and autonomous *chou*, and the Party committees of the counties, autonomous counties, and municipalities shall set up control commissions. The Central Control Commission shall be elected by the Central Committee at its plenary session. A local control commission shall be elected by a plenary session of the Party committee for that locality, subject to approval by the next higher Party committee.

ARTICLE 53 — The tasks of the central and local control commissions are as follows: regularly to examine and deal with cases of violation of the Party Constitution, Party discipline, communist ethics and the state laws and decrees on the part of Party members; to decide on or cancel disciplinary measures against Party members; and to deal with appeals and complaints from Party members.

ARTICLE 54 — The control commissions at all levels function under the direction of the Party committees at corresponding levels.

Higher control commissions have the power to check up on the work of lower control commissions, and to approve or modify their decisions on any case. Lower control commissions must report on their work to higher control commissions, and present accurate reports on violations of discipline by Party members.

CHAPTER 8 — RELATION BETWEEN THE PARTY AND THE COMMUNIST YOUTH LEAGUE

ARTICLE 55 — The Communist Youth League of China carries on its activities under the guidance of the Communist Party of China. The Central Committee of the Communist Youth League accepts the leadership of the Party's Central Committee. The Communist Youth League's local organizations are simultaneously under the leadership of the Party organizations at the corresponding levels and of higher League organizations.

ARTICLE 56 — The Communist Youth League is the Party's assistant. In all spheres of socialist construction Communist Youth League organizations should play an active role in publicizing and carrying out Party policy and decisions. In the struggle to promote production, improve work, and expose and eliminate shortcomings and mistakes in work, the Communist Youth League organizations should render effective help to the Party and have the duty to make suggestions to the Party organizations concerned.

ARTICLE 57 — Party organizations at all levels must take a deep interest in the Communist Youth League's ideological and organizational work, give guidance to the Communist Youth League in imbuing all its members with communist spirit and educating them in Marxist-Leninist theory, see to it that close contact is maintained between the Communist Youth League and the broad masses of young people, and pay constant attention to selecting members for the leading core in the Communist Youth League.

ARTICLE 58 — Members of the Communist Youth League shall withdraw from the League when they have been admitted to the Party and have become full Party members, provided they do not hold leading posts or engage in specific work in the League organizations.

CHAPTER 9 — LEADING PARTY MEMBERS' GROUPS IN NON-PARTY ORGANIZATIONS

ARTICLE 59 — In the leading body of a state organ or people's organization, where there are three or more Party members holding responsible posts, a leading Party members' group shall be formed. The tasks of such a group in the said organ or organization are: to assume the responsibility of carrying out Party policy and decisions, to fortify unity with non-Party cadres, to cement the ties with the masses, to strengthen Party and state discipline, and to combat bureaucracy.

ARTICLE 60 — The composition of a leading Party members' group shall be decided by a competent Party committee. The group has a secretary, and may, in case of need, also have a deputy secretary.

A leading Party members' group must in all matters accept the leadership of the competent Party committee.

CHINESE-AMERICAN MUTUAL DEFENSE TREATY (Signed December 2, 1954; effective March 3, 1955)

ARTICLE 1 — The Parties undertake, as set forth in the Charter of the United Nations, to settle any international dispute in which they may be involved by peaceful means in such a manner that international peace, security, and justice are not endangered and to refrain in their international relations from the threat or use of force in any manner inconsistent with the Purposes of the United Nations.

ARTICLE 2 — In order more effectively to achieve the objective of this Treaty, the Parties separately and jointly by self-help and mutual aid will maintain and develop their individual and collective capacity to resist armed attack and Communist subversive activities directed from without against their territorial integrity and political stability.

ARTICLE 3 — The Parties undertake to strengthen their free institutions and to cooperate with each other in the development of economic progress and social well-being and to further their individual and collective efforts towards these ends.

ARTICLE 4 — The Parties, through their foreign ministers or their deputies, will consult together from time to time regarding the implementation of this Treaty.

ARTICLE 5 — Each Party recognizes that an armed attack in the West Pacific area on the territories of either of the Parties would be dangerous to its own peace and safety and declares that it would act to meet the common dangers in accordance with its constitutional processes.

Any such armed attack and all measures taken as a result thereof shall be immediately reported to the Security Council of the United Nations. Such measures shall be terminated when the Security Council has taken the measures necessary to restore and maintain international peace and security.

ARTICLE 6 — For the purposes of Articles 2 and 5, the terms "territorial" and "territories" shall mean in respect of the Republic of China, Taiwan and the Pescadores; and in respect of the United States of America, the island territories in the West Pacific under its jurisdiction. The provisions of Articles 2 and 5 will be applicable to such other territories as shall be determined by mutual agreement.

ARTICLE 7 — The Government of the Republic of China grants, and the Government of the United States of America accepts, the right to dispose such United States land, air, and sea forces in and about Taiwan and the Pescadores as may be required for their defense, as determined by mutual agreement.

ARTICLE 8 — This Treaty does not affect and shall not be interpreted as affecting in any way the rights and obligations of the Parties under the Charter of the United Nations or the responsibility of the United Nations for the maintenance of international peace and security.

ARTICLE 9 — This Treaty shall be ratified by the Republic of China and the United States of America in accordance with their respective constitutional processes and will come into force when instruments of ratification thereof have been exchanged for them at Taipei.

ARTICLE 10 — This Treaty shall remain in force indefinitely. Either Party may terminate it one year after notice has been given to the other Party.

CHINESE-SOVIET TREATY OF FRIENDSHIP AND ALLIANCE (Effective February 14, 1950)

ARTICLE 1 — Both High Contracting Parties undertake jointly to take all necessary measures at their disposal for the purpose of preventing a repetition of aggression and violation of peace on the part of Japan or any other state which should unite with Japan, directly or indirectly, in acts of aggression. In the event of one of the High Contracting Parties being attacked by Japan or states allied with it, and thus being involved in a state of war, the other High Contracting Party will immediately render military and other assistance with all the means at its disposal.

The High Contracting Parties also declare their readiness in the spirit of sincere cooperation to participate in all international actions aimed at insuring peace and security throughout the world, and will do all in their power to achieve the speediest implementation of these tasks.

ARTICLE 2 — Both the High Contracting Parties undertake by means of mutual agreement to strive for the earliest conclusion of a peace treaty with Japan, jointly with the other Powers which were allies during the Second World War.

ARTICLE 3 — Both High Contracting Parties undertake not to conclude any alliance directed against the other High Contracting Party, and not to take part in any coalition or in actions or measures directed against the other High Contracting Party.

ARTICLE 4 — Both High Contracting Parties will consult each other in regard to all important international problems affecting the common interests of the Soviet Union and China, being guided by the interests of the consolidation of peace and universal security.

ARTICLE 5 — Both the High Contracting Parties undertake, in the spirit of friendship and cooperation, and in conformity with the principles of equality, mutual interests, and also mutual respect for the state sovereignty and territorial integrity and non-interference in internal affairs of the other High Contracting Party—to develop and consolidate economic and cultural ties between the Soviet Union and China, to render each other every possible economic assistance, and to carry out the necessary economic cooperation.

ARTICLE 6 — The present Treaty comes into force immediately upon its ratification; the exchange of instruments of ratification will take place in Peking.

The present Treaty will be valid for 30 years. If neither of the High Contracting Parties gives notice one year before the expiration of this term of its desire to denounce the Treaty, it shall remain in force for another five years and will be extended in compliance with this rule.

Done in Moscow on February 14, 1950, in two copies, each in the Russian and Chinese languages, both texts having equal force.

RECOMMENDED READINGS

GENERAL WORKS

Ch'ien Tuan-sheng, *The Government and Politics of China*, Cambridge, 1950.
Fairbank, J. K., *The United States and China*, Cambridge, 1958.
Fitzgerald, C. P., *China, A Short Cultural History*, London, 1950.
Hu Chang-tu and others, *China: Its People, Society, Culture*, New York, 1960.
Latourette, K. S., *The Chinese, Their History and Culture*, New York, 1946.
Peffer, N., *The Far East: A Modern History*, Ann Arbor, 1958.
Smith, A. H., *Chinese Characteristics*, New York, 1894.
Vinacke, H. M., *A History of the Far East in Modern Times*, New York, 6th ed., 1959.

EARLY POLITICAL THOUGHT

Bodde, Derk, "Authority and Law in Ancient China," *Journal of American Oriental Society*, July–September, 1954.
Creel, H. G., *Chinese Thought from Confucius to Mao Tse-tung*, Chicago, 1953.
Lin Mou-sheng, *Men and Ideas: An Informal History of Chinese Political Thought*, New York, 1942.
Soothill, W. E., *The Analects of Confucius*, London, 1937.
Thomas, E. D., *Chinese Political Theories*, New York, 1927.

IMPERIAL GOVERNMENT

Backhouse, E. and J. O. P. Bland, *Annals and Memoirs of the Court of Peking*, London, 1914.
Chang Chung-li, *The Chinese Gentry*, Seattle, 1955.
Grousset, René, *The Rise and Splendor of the Chinese Empire*, Berkeley, 1958.
Morse, H. B., *The Trade and Administration of China*, New York, 1921.
Smith, A. H., *Village Life in China*, New York, 1899.

TRANSITION AND REVOLUTION: THE COLLAPSE OF MONARCHY

Backhouse, E. and J. O. P. Bland, *China under the Empress Dowager*, London, 1921.
Buck, Pearl, *Imperial Woman* (Cardinal edition), New York, 1958.
Chün Tu-Hsüeh, *Huang Hsing and the Chinese Revolution*, Palo Alto, 1961.
Kent, P. H. B., *The Passing of the Manchus*, London, 1912.
Levi, Werner, *Modern China's Foreign Policy*, Minneapolis, 1953.

POLITICAL IDEAS OF SUN YAT-SEN

Hsü, Leonard, *Sun Yat-sen: Political and Social Ideals*, Los Angeles, 1933.
Leng Shao-chuan and N. D. Palmer, *Sun Yat-sen and Communism*, New York, 1961.

Mao Tse-tung and others, *Dr. Sun Yat-sen*, Peking, 1957.
Sharman, L., *Sun Yat-sen: His Life and Its Meaning*, New York, 1934.
Sun Yat-sen, *San Min Chu I* (*The Three Principles of the People*, transl. by F. W. Price), Shanghai, 1927.
William, Maurice, *Sun Yat-sen v. Communism*, Baltimore, 1932.

THE PARLIAMENTARY REPUBLIC

Ch'en, Jerome, *Yuan Shih-k'ai*, Palo Alto, 1961.
Houn, F. W., *The Central Government of China, 1912–1928*, Madison, 1957.
MacNair, H. F., *China in Revolution*, Chicago, 1931.
T'ang Leang-li, *The Inner History of the Chinese Revolution*, London, 1930.
T'sao, W. Y., *The Constitutional Structure of Modern China*, Victoria, 1947.
Wang Ch'ing-wei, *The Chinese National Revolution*, Peiping, 1931.
Weale, Putnam, *The Fight for the Republic in China*, New York, 1917.

ERA OF THE WARLORDS

Hu Shih, *The Chinese Renaissance*, Chicago, 1934.
Linebarger, P. M. A., *Government in Republican China*, New York, 1938.
MacNair, H. F., *China in Revolution*, Chicago, 1931.
Powell, J. B., *My Twenty-Five Years in China*, New York, 1945.
Vinacke, H. M., *Modern Constitutional Development in China*, Princeton, 1920.

REVIVAL OF THE KUOMINTANG

Bisson, T. A., *Ten Years of the Kuomintang*, New York, 1933.
Kiang Wen-han, *The Chinese Student Movement*, New York, 1948.
Peake, C. H., *Nationalism and Education in Modern China*, New York, 1932.
Woo, T. C., *The Future of the Chinese Revolution*, London, 1928.

THE RISE OF COMMUNISM IN CHINA

Chen Han-seng, *Landlord and Peasant in China*, New York, 1936.
Hu Ch'iao-mu, *Thirty Years of the Communist Party of China*, Peking, 1951.
Isaacs, Harold, *The Tragedy of the Chinese Revolution*, Stanford, 1961.
Malraux, André, *Man's Fate* (Modern Library edition), New York, 1934.
Schwartz, B. I., *Chinese Communism and the Rise of Mao*, Cambridge, 1952.
Snow, Edgar, *Red Star over China*, New York, 1944.
Taylor, G. E., *The Struggle for North China*, New York, 1940.
Union Research Institute, *Communism in China*, Hong Kong, 1960.
Wint, Guy, *Dragon and Sickle: How the Communist Revolution Happened in China*, New York, 1959.

THE NATIONAL GOVERNMENT OF THE KUOMINTANG

Bate, Don, *Wang Ch'ing-wei, Puppet or Patriot?* Chicago, 1941.
Ch'ien Tuan-Sheng, *The Government and Politics of China*, Cambridge, 1950.
Fei Hsiao-tung, *Peasant Life in China*, London, 1937.
Linebarger, P. M. A., *The China of Chiang Kai-shek*, Boston, 1942.

WAR-TIME PROBLEMS AND POLICY

Chiang Kai-shek, *China's Destiny*, New York, 1947.
Department of State, *United States Relations with China*, Washington, 1949.

Peck, Graham, *Two Kinds of Time*, Boston, 1950.
Quigley, H. S., *Far Eastern War, 1937–1941*, Boston, 1942.
Rosinger, L. K., *China's War-Time Politics*, Princeton, 1945.

THE PEOPLE'S GOVERNMENT AT PEKING

Agarwala, A. N., *The Government and Politics of China*, Delhi, 1959.
Asian Annual, London, 1960.
Cameron, James, *Mandarin Red*, New York, 1955.
Clark, Gerald, *Impatient Giant: Red China Today*, New York, 1959.
Department of State, *United States Relations with China*, Washington, 1949.
Epstein, I., *The Unfinished Revolution in China*, New York, 1949.
Feis, Herbert, *The China Tangle*, Princeton, 1953.
Kirby, E. S., *Contemporary China*, I, III, Hong Kong, 1956, 1960.
Mallory, Walter, editor, *Political Handbook of the World*, New York, 1961.
Mao Tse-tung, *China's New Democracy*, New York, 1949.
Tang, Peter, *Communist China Today*, New York, 1957.
Union Research Institute, *Communism in China*, Hong Kong, 1959.

THE IDEOLOGY OF MAO TSE-TUNG

Barnett, A. D., *Communist China and Asia*, New York, 1960.
Mao Tse-tung, *China's New Democracy*, New York, 1949.
Mao Tse-tung, *Selected Works*, Volume IV, English ed., Peking, 1961.
Schwartz, B. I., *Chinese Communism and the Rise of Mao*, Cambridge, 1952.
Snow, Edgar, *Red Star over China*, New York, 1938.

COMMUNIST SOCIAL POLICY

Barnett, A. D., *Communist China and Asia*, New York, 1960.
Cameron, James, *Mandarin Red*, New York, 1955.
Chandrashka, S., *China's Population*, London, 1959.
Chen, T. H. E., *Thought Reform of the Chinese Intellectuals*, New York, 1960.
Clark, Gerald, *Impatient Giant: Red China Today*, New York, 1959.
Mills, H. C., "Thought Reform: Ideological Remolding in China," *Atlantic Monthly*, December, 1959.
Orleans, L. A., *Professional Manpower and Education in Communist China*, National Science Foundation, Washington, 1961.
Schurman, H. F., "Organization and Response in Communist China," *Annals of the American Academy of Political and Social Science*, January, 1959.
Union Research Institute, *Communist China 1958*, Hong Kong, 1959.
Walker, R. L., *China under Communism: The First Five Years*, New Haven, 1955.
Wang, Y. C., "Intellectuals and Society in China, 1860–1949," *Comparative Studies in Society and History*, The Hague, July, 1961.
Welch, Holmes, "Buddhism under the Communists," *China Quarterly*, April–June, 1961.

COMMUNIST ECONOMIC POLICY

Adler, S., *The Chinese Economy*, New York, 1947.
Clark, Gerald, *Impatient Giant: Red China Today*, New York, 1959.

Doi, Akira, "The Chinese Communes Today," *Japan Quarterly*, April–June, 1960.

Greene, Felix, *Awakened China, The Country Americans Don't Know*, New York, 1961.

Hsia, Ronald, "China's Industrial Growth," *Annals of the American Academy of Political and Social Science*, January, 1959.

Hudson, G. F., and others, *The Chinese Communes*, London and New York, 1960.

Hughes, T. J. and D. E. T. Luard, *Economic Development of Communist China*, London, 1959.

Kamekichi, T., "The Chinese Economy as I Saw It," *Japan Quarterly*, January–March, 1960.

Kirby, E. S., editor, *Contemporary China*, I, 1956; II, 1958. Hong Kong.

Ladejinsky, W., "Carrot and Stick in Rural China," *Foreign Affairs*, October, 1959.

Union Research Institute, *Communist China, 1958*, Hong Kong, 1959.

Walker, R. L., *China under Communism: The First Five Years*, New Haven, 1955.

COMMUNIST FOREIGN POLICY

Anonymous, "Peking on Co-existence," *Foreign Affairs*, July, 1960.

Barnett, A. D., *Communist China and Asia*, New York, 1960.

Boorman, H. L., and others, *The Moscow-Peking Axis*, New York, 1957.

Salisbury, Harrison, "Red China against Russia," *Saturday Evening Post*, March 19, 1960.

Snow, Edgar, "A Report from Red China," *Look*, January 31, 1961.

Steiner, Arthur, *Communist China in the World Community*, Carnegie Endowment for World Peace, 1961.

Warner, Denis, *Hurricane from China*, New York, 1961.

Wright, Quincy, "The Status of Communist China," *Journal of International Affairs*, Vol. XI, No. 2.

THE NATIONAL GOVERNMENT ON TAIWAN

Asian Annual, London, 1960.

Barnett, A. D., *Communist China and Asia*, New York, 1960.

Bate, H. M., *Report from Formosa*, New York, 1952.

Clark, Gerald, *Impatient Giant: Red China Today*, New York, 1959.

Khu, Eng-han, "Formosa: A Formosan View," *Japan Quarterly*, January–March, 1959.

Kirby, E. S., *Rural Progress in Taiwan*, Taipei, 1960.

Li, Thian-hok, "The China Impasse," *Foreign Affairs*, April, 1958.

Mallory, Walter, editor, *Political Handbook of the World*, New York, 1961.

Ravenholt, A., "Formosa Today," *Foreign Affairs*, July, 1952.

Scalapino, Robert, "United States Relations with Asia," U. S. Senate, November 1, 1959.

Walker, R. L., "Taiwan's Development as Free China," *Annals of the American Academy of Political and Social Science*, January, 1959.

Whiting, A. S., "Formosa's Future: Neither China?" *Bulletin of Foreign Policy Association*, New York, September 15, 1956.

DEMOCRACY'S CHANCE IN CHINA

Chandra-Sekhar, Sripati, *Red China: An Asian View*, New York, 1961.

"Contemporary China and the Chinese," *Annals of the American Academy of Political and Social Science*, January, 1959.

Elegant, R. S., *The Center of the World: Communism and the Mind of China*, New York, 1962.

Hu Shih, "Historical Foundations for a Democratic China," Edmund J. James Lectures on Government. University of Illinois, 1941.

Levenson, J. R., *Confucian China and Its Modern Fate*, Berkeley, 1958.

Liang, Ch'i-ch'ao, *History of Chinese Political Thought*, New York, 1930.

Lin Mou-sheng, *Men and Ideas*, New York, 1942.

"Report on Contemporary China," *Current History*, December, 1958.

WHAT POLICY FOR THE UNITED STATES?

Acheson, Dean, *Power and Diplomacy*, New York, 1960.

Barnett, A. D., *Communist China and Asia*, New York, 1960.

Bowles, Chester, "The China Problem Reconsidered," *Foreign Affairs*, April, 1960.

Hornbeck, S. K., *"China" and United States "China Policy,"* New York, 1961.

Knowland, W. F., "The United States Should Not Recognize Communist China," *Current History*, December, 1958.

Koen, R. Y., *The China Lobby in American Politics*, New York, 1960.

Levi, Werner, "American Foreign Policy toward China," *Journal of International Affairs*, Vol. XI, No. 2.

Quigley, H. S., "Trade with Communist China," *Current History*, December, 1958.

Rusk, Dean, Press release of interview with Robert Kee, BBC, Washington, March 6, 1961.

Scalapino, R. L., "United States Relations with Asia," Senate Committee on Foreign Relations, November 1, 1959.

Snow, Edgar, "A Report from Red China," *Look*, January 31, 1961.

Thompson, K. W., *Political Realism and the Crisis of World Politics*, Princeton, 1960.

Whelan, J. G., "The United States and Diplomatic Revolution: The Contrasting Cases of Russia and Red China," *China Quarterly*, January–March, 1961.

Wright, Quincy, "The Status of Communist China," *Journal of International Affairs*, Vol. XI, No. 2.

Periodicals

American, Asian, and European periodicals, both scientific and literary, carry helpful factual and interpretative articles on contemporary China. Their back files are essential sources for historical data. Listed here are those especially concerned with East Asia. For coverage of news and documents no other Western newspaper is comparable with the *New York Times*.

Asian Survey, Berkeley
China Quarterly, London
China Reconstructs, Peking
Contemporary Japan, Tokyo
Eastern World, London

Extracts from China Mainland Press, U.S.
Consulate General, Hong Kong
Far Eastern Economic Review, Hong Kong
Free China Review, Taipei
Japan Quarterly, Tokyo
Journal of the Asian Association, Ann Arbor
Pacific Affairs, Vancouver, B.C.
Peking Review, Peking

INDEX

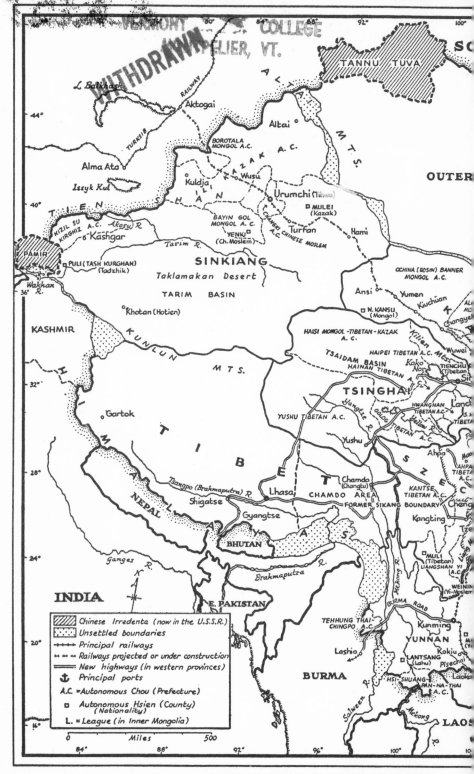

CHINA IN 1956 (FROM *COMMUNIST CHINA TODAY*, BY